The World
in Depression
1929–1939

Charles P. Kindleberger

UNIVERSITY OF CALIFORNIA PRESS
BERKELEY AND LOS ANGELES

History of the World Economy
in the Twentieth Century

Volume 4

Copyright © Charles P. Kindleberger, 1973
California Library Reprint Series Edition, 1975

University of California Press
Berkeley and Los Angeles

ISBN: 0-520-02423-0 cloth-bound
       0-520-02514-8 paper-bound
Library of Congress Catalog Card Number 72-97743

Printed in the United States of America

To the memory of E.C.K.

Contents

List of Text Figures

List of Tables

Preface

'This is where I came in.' When Dr Wolfram Fischer asked me to write on the world economic history of the 1930s, I was delighted to comply. This was partly because of the surging intellectual interest in the world depression which may be encountered among scholars everywhere. It was also partly to work out for myself the complex events of my youth and early professional life: events which brought me and many others into economics.

The October 1929 crash of the stock market strikes no chords in my memory. With the rest of the world, I was aware of it, but to a sophomore in college it meant little. The family's few stocks were owned outright rather than on margin. Despite the decline of business, and with the help of an uncle in shipping, I got a job the next summer working on a freighter delivering heavy equipment from Copenhagen to Leningrad and bringing back wood-pulp from Kotka, Raumo and Kemi in Finland. I don't think this was ordinary dumping, but I don't know. It was not the kind of exchange-dumping which occurred after 1932 and is discussed in Chapter 8. It was memorable mainly for the fact that one could drink beer and spirits against one's pay after the ship reached Copenhagen. (My wages as a deck-boy were $20 a month.) The trip cultivated an interest in international trade and a taste for Tuborg beer which have lasted all my life. (A friend of mine got a job working on ships in 1940 through his uncle. The uncle who helped me was a vice-president of a shipping company; his was vice-president of a seamen's union. Nepotism continued through the 1930s, but its locus shifted.)

Falling family income was still sufficient to pay both college expenses and my fare to Europe in the summer of 1931 to take

13

advantage of a summer scholarship to the Students International Union. Salvador de Madariaga, who normally ran the seminar, had just been appointed ambassador to the United States from Spain, so we undergraduates from the United States and Europe were thrown in with older students at the Geneva School for International Studies, run by Professor (later Sir) Alfred Zimmern. It was an exciting experience, from the visiting lecturers to the farewells for Patrick Sloan at the end of the summer as he made his way, equipped with stacks of toilet paper and needles, to spend a year in the Soviet Union.

I cannot say, however, that I formed a very clear idea of the events described in Chapter 7. I have run across a notebook I kept that summer, which records lectures by Paul Douglas, E. M. Patterson from the United States, Maurice Bonn, Henri Hauser, Douglas Copland and a host of others. There is even an outline of a seminar I myself gave in the economics group, entitled 'Economic Conditions in the United States'. None of these scribbles were helpful in what follows. I was aware of the Bank for International Settlements mainly because of a young employee who came down frequently from Basle to court one of the delightful Smith girls among the American colony in Geneva.

In February 1932, after graduating from college, I had the strengthening experience of being unemployed, but only for a limited period of eight or ten weeks. Again through influence, I got a job as an office boy (complete with B.A. honours and a Phi Beta Kappa key), in what I am now, as a Keynesian, ashamed to reveal was the National Economy League, a pressure group founded by Archibald Roosevelt and other conservatives to insist on balancing the national budget. In July 1932, again through nepotism, I obtained another job as office boy with Johnson & Higgins, marine insurance brokers. The two memorable incidents of the next year in that capacity included the increase in first-class postage from 2c. to 3c., which induced the firm to shift its downtown Manhattan communication system from the United States post office to its own staff (it was my first and painful acquaintance with an elastic demand schedule); and a slip of paper from the office manager stating that because of N.R.A. (the National Recovery Administration) – and, I could read between the lines, 'and for no other reason' – my salary would be increased from $12 to $15 a week.

By February 1933 I had arranged to study graduate economics at Columbia University the following autumn. As an introduction, I took an evening course in money and banking from Ralph W. Robey, the financial editor of the *New York Evening Post*. In the early weeks of February and March 1933, he regaled the class with day-to-day accounts of the collapse of the American banking system which made economics as exciting as *The Perils of Pauline*.

By some intellectual process which I cannot reconstruct, a term paper in the autumn term of 1933–4 in a class on international banking lit on the topic of competitive exchange depreciation between Denmark and New Zealand. Professor Benjamin H. Beckhart encouraged me to revise it for publication, and a reference to this, my professional baptism, may be found in Chapter 8. The early prejudice against flexible exchange rates remains.

After finishing class work and making a start on the dissertation in June 1936, I went to work in the International Research Division of the U.S. Treasury, under Harry D. White and Frank V. Coe, calculating purchasing-power parities for various currencies, especially including those of the gold bloc. This was a temporary position; a permanent one opened up at the Federal Reserve Bank of New York on 1 October 1936. I was paid $200 a month in each job, or $2,400 a year. Mr White asked me whether I would consider staying on at the Treasury. I allowed that I would be willing to consider an offer of a P-2 rating – professionals being rated in a scale from P-1 to P-6 – which paid $2,600 a year. He regarded this as excessive, and I moved on, going to work in New York on 1 October 1936, four days after the formation of the Tripartite Monetary Agreement of 26 September.

At the Federal Reserve Bank of New York I analysed events in European economies and the New York exchange market, going through the gold scare of April 1937 and the dollar scare which followed in the autumn. In February 1939, before Hitler's march into Prague, I agreed to go to the Bank for International Settlements in the summer. With the help of friends at the Board of Governors of the Federal Reserve System, I was called home after the fall of Paris in June 1940.

All this interests me far more than it will the reader, but it explains that this is where I came into economics, and the extent to which this book is *recherche du temps perdu*. Perhaps more than the biases of youthful experience, however, the book reflects the intellectual idiosyncrasies developed during a score of years spent teaching after the war. The reader is duly warned against both sources of distortion.

Commissioned to be about the 1930s, the book concerns the world economy in depression. It is written from an American point of view, in so far as that is inescapable, but I have used where I could materials from Europe. The editor is unhappy that there is not more about the Soviet Union and Asia. The picture is distorted on these accounts, but one should not pretend to know what one does not know.

I am also conscious that there is little of the social, political and personal drama with which the depression is rife or fraught, and which has been brought out in recent books by Studs Terkel, John Brooks and Kenneth Galbraith. In reviewing a book in economic history using econometric methods, I once said I missed the sweat of the men handling the cotton, and the sea shanties of the men aboard the ships. This book is short on colourful anecdotes on stockbrokers or applesellers beyond the autobiographical notes above. Neither is it econometric in the manner of the new economic history which tries to prove hypotheses rigorously with multiple regressions of lagged variables. It is history with a narrative, instead of tables of R squares, Durbin-Watson tests and the like. So much the worse for it.

Finally, by way of apology, I find the key to why the depression was so wide, so deep and so long in my speciality, the international monetary mechanism. This should surprise no one.

As a non-historian I have accumulated a series of debts to the profession and to those, like me, who are on its fringes. I am deeply impressed by the hospitality of the historical profession to outsiders, offering them help rather than protecting jurisdictional boundaries. First and foremost, I should like to thank D. E. Moggridge of Clare College, Cambridge, and Peter Temin, my colleague at M.I.T. Both read the manuscript with care, and divided by specialization in improving it. Temin asked the big

16

searching questions about proof and demonstration. Moggridge went way beyond the call of duty in calling attention to other evidence, questioning interpretations, and especially digging in the public records to provide additional material on a number of points on which the evidence was scanty.

If Moggridge and Temin belong in a non-competing group, the list of my other intellectual creditors is given alphabetically to avoid invidious and impossible distinctions. Professor Lester V. Chandler of Princeton and Atlanta Universities started me in business with a mountain of carbons of his notes from the Federal Reserve Bank of New York files, and has been provocative and suggestive in a number of discussions. Stephen V. O. Clarke of the Federal Reserve Bank of New York read the manuscript and provided much useful comment, and, additionally, has searched the bank's files on several points. Professor Heywood Fleisig of Cornell University, who is also working on the depression, shared with me his dissertation before publication and another important paper in draft and corrected an important error in my manuscript. George Garvy, Vice-President of the Federal Reserve Bank of New York, drew my attention to the work of Woytinsky in seeking to promote public works in Germany in 1931 and 1932, and lent me the bank's copy of Grotkopp's *Die grosse Krise* before I obtained one of my own. Closely allied to the same subject, Professor Alexander Gerschenkron of Harvard University insisted upon the importance of the expansionary ideas of Wilhelm Lautenbach, an *Oberregierungsrat* in the German Economics Ministry in 1930 and 1931.

Dr Helen Hughes, now of the International Bank for Reconstruction and Development, was kind enough to lend me two draft chapters of her unpublished economic history of Australia. Professor Ryutaro Komiya at my request dug about in Japanese sources to try to find the answer to the riddle as to how Japan produced Keynesian policies as early as 1932 without a Keynes. Professor Peter H. Lindert of the University of Wisconsin commented on the first draft with incisiveness. James R. Moore, a graduate student at the State University of New York in Stony Brook, writing a dissertation on the World Economic Conference of 1933, was kind enough to furnish me with a bibliography of sources consulted by real historians. Professor Adolph Sturmthal of the University of Illinois provided fascinating material on the antipathy of Marxists in Germany to exchange devaluation.

The production process of a book of this sort also involves trying out various ideas in seminars and lectures. This I have done at the University of Alabama, the Cambridge Economic History group, Columbia University, Cornell University, as a participant in discussion groups in the Council on Foreign Relations, at the Institute of World Affairs at Salisbury, Conn. (successor to the Students International Union of 1931), and the New York Metropolitan Economists group. The interchanges and discussions on these occasions, in which some of those named above took part, have been highly stimulating and suggestive.

Harvard University has hit upon the generous courtesy of allowing neighbouring scholars access to the bountiful stacks of the Widener Library free of charge for a month each year. I have availed myself twice of this valued privilege and am grateful to the university and to the Librarian. If I occasionally consort with the rich library up the street, however, it does not mean that I am not devoted and faithful to the Dewey Library of M.I.T. Its friendliness and eagerness to help almost make up for the gaps in the collection, and I continue to be grateful to Barbara Klingenhagen, William Presson and the others.

Mary Ann Reardon, now Mrs Bailey, assisted me in the early summer of 1970 by ferreting out piles of statistics, many more than I could use. Anne Pope distinguished herself in organizing all and undertaking much of the typing of the first draft. The final draft was produced by another old-timer, like Miss Klingenhagen and me, Mrs Inez Crandall, now retired, who was a departmental secretary at M.I.T. for some twenty years.

The book is dedicated to the memory of my father, E. Crosby Kindleberger, who struggled with great courage against a physical handicap, and against the Great Depression.

Massachusetts Institute of Technology   C.P.K.

1. Introduction

The 1929 world depression raises a series of issues for economic analysis and historical methodology which can perhaps be summed up most concisely in the difference of view precipitated in a television debate in May 1969 between two American economists, Milton Friedman and Paul Samuelson. Friedman insisted then, as he has done on other popular and professional occasions,[1] that the depression had a single cause: errors in carrying out monetary policy in the United States. Samuelson maintained it was the result of a series of historical accidents. The Friedman position disposes of a series of lesser analytical issues which emerge if the original question of system *v.* accident is resolved in favour of system. He finds the origin in the United States rather than in Europe or the periphery; in monetary rather than real factors; in policy rather than in the nature of institutions or in the tasks required of them; in a national economy rather than in the operation of the international system. Within the limits of United States monetary policy, moreover, which excludes the villain of many another analysis – structural dislocation in Europe after the First World War or the failure of the United States to act like a creditor nation, particularly the imposition of the Smoot-

1. See, for example, *The Balance of Payments: Free versus Fixed Exchange Rates*, American Enterprise Institute for Public Policy Research, Washington, D.C., 1967, p. 90: 'When the United States embarked on deflation and proceeded to reduce its money stock, the rest of the world was forced into a major catastrophe.' Professor Friedman's scholarly treatment of the subject is in Milton Friedman and Anna Jacobson Schwartz, *A Monetary History of the United States, 1867–1960*, Princeton University Press, 1963, esp. Chapter 7, 'The Great Contraction, 1929–33'. This is also published separately in *The Great Contraction*, Princeton University Press, Princeton, 1966.

Hawley Tariff Act of 1930 – he rules out stock-market speculation, and the delay in passing the Glass-Steagall Act of 1932 which overcame a domestic shortage of monetary gold by allowing the Federal Reserve System to substitute government securities instead of gold for the lacking eligible paper needed as backing for the central bank's liabilities. There would doubtless have been a recession or a depression with perfect monetary policy, or a money supply which grew in the United States at some optimal pace. But Friedman's explanation of the 1929 world-wide great depression is national, monetary, related to a policy decision. It is uni-causal. In my judgement it is wrong.

There is a host of similar explanations which rely mainly on a single root cause of the depression, or a single origin. President Hoover was persuaded throughout his career in the White House and in writing his memoirs on the depression twenty years later that the origin of the trouble lay in Europe, starting with the difficulties of adjusting to the consequences of the First World War and accentuated by a financial crisis in 1931.[2] The widest-held European view is that the depression started in the United States: fundamentally in that country's unwillingness to write off war debts; more precisely in the stock-market crash of 1929 or the frenzied lending of 1927 and 1928. More subtle analysts look to the failure to operate the gold standard properly, converting it to the gold-exchange standard on some showings, lowering interest rates unduly in the United States in 1927 on others.

But Samuelson's explanation of 'a series of historical accidents' is perhaps no more satisfactory. Great depressions recur. The great depression of 1873 to 1896, sometimes regarded by economic historians as *the* great depression, was perhaps different in origin, characteristics and effects, so that on these scores one can regard the period from 1929 to 1939 as unique.[3] Going further back,

2. *The Memoirs of Herbert Hoover*, vol. III: *The Great Depression, 1929–1941*, Macmillan Co., New York: Hollis & Carter, London, 1952. For a contemporary statement, see his Foreign Affairs Message to Congress, 10 December 1932, in Department of State, *Foreign Relations of the United States, 1931*, vol. I, Washington, D.C., 1946, pp. x ff.

3. But note that J. T. W. Newbold, 'The Beginnings of the World Crisis, 1873–1896', *Economic History*, vol. II, No. 7 (January 1932), pp. 437 and 439, found the origin of that depression in the 'profound unsettlement of short-

however, produces the uniformities that the social scientist searches for. Like the First World War, the Napoleonic Wars were followed by a short, sharp deflation in 1816, comparable to that of 1920–21, and a period of monetary adjustment culminating in the restoration of the pound to par in 1819 and 1821. Then came a spurt of foreign lending, from 1821 to 1825, followed by a stock-market crash in 1826 and a depression. If one subtracts 100 plus three to five years from the major economic events of the 1920s and 1930s, interesting parallels emerge. The 1826 depression was not perhaps as deep or as widespread as that of 1929, or as those of 1837 and 1848 which followed it. But the timing is disconcertingly similar.[4]

Moreover, the European depression of the 1840s, not deeply shared in the rest of the world, presents the same issues as the 1930s as to origin and the role of accidental factors. British historians think of the 'commercial crisis of 1847–8' as largely the result of the railway mania, with an admixture of money panic associated with the failure of a series of grain dealers. On the Continent there was considerable difference of opinion. Cameron calls it 'first and foremost a financial and banking crisis',[5] whereas other economic historians direct attention to real causes, including the smallest wheat crop in fifty years in 1846, followed in 1847 by the largest crop in fifty years. Fohlen, more or less ignoring financial aspects, calls the 'crisis of 1848 . . . in effect a series of economic and political accidents'.[6] At a deeper level, it may be possible to detect a parallel between the crisis of 1848 on the European Continent and the 1929 depression; both represented failures of the economic system at a transitional stage from one set of institutions and forms to another. But this is to anticipate.

term money markets', arising from a withdrawal of £90 million from London in twelve months. These funds had been accumulated by Germany as part of its receipts of the Franco-Prussian indemnity of 1872. See also Walter Bagehot, *Lombard Street*, new edition, John Murray, London, 1917, pp. 291 ff.

4. Alexander Dana Noyes, *The Market Place: Reminiscences of a Financial Editor*, Little Brown, Boston, 1938, pp. 338–40.

5. Rondo E. Cameron, *France and the Economic Development of Europe*, Princeton University Press, Princeton, 1961, p. 125.

6. Claude Fohlen, *Une Affaire de famille au XIXe siècle: Méquillet Noblot*, Colin, Paris, 1955, p. 62.

Another form of 'historical accident' might be the pure fortuitousness of regularly recurring cycles of three different periodicities reaching their depression phases simultaneously. The depression of a Kondratieff long cycle covering as much as fifty years arrived simultaneously with the depressions of a Juglar intermediate nine-year cycle and of a short-range Kitchin cycle in inventories. Vastly oversimplified, this is the Schumpeter view.[7] It is difficult, however, for most economists to think of these sorts of cycle as independent of each other, like celestial bodies in orbit, and of the great depression as a random but predictable event like an eclipse.

If we reject both the single or dominant cause and the series of historical accidents as the explanation of the great depression, we are left with a host of issues. In one perspective, we may ask how and where the depression originated, why it spread so widely, why it went so deep and lasted so long. Questions about where and how it originated have an obvious interest apart from political recrimination, but in their turn they open up new conundrums about *causa proxima* and *causa remota* as well as *causa causans*. Assume that the answer to the question of where the depression originated is limited to the United States, Europe, the periphery or to the relations among any two or three of them. We then need to know, first, what happened to produce the trouble, and secondly, why the economic system failed to respond to deal with the trouble, either automatically, through the microeconomic mechanism of adjustments in supply and demand, or through macroeconomic response through monetary and fiscal systems; or through policy reactions in which the automatic economic forces set in motion are reversed or supported in the interest of stability. Take, for example, the view that the depression originated in the recovery of European production in foodstuffs, raw materials, textiles and so forth, the output of which had been expanded overseas during the First World War. This would be a real explanation instead of a monetary one, but it is not complete unless we can explain why

7. Joseph A. Schumpeter, *Business Cycles: A Theoretical, Historical and Statistical Analysis of the Capitalist Process*, 2 vols., McGraw-Hill, New York and London, 1939. Schumpeter also makes allowance for 'non-essential events which explain particular circumstances' (p. 908), and for 'incidents, accidents and policy' (pp. 937 ff.).

over-expansion in one or more lines did not produce price declines which cut back output and redirected resources. Or, if the blame is laid on the halt in United States lending to Germany and the periphery in 1928, perhaps owing to the attraction of funds into the call-money market supporting the rise in New York stock prices, it is necessary to explain not only how the halt in lending set the world economy into reverse gear, but why other forces did not move into action to offset the impact – either borrowing from a different source or in a different form through the automatic market mechanism; or why monetary or fiscal measures were not taken to offset the impact as a result of policy decision. The initial force may be contained in two ways – automatically or by policy decision – and to explain its consequences one has to account both for the failure of automatic forces in the economy to act and for the failure of decision-making machinery.

The failure of economic policy is relatively easy. Throughout the chronological account of the depression which follows, we shall cite instance after instance of what, with hindsight, appears as economic illiteracy. There is no monopoly. Deflationists are found everywhere – Hoover, Brüning, Snowden, Laval. Examples abound of bad judgement – the British decision to return to the gold standard at par in 1925, and the similar Japanese decision taken in July 1929 and carried out in January 1930; of ill-conceived nostrums – the Roosevelt-Morgenthau-Warren attempt to raise commodity prices by changing the price at which the Reconstruction Finance Corporation bought newly mined gold in the United States, and the Blum experiment with the forty-hour week in France in 1936; of too little and too late, such as the 50 million schilling ($7 million) loan for Austria on 16 June 1931 which the Bank of England made for a week (but was forced to renew many times). Often no one in authority had any positive idea of what to do, and responded to disaster in the policy clichés of balancing budgets, restoring the gold standard and reducing tariffs. Hobsbawm puts it too strongly perhaps: 'Never did a ship founder with a captain and a crew more ignorant of the reasons for its misfortune or more impotent to do anything about it.'[8]

8. E. J. Hobsbawm, *Industry and Empire· an Economic History of Britain.*

There were many economists and a few public figures in Britain (Keynes, H. D. Henderson, Mosley), in France (Reynaud), in Germany (Lautenbach, Woytinsky), and perhaps in the United States, who had domestic remedies which made sense in modern terms; and a number of suggestions put forward for the World Economic Conference of 1933 anticipated the decisions of Bretton Woods a calendar decade and intellectual light-years later. Roosevelt frequently confessed to his ignorance, but had the virtue of not being doctrinaire and, more positively, of insisting on trying one thing after another until he found something which would help.[9]

The emphasis on doctrine in policy formation may be too simple. In many instances, policy was constrained not by official understanding of economic principles but by public attitudes. The classic example was perhaps war debts, the American public being 'more unanimous on this one question of foreign policy than on any other'[10] in wanting debts collected; even if Hoover and Roosevelt had wanted to cancel the debt – which they did not –

since 1750, Weidenfeld & Nicolson, London: Pantheon, New York, 1968, p. 179.

9. See Raymond Moley, with the assistance of Elliott Rosen, *The First New Deal*, Harcourt Brace & World, New York, 1966, p. 6: 'Roosevelt's knowledge of economics was limited'; and p. 244: 'I doubt that Roosevelt or I could have passed an examination such as is required of college students in elementary economics.... We were rank amateurs in the very domain of knowledge that was of paramount importance.' See also John Morton Blum, *From the Morgenthau Diaries*, vol. I: *Years of Crisis, 1928–38*, Houghton Mifflin, Boston, 1959, p. 141: 'Roosevelt said [to Morgenthau]: "You and I, of course, started with no knowledge of this subject, but the two of us have done well and have been able to more than hold up our end."' Schlesinger quotes Roosevelt as likening himself to a quarter-back who would try a variety of plays to find one that succeeded. See Arthur M. Schlesinger, Jr, *The Age of Roosevelt*, vol. II: *The Coming of the New Deal*, Houghton Mifflin, Boston, 1959; Heinemann, London, 1960, p. 193. But see Rexford G. Tugwell, *The Brains Trust*, Viking Press, New York, 1968, p. 73, who insists that Roosevelt had had courses in economics, 'not only in such specialties as finance, transportation, taxation and insurance, [but] he was far from a beginner in economic theory'.

10. See Robert H. Ferrell, *American Diplomacy in the Great Depression: Hoover-Stimson Foreign Policy, 1929–1933*, Yale University Press, New Haven, 1957, p. 33.

they would have had no easy time doing it. (Hoover's failure to understand is reflected in his insistence that, because the French had deposits in New York in excess of the amount due in, say, December 1932, they were able to pay, thus ignoring the distinction between capital and income or how the French Treasury was to gain command of the dollars or gold from the Bank of France without violating its statutes or the budgetary process.)[11] Equally adamant in its unwillingness to pay in December 1932 was the French Chamber, as was evidenced by Herriot's fall from power on 14 December 1932, when he proposed the payment of the instalment due the next day.[12]

The failure of automatic forces to offset events which pushed the system in the direction of depression has received some attention with regard to the gold standard, but less in other respects. The claim is widely made that it was not the gold standard which failed, but the way it was operated.[13] Countries which lost gold did not always deflate, and those which gained it, notably France and the United States, expanded too much or too little. It is not so universally recognized that other aspects of the international monetary mechanism are supposed to work symmetrically; if the

11. *The Memoirs of Herbert Hoover*, vol. III, p. 185. Hoover claims that the French would have paid in December 1932 had it not been for an unfortunate statement by Roosevelt at Warm Springs to the effect that he did not regard payment of the 15 December instalment as a necessary condition for opening further negotiations. The amount due was $50 million and French holdings in New York were $500 million.

12. See Henry L. Stimson and MacGeorge Bundy, *On Active Service in Peace and War*, Harper & Brothers, New York, 1947, p. 217. Herriot was a real hero to Stimson for opposing his own people in the interests of international understanding – much bigger than anyone on the United States side of the Atlantic. Stimson was one of the few cancellationists in the United States government. See Elting E. Morison, *Turmoil and Tradition: A Study of the Life and Times of Henry L. Stimson*, Houghton Mifflin, Boston, 1960, p. 433, when Stimson and Mills went to the White House in January 1933 to ask President Hoover to take some bold step. 'For a time the President was roused by the possibility of a "great state paper", but then he changed his mind. Stimson, he said, was "ten million miles away from his position" – the "debts were merely a chip on the current of ordinary prosperity".'

13. See Lionel Robbins, *The Great Depression*, Macmillan, London, 1934, esp. pp. 97 ff.

flow of capital stops, for example, it may be deflationary for the countries which cease to import capital, though it should be expansionary for those which no longer send savings abroad. Equally, the imposition of tariffs should be expansionary for the importing country if contractive for the countries losing export markets. If prices of particular internationally traded commodities fall, the income and spending of countries specialized in these goods evidently also fall, but those of countries which regularly buy them should rise. Again, currency appreciation is deflationary, but the counterpart of depreciation in other countries pushes in the opposite direction. It is therefore inadequate to explain world depression by referring to losses of gold or markets, a fall of prices, or currency appreciation, without specifying why the expansionary force, which is a counterpart to the depressive factor specified, did not function properly. There are a number of factors which can be pointed to, which will be explained as the occasions arise: accelerators, money illusion, elastic expectations, the dynamic spread of deflation to the banking system and the like. Without some such asymmetry or positive feedback, however, no substantial depression is possible.

A symmetrical system with rules for counterbalancing, such as the gold standard is supposed to provide, may give way to a system with each participant seeking to maximize its short-run gain. This is the competitive system envisaged by Adam Smith where each man (or country), in advancing his own welfare, advances that of the total, either because of an absence of inter-actions or because of external economies. But a world system of a few actors (countries) is not like this, and the fallacy of com-position – that the total often differs from the sum of the parts – enters to affect the outcome. In advancing its own economic good by a tariff, currency depreciation or foreign-exchange control, a country may worsen the welfare of its partners by more than its own gain. Beggar-thy-neighbour tactics may lead to retaliation, so that each country ends up in a worse position from having pursued its own gain.[14] National economic interests are some-

14. See President Roosevelt's First Inaugural Speech: 'Our international trade relations, though vastly important, are in point of time and necessity secondary to the establishment of a sound national economy. I favour as a

times complementary, sometimes opposed, with no one or two countries controlling the outcome, which rather depends upon the actions of them all.[15] This is a typical non-zero sum game, in which any player undertaking to adopt a long-range solution by itself will find other countries taking advantage of it. Agreement that all should adopt a long-range strategy may be conceptually satisfactory, but is likely to involve different degrees of sacrifice from different players at a given moment in time. Britain wants to stabilize currencies at \$3·40 to the pound, while the United States lacks interest in the subject until the rate is nearer \$4·86. Or postulate a network of reparations, war debts and commercial loans in which Germany owes reparations to Britain and France and commercial debts to the United States; Britain owes to the United States about what it receives from Germany, and is owed in war debts from France; France is to receive the lion's share of reparations, well in excess of its war debts to Britain and the United States. In this circumstance, Germany is more ready to cancel reparations than to default on commercial debts, since it owns some assets abroad and is interested in maintaining its credit. Britain is willing to cancel reparations, but only if war debts are excused. France insists on receiving reparations, wants war debts cancelled, and is relatively indifferent to commercial loans. The United States can see no connection between war debts and reparations, is

---

practical policy the putting of first things first. I shall spare no effort to restore world trade by international economic adjustment; but the emergency at home cannot wait on that accomplishment' – *The Papers and Addresses of Franklin D. Roosevelt*, vol. II: *The Years of Crisis*, Random House, New York, 1938, p. 14. See also Blum in *From the Morgenthau Diaries*, vol. I, p. 75: 'European nations on the whole resented the gold-buying policy, but no nation had for several years shown much regard for the economic convenience of others, and in 1933 the pressure on the President was such that he had to do something'; and Hugh T. Patrick, 'Some Aspects of the Interwar Economy', prepared for Sixth Conference on Modern Japan: 'Dilemmas of Growth in Prewar Japan', a conference held in Puerto Rico, 2–7 January 1968 (mimeographed), p. 43: 'There is some merit to criticism that Japan pursued a beggar-thy-neighbour policy; in the world economy at that time though, neighbours had to look out for themselves.'

15. See Oskar Morgenstern, *International Financial Transactions and Business Cycles*, Princeton University Press, Princeton, 1959, p. 572.

prepared *in extremis* to accept a moratorium on reparations and war debts, but seeks to safeguard the sanctity of commercial debts and wants to revive war-debt payments after the year's moratorium is over. No equitable solution is possible. Inevitably the system runs down to wipe the slate clean of reparations, debts and service on commercial lending. In exactly the same way, the attempt of a system of countries with interlocking multilateral trade to achieve export surpluses tends to wipe out all trade as successive trading partners cut imports from the next country.

In these circumstances, the international economic and monetary system needs leadership, a country which is prepared, consciously or unconsciously, under some system of rules that it has internalized, to set standards of conduct for other countries; and to seek to get others to follow them, to take on an undue share of the burdens of the system, and in particular to take on its support in adversity by accepting its redundant commodities, maintaining a flow of investment capital and discounting its paper. Britain performed this role in the century to 1913; the United States in the period after the Second World War to, say, the Interest Equalization Tax in 1963. It is the theme of this book that part of the reason for the length, and most of the explanation for the depth of the world depression, was the inability of the British to continue their role of underwriter to the system and the reluctance of the United States to take it on until 1936.

This game-theoretic interpretation of the international economic and monetary system, plus the insistence on an asymmetry in the operation of the system, also contributes to the general conclusion that the conventional wisdom of the period was not as wrong as most modern economists believe in its concern with the dangers of speculation, the necessity to raise prices, the desirability of lowering tariffs and the need to stabilize exchange rates. It is true that stock-market speculation was no longer a problem after 1929, and that no one knew how to raise world prices, or even to raise national prices through exchange depreciation which might only lower gold prices abroad. Programmes for tariff truce or halting competitive exchange depreciation were purely negative, stopping forces which were making the world economy continue to run down, without doing anything positive to reverse the positive-

28

feedback mechanism. It is clear that the leading theorists and practitioners of the 1930s were wrong on a number of issues, such as budget-balancing, and poor on therapy, but their diagnosis was not as weak as is widely believed.

In the inescapable choice between chronological and functional organization, the book adopts mainly the former but associates each year or pair of years with a particular set of problems or occurrences. Chapter 2 sets the stage by discussing the recovery from the First World War to about 1926 and the position of war debts, reparations, stabilization of exchange rates and foreign lending. Chapter 3 concentrates on 1927 and the approach of difficulties in central-bank cooperation, the international capital market, the rise in New York stock prices. The fourth chapter looks at the position in major foodstuffs and raw materials, which can be said to have turned between 1925 and 1928. And 1929 is, of course, the year of the stock-market crash, the title of Chapter 5.

The years from 1930 to 1933 are each the subject of separate chapters dealing with 'The Slide to the Abyss' (Chapter 6), '1931' (Chapter 7), 'More Deflation' (Chapter 8), and 'The World Economic Conference' (Chapter 9) respectively. Thereafter the chronological pace speeds up. Chapter 10 deals with 1934 and 1935 and is entitled 'The Beginnings of Recovery'. In 1936, and Chapter 11, 'The Gold Bloc Yields'. Chapter 12 deals with 1937 and the recession. 'Rearmament in a Disintegrating World Economy' covers the final period of 1938 and 1939 and Chapter 13. A final chapter, 'An Explanation of the 1929 Depression' (Chapter 14), brings the threads of the analysis together into conclusions.

To the extent that the organization is analytical rather than chronological, there are difficulties in following issues in the years before and after their holding of the centre stage. Less developed countries are treated mainly in Chapter 4 on primary product prices, for example, but must not be lost sight of either at the depths of the depression in 1932 and 1934 or in the later stages of recovery.

In this chronological treatment a number of turning-points deserve emphasis: 1929, 1930, 1931 and 1933 – the stock-market crash, the financial crisis, the failure of revival in the spring of

1930 and the missed opportunity of the World Economic Conference to organize recovery. Most analysis concentrates on October 1929 and May–June 1931.[16] The baffling second quarter of 1930 and June–July 1933, covering the World Economic Conference, are, however, important in explaining why the depression went so deep, lasted so long and why recovery was so incomplete.

16. See, for example, Herbert Hoover's division of the depression into five phases: (1) October 1929 to April 1931; (2) April 1931 to July 1931 (the quake from Europe); (3) August 1931 to December 1931 (the collapse of sterling); (4) December 1931 to July 1932 (reaching bottom); (5) the electoral campaign in the United States, leading to the bankers' panic of March 1933 – *The Memoirs of Herbert Hoover*,vol. iii, p. 38.

2. Recovery from the First World War

The year 1925 generally marks the transition from postwar recovery to the brief and limited boom which preceded the depression. This was the year of the stabilization of sterling and of the other currencies which followed it back to the gold standard. (In the United States, it also marked the peak of the boom in a number of important respects: the collapse of Florida land speculation, the peak for postwar housing starts, and the highest price of wheat.) But 1924, with the stabilization of the mark and the Dawes Plan, or 1926, when the last war-debt settlements with the United States were reached and the French franc was stabilized *de facto*, would do as well.

Recovery from the First World War was never achieved in a number of important respects, such as the loss of the cream of its youth by the countries of Europe, or the relative setback to the European position owing to the stimulus to economic growth in the dominions, Japan and the United States. By 1925 or 1926, however, Europe stopped looking back to 1914 and began to contemplate the future more confidently. The state of recovery achieved contained certain seeds of trouble, initial conditions from which the world depression of 1929 emerged. These concerned especially an increased reluctance by labour to accept wage decreases after about 1921, making for an irreversibility of wage and price increases;[1] reparations and war debts which, however much they appeared to have been settled by the Dawes

1. Peter Temin asserts that the First World War marks a watershed, before which entrepreneurs regarded wages as a fixed cost, and after which as marginal. See his 'Three Problems in Economic History', in *Journal of Economic History*, vol. XXXI, No. 1 (March 1971), p. 67.

Plan and the interallied debt settlements, were to prove destabilizing; the system of exchange rates, with the pound overvalued and the franc undervalued, resulting in the substantial accumulation of French claims on Britain; and the entry into world lending of the United States, substituting in part for Britain, with much enthusiasm, no experience, and little in the way of guiding principles.

The 1920–21 boom and collapse

In 1919 and 1920 a short, sharp world-wide boom took place, reflecting mainly a scramble for goods to replace the inventories drawn down during five years of war. It was especially marked in Britain and the United States.[2] Pent-up financial accumulations were let loose on limited stocks, and prices soared. France, Germany and the rest of the European Continent stood largely aside, lacking the financial resources to participate in the bidding. After a sharp rise in prices, however, there was a sharp fall as production started up and supplies emerged on the market. The swift rise and fall traced out a hairpin shape in the price indexes. In all cases, however, the fall, when it came in the summer of 1920, and especially the spring of 1921, left prices well above 1914.

It was the last time, however, that wages could be depressed so far and so fast. In Britain, average weekly wages fell 38 per cent (and the cost of living 50 per cent) between January 1921 and December 1922. Much of the compression was the consequence

2. Milton Friedman and Anna Jacobson Schwartz, *A Monetary History of the United States, 1867–1960*, Princeton University Press, Princeton, 1963, p. 360, assert that the 1920 and 1929 contractions both originated in the United States, despite their world-wide character, and cite the evidence of leading U.S. gold movements. Their opinion on both scores is not universally shared. For a somewhat different point of view which ascribes importance to monetary policy in the early 1920s and blames both the United States and Britain, see Jørgen Pedersen, 'Some Notes on the Economic Policy of the United States during the Period 1919–1932', in Hugo Hegeland, ed., *Money, Growth and Methodology*, In Honor of Johan Åkerman, Lund Social Science Studies, Lund, 1961, pp. 474 ff.

of sliding-scale wage agreements.[3] These quickly fell into disfavour. When real wages in a few industries reached prewar levels, trade unions turned away from this device adopted during the wartime rise of prices. For the first time on any substantial scale, the economic system developed an asymmetry: with expansion from full employment, one encountered price and wage increases in the manufacturing sector; with contraction, stubborn resistance of prices and wages and unemployment. The British example was the sharpest. But in Germany, too, it was noted that a new phenomenon – unemployment – showed up after the war.[4]

It was not only wage rates which resisted compression. The boom of 1919–20 produced a rise in the price of capital assets, which in turn added to fixed charges. Houses, ships and especially the equities of firms were sold at fancy prices, with a flurry of mergers, combines and public flotations of private companies, with heavy burdens for the future in debt service to bond holders, especially banks, and in customary dividends. In Britain, the boom was fed by the prospect of the destruction of German competition in coal, steel, shipping, textiles. British dominance in these fields proved to be cruelly short-lived. Hopes in coal were crushed by the disastrous strike of April–June 1921. Shipbuilding was hit by technological advances elsewhere, especially Scandinavia, and by the later overvaluation of the pound. In cotton textiles, Japan's and India's invasion of profitable colonial markets emerged quickly.[5]

In Germany, the inflation of 1922–3 induced a number of entrepreneurs, notably Hugo Stinnes, to build up huge combines based on debt, which were in difficulties once the mark was stabilized.[6] The Stinnes empire collapsed. Other firms which had managed to pay off indebtedness during the inflation lacked working capital, and after stabilization had to borrow substantial accounts

3. D. E. Moggridge, *The Return to Gold, 1925: The Formulation of Economic Policy and its Critics*, Cambridge University Press, Cambridge, 1969, p. 78.

4. Wilhelm Grotkopp, *Die grosse Krise, Lehren aus der Überwindung der Wirtschaftskrise, 1929–32*, Econ-Verlag, Düsseldorf, 1954, p. 14.

5. A. C. Pigou, *Aspects of British Economic History, 1918–25*, Macmillan, London, 1948.

6. Gustav Stolper, *German Economy, 1870–1940, Issues and Trends*, Reynal & Hitchcock, New York: Allen & Unwin, London, 1940, p. 159.

at high rates of interest. The major complaint of German enterprise was of 'capital shortage'.[7]

Reparations

Viewed from the 1970s, the attempt by the Allies to exact reparations from Germany make little sense. The notion that Germany could be saddled at the same time with the costs of the war and reconstruction made even less. At the time, however, there was ample precedent for taking this course. Germany had collected 5,000 million marks in reparations in 1871, without involving France in any great difficulty.[8] Britain had led the victors at Waterloo in exacting 700 million francs from France after 1815. Now it was the turn of the French. Having paid twice, they were ready to receive.

The history of the unsuccessful attempt by the Allies, especially the French, to collect reparations from Germany is familiar and dolorous. It falls into three periods: the first, from Versailles in 1919 to the Dawes Plan in September 1924; the second from the Dawes Plan to the Young Plan (1924 to 1930); the third, the little over fourteen months from the initiation of the Young Plan in April 1930 to the Hoover moratorium in June 1931. Unlike the war debts on which Britain paid instalments to the United States in December 1932 and June 1933, reparations were moribund in June 1931, although they were not finally declared dead until

7. Karl Erich Born, *Die deutsche Bankenkrise, 1931, Finanzen und Politik*, R. Piper, Munich, 1967, p. 15.

8. *À propos* of the inflation caused in Germany by the receipt of reparations, Bismarck is reported to have said: 'The next time we win a war against France, we'll demand that we pay her an indemnity.' And in a contemporaneous dialogue between a German and a French diplomat, the former said, 'It doesn't seem that we received those billions', to which the latter replied, 'Nor that we paid them' – see Alfred Sauvy, *Histoire économique de la France entre les deux guerres*, vol. I: *1918–31*, Fayard, Paris, 1965, pp. 131–2. For an account of why the 1871 reparations were successfully transferred, while those after the First World War were not, see my *International Economics*, 4th edition, Irwin, Homewood, Ill., 1968, pp. 326–9. A description of the French payment to England after the Napoleonic Wars is found in Rondo E. Cameron, *France and the Economic Development of Europe, 1800–1914*, Princeton University Press, Princeton, 1961, p. 76.

the Lausanne Conference of July 1932. Certainly the depression finished reparations. Étienne Mantoux, the French economist, who reacted belatedly but with sharp anger to Keynes's *Economic Consequences of the Peace*, insists that the reparations settlement of Versailles was in no way directly responsible for the depression. Perhaps this is so. But the history of reparations is bound up with the origins of the depression in so many indirect ways that its main outlines must be borne in mind.[9]

The Treaty of Versailles had been unable to fix an amount for German reparations. Any stated sum would have seemed too large to the Germans (and the Americans and possibly the British), and too small to the French. The treaty was content to deal with establishing general principles for paying in foreign securities, in payments in kind (i.e. exports), and in foreign exchange, while setting up a Reparations Commission to work out detailed sums. This body produced a figure of 132,000 million gold marks in April 1921. The Allied members of the commission calculated that 7,900 million had thus far been paid in securities, ships and deliveries, while the Germans claimed credit for having paid 20,000 million. The difference at this stage was largely 12,000 million marks, which the Germans claimed as the value of state works in ceded territories.[10] The French rejected a proposal for

9. Étienne Mantoux, *The Carthaginian Peace or the Economic Consequences of Mr Keynes*, Charles Scribner's Sons, New York, 1952, pp. 168–9; J. M. Keynes, *The Economic Consequences of the Peace*, Macmillan, London, 1919; Harcourt Brace, New York, 1920.

10. Mantoux presents a table of reparation payments by periods, as calculated separately by the Reparations Commission and the German government (*The Carthaginian Peace*, p. 152):

Payments made	Reparations Commission	German government
	(in billions of gold marks)	
11 November 1918 to 31 August 1921	9·7	42·1
under the Dawes Plan	7·6	8·0
under the Young Plan	2·8	3·1
other	0·8	14·6
TOTAL	20·9	67·8

Differences between the two figures turn on particular interpretations;

using German labour to reconstruct the Nord; proposed by Loucheur, the Commissioner for the Reconstruction of the Devastated Areas, and worked out with the cooperation of Walter Rathenau, it gave rise to objections from the French public, for reasons of sentiment, as well as from the construction industry, which wanted the orders.[11] The Germans, on the other hand, found it difficult to pay reparations in kind, especially in coal, though when the British coal strike took place in 1926, their exports of coal rose briskly. Payments in foreign exchange and deliveries in kind to France dwindled in 1922 to such an extent that the French and Belgian troops entered the Ruhr in January 1923.

Occupation of the Ruhr did not help. German employers and workers sabotaged output and distribution in a massive exhibition of passive resistance or non-violent warfare. There was even violence: on 31 March 1924, Easter Saturday, a French squad of soldiers searching Krupps was 'threatened' by a crowd of workers, and, firing into them, killed thirteen, including five teenagers, and wounded fifty-two. The funeral was a highly emotional one. Throughout the occupation, the strain was said to be harder on French troops than on the German populace.[12] The German government paid subventions to industry and discounted securities for banks to maintain payrolls. The inflation well under way in 1922 gave way to hyperinflation. By June, the mark was 100,000 to the dollar; by November 4,000 million. Grigg thought that the occupation of the Ruhr was 'the most effective and direct cause

---

Mantoux states that the earliest German figure includes 8·5 billions for the German naval vessels scuttled at Scapa Flow.

To 29 billion for repayments made to the occupation of the Ruhr, Schacht adds 11 billion of seized foreign assets, 8 billion paid under the Dawes Plan as above, and 80 to 100 billion, representing the value of German colonies lost at Versailles. See Hjalmar Schacht, *The End of Reparations*, Jonathan Cape, London: Jonathan Cape and Harrison Smith, New York, 1931, p. 22. As we shall see below, when Schacht thought reparations, he thought colonies.

11. See P. J. Grigg, *Prejudice and Judgement*, Jonathan Cape, London, 1948, p. 71; Lord Salter, *Memoirs of a Public Servant*, Faber & Faber, London, 1961, p. 164. For a similar German suggestion of July 1919, see Sauvy, *Histoire économique de la France entre les deux guerres*, vol. I, p. 140.

12. Grigg, *Prejudice and Judgement*, p. 160.

of Hitler, and but for this there would have been no Second World War'.[13] Most observers blame the inflation and the consequent pauperization of the middle class rather than the occupation of the Ruhr itself.[14] Whether one inevitably involved the other is perhaps an open question. But hyperinflation had one delayed result in making it difficult, after 1930, to fight deflation in the midst of depression. By demonstrating the devastation that could be caused by inflation, it furnished those who believed in putting the economy through the purifying fires of deflation with an inexhaustible supply of ammunition against programmes of even moderate monetary or fiscal expansion.[15]

In their occupation of the Ruhr, the French collected £128,000 over costs in the first four months of 1923, compared with £10½ million in the similar period of 1922. A British attempt at mediation begun in May produced little immediate result. The hyperinflation raced on. Its effects suited almost no one.

Finally, in December, the British, French and Germans agreed to appoint two commissions, one of no importance, save for French *amour propre*, under Reginald McKenna, to determine how much capital German citizens had managed to expatriate from under Allied noses (as well as the chances of getting it back); the second, to consider means of balancing the German budget, stabilizing the currency and fixing a new and viable level of annual reparations. This was under the chairmanship of Charles G. Dawes, the first director of the United States Bureau of the Budget. The United States had neither signed the Treaty of Versailles, nor joined the League of Nations, having turned in revulsion from the intrigues of Europe after the war. The Secretary of State, Charles E. Hughes, was, however, willing to assist unofficially in the attempt to untangle reparations, albeit insisting that such reparations had no connection with war debts owed by the Allies to the United States. With Dawes was an American financier, Owen D. Young, and a few American assistants from J. P. Morgan & Co. The bulk of the work, however, was done

13. ibid., p. 172.

14. Mantoux, *The Carthaginian Peace*, p. 144.

15. P. Einzig, *World Finance Since 1914*, Kegan Paul, London: Macmillan Co., New York, 1935, p. 177.

by the British staff, including Sir Josiah Stamp and Sir Robert Kindersley.

The Dawes Plan involved a schedule of annual payments starting at 1,000 million gold marks in the first year and rising to 2,500 million in the fifth, varying thereafter somewhat according to changes in world prosperity (if gold prices changed upward or downward by more than 10 per cent). There was to be a Reparations Agency in Berlin, to oversee the raising of the necessary amounts in marks, and to intervene to postpone payments in the event of serious transfer difficulties. A loan of 800 million marks was to be floated in various financial capitals, against the collateral of German railroad securities. This last provision was to satisfy Poincaré, who had continuously demanded *gages productifs* in the form of mines, forests, industrial plant and the like.

The Dawes loan played a fateful role. One hundred and ten million dollars of it were sold in New York, underwritten by Morgan's. It was oversubscribed ten times. More than anything else, this was the spark that ignited foreign lending from New York, first to Germany, and shortly thereafter to Latin America and much of the rest of Europe.[16] An initial success with a loan floated for political ends connected with reparations has, on previous occasions, been followed by a spurt of foreign lending. In the settlement after Waterloo, French reparations were paid through discounting *rentes* with Baring Brothers of London. The success of that venture stimulated British foreign lending in the 1820s. The French indemnity to Germany after

16. See Herbert Feis, *The Diplomacy of the Dollar, 1919–1939*, W. W. Norton, New York, 1950, p. 42. This may overstate the case somewhat, since J. P. Morgan & Co. had arranged a $150 million loan for Japan in February 1924, and one of $100 million to assist French stabilization in March 1924. But the Dawes loan was quickly followed up by similar bond issues for Krupp and Stahlverein, Thyssen, Krupp twice again, and subsequently by German municipalities.

Ilse Mintz makes it clear that the quality of foreign government bonds issued in New York deteriorated after 1924. Of those issued from 1920 to 1924, only 18 per cent were in default on 31 December 1937, while of those issued from 1925 to 1929, the ratio of default on the same date was 50 per cent. See Ilse Mintz, *Deterioration in the Quality of Foreign Bonds Issued in the United States, 1920–1930*, National Bureau of Economic Research, New York, 1951, p. 6.

the Franco-Prussian War was raised to the extent of 3,500 million francs by the famous Thiers *rente*, issued at a substantial discount. This made large profits for French commercial banks, *banques d'affaires* and private individuals, and diverted investment attention from industry to speculation in bonds, including foreign bonds, down to the outbreak of the First World War.

Reparations may not have been directly responsible for the depression, as Mantoux claims they were not, but together with war debts they complicated and corrupted the international economy at every stage of the 1920s and during the depression through to 15 June 1933, three days after the opening of the World Economic Conference. Keynes's brilliant polemic, *The Economic Consequences of the Peace*, may have been distorting in many respects; self-confirming in its contention that if the Germans heard a reasonable argument to the effect that they could not pay, they would not; and devastatingly encouraging to American isolationists in its attacks on President Wilson as an incompetent invalid; but it was surely right in thinking it useful to cancel war debts, set a small figure for reparations such as $10,000 million and clear the issue off the international agenda.[17]

17. See J. M. Keynes, *The Economic Consequences of the Peace*, pp. 135, 147 and 200. For criticisms of Keynes's observations at the Paris conference, see Mantoux, *The Carthaginian Peace*, *passim*, and esp. p. 45, citing E. M. House and Charles Seymour, *What Really Happened in Paris: the Story of the Peace Conference 1918–1919*, Charles Scribner's Sons, New York: Hodder & Stoughton, London, 1921; J.-B. Duroselle, *De Wilson à Roosevelt*, Colin, Paris, 1960, p. 115; and Sir Arthur Salter, *Slave of the Lamp*, Weidenfeld & Nicolson, London, 1967, pp. 85 and 86. Salter thought the book mistaken in its main theme and fraught with disastrous consequences. He tried especially to persuade Keynes to omit the passage about 'debamboozling the old Presbyterian'. Another suggestion that war debts be abolished and reparations cut to 53,000 million marks – not far from Keynes's $10,000 million – came from Loucheur, originally a commissioner for devastated areas, later a French negotiator on reparations, ultimately Minister of Finance. The same politician later grew very cynical and said, after a day in the Chamber of Deputies, 'I am unable to tell the truth; they would kill me' – see Sauvy, *Histoire économique de la France entre les deux guerres*, I, pp. 144 and 148.

War debts

Reparations and war debts were joined in the minds of the British, French, Italians, Belgians, but not in that of the United States, which disassociated them 'with the obstinacy worthy of a better cause'.[18] The United States refused to accept reparations from Germany. It wanted to be repaid for loans and advances to the

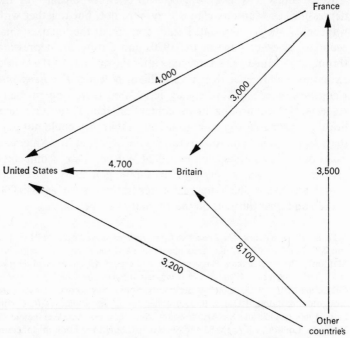

Figure 1. Inter-Allied debts at the end of the First World War (in millions of dollars).

SOURCE: A. Sauvy, *Histoire économique de la France*, I: *1918–1931*, Fayard, Paris, 1965, p. 169.

Allies for wartime assistance, prior to the Armistice, and for grain, cotton and similar supplies – involving lesser sums – afterwards. It was opposed to mixing political and economic questions, but frowned on loans by Wall Street to countries which had not made and ratified their debt settlements with the United States.

18. ibid., p. 167.

Smaller amounts were involved in the wartime obligations among the European Allies, with Britain being owed substantial debts by France, Italy and (less usefully) Russia; France by Belgium, Yugoslavia and so on. A schematic diagram with figures in dollars is given by Sauvy, but includes the larger amounts owed by Russia to Britain and France ($2,500 million and $900 million respectively).

The British suggestion for cancellation of war debts, originally advanced in Keynes's book, was put forward in a series of formal exchanges of 1920 ending up in letters between Lloyd George and President Wilson, and especially in the Balfour note of 1 August 1922 addressed to the other Allies. The last stated that, in as much as the United States insisted on collecting its war debts, the British had no choice but to collect debts owed to her, but would do so only up to the limit of the British debt to the United States. United States policy was set out time and again. It was prepared to negotiate, but insisted on doing so with the debtors one at a time, with separate settlements taking into account ability to pay. The executive branch of the government had no authority to cancel any obligations; this was a matter for Congress. Under legislation approved on 9 February 1922, though not conformed to it strictly, United States settlements were made with thirteen countries in all, beginning with Finland and Great Britain in 1923, and ending with France and Yugoslavia in 1926.[19] A typical settlement, that of 19 June 1923 between the United States and Great Britain, provided for payments over sixty-two years with interest at 3 per cent for the first ten years and $3\frac{1}{2}$ per cent thereafter. The principal sum was made up of the monies actually advanced, plus interest at $4\frac{1}{2}$ per cent to the date of settlement, plus and minus certain adjustments. In the French, Italian and Yugoslav agreements, considerably lower interest rates were charged, on the principle of lesser ability to pay. These averaged 1·6 per cent, 0·4 per cent and 1 per cent respectively.

Like reparations, war debts exacerbated international economic

19. For a detailed account, see Harold G. Moulton and Leo Pasvolsky, *War Debts and World Prosperity*, The Brookings Institution, Washington, D.C., 1932. The lists of settlements are given on p. 82 for the United States and p. 115n. for Great Britain.

relationships during the 1920s and the depression. The United States, for example, tried to use other economic considerations, such as access to the New York capital market, as a means of applying pressure to collect the debts, and to use the debts to accomplish other economic ends, such as the stabilization of the pound in 1932.[20]

War debts, along with reparations, raised a transfer problem, and hence became an issue of commercial policy. They had to be provided for in the budgets of debtors, and were needed on occasion to balance the budgets of creditors. The United States contemplated paying a bonus to veterans out of its receipts. Like an aching tooth, war debts distracted attention.

20. After obtaining a loan from J. P. Morgan in March 1924, the French tried to borrow in New York again in November 1924, but were prevented from doing so by the informal ban maintained by the Department of State which responded to investment banker requests for its views on bond issues. Since no attempt had been made to settle the war debts, it told the bankers and the French that it could not look on such a loan with favour. The ban was renewed in September 1925, when a French delegation in Washington failed to reach agreement with the United States; and once again, in April 1926, after agreement had been reached but no French government dared to submit it to the Chamber for ratification. In this instance it was not needed, since stabilization was accomplished without the normal precaution of a foreign loan. See Feis, *The Diplomacy of the Dollar*, pp. 21–3. It is to be noted that Poincaré told Moreau that the United States spent 'enormous sums' on the French press to persuade French public opinion to ratify the accords. This would appear to be a case of the pot calling the kettle black – Émile Moreau, *Souvenirs d'un gouverneur de la Banque de France, Histoire de la stabilisation du franc, 1926–1928*, Génin, Paris, 1954, p. 140. (I have recommended this book on other occasions for its general interest, and in particular for its picture of a laconic and shrewd, if suspicious, central banker. Those who read it straight through are urged to keep an eye out for M. Aupetit. It is almost, but not quite, as enjoyable to track down the twenty or so references to him in the index.)

For the continued insistence of Hoover that he would not cancel war debts without getting something for it, see Raymond Moley, with the assistance of Elliott Rosen, *The First New Deal*, Harcourt Brace & World, New York, 1966, p. 50. Moley called the cancellation of war debts exchanging 'a definite quid for an illusory quo – tariff concessions or the stabilization of the French and British currencies'. This was in January 1933, after the Hoover moratorium, when the definite character of war debts was subject to some dispute.

Stabilization of currencies

Stabilization waited on some settlement of war debts and reparations. Or, at least, some start towards it. In Germany, mortgages had been wiped out in the hyperinflation of 1922–3. A new currency, the Rentenmark, was introduced on the basis of the security of German land and buildings in November 1923. This was done slowly, alongside the old mark, but by restoring confidence succeeded in halting and even reversing the inflation. Bankruptcies took place in increasing number after April 1924. Schacht, who became head of the Reichsbank in December 1923, negotiated British aid for the establishment of the Golddiskontobank to finance foreign trade in gold marks in early 1924.

In August 1924, with the acceptance of the Dawes Plan, the Rentenmark gave way to the Reichsmark converted from the old mark at a million millions to one. As part of the Dawes Plan, the Reichsbank became independent of the German government and was strengthened with the 800 million R M Dawes loan. It was required by Article 5 to maintain reserves, three quarters gold, one quarter foreign exchange, at a 40 per cent ratio to note and deposit liabilities. Schacht maintained the deflationary pressure. High interest rates and the success of the Dawes loan attracted more foreign loans. The inflow of capital can hardly be thought of as a monetary phenomenon, responding to short-term interest rates and liquidity or associated with an overvalued exchange rate. Germany still lacked real capital as a result of the war and inflation, despite some considerable capital formation during the inflation. In the first stages, the borrowing was largely for industry. Thereafter it spread to states and municipalities. Schacht conducted a campaign against unproductive borrowing. In November 1927, for example, he made a speech excoriating German cities for building 'stadiums, swimming pools, public squares, dining halls, convention halls, hotels, offices, planetariums, airports, theatres, museums, etc., and the purchase of land'.[21] This sort of

21. Schacht, *The End of Reparations*, p. 33. However, in 1926 Schacht told Strong that if he could borrow $200 million to $400 million in long-term loans from the United States, for German industrial establishments and including possibly German municipalities in good credit standing, he could maintain

inflow can hardly be described as the consequence of a shortage of capital. The original shortage of capital, however, led to high interest rates, which stimulated the capital inflow. And in time this acquired a momentum of its own.

Stabilization of sterling at par in the spring of 1925 was more debatable. It was debated at the time, and is debated still. The issues in the discussion are to what extent it was accidental – the result of destabilizing speculation in the pound which pushed it within shooting distance of parity in the autumn of 1924 – or of deep-seated forces which were inexorably tending in this direction. Such forces were strong: the return to par has been characterized 'as a question of prestige, a question of dogma, . . . almost a question of religion'.[22] Another French view calls the return to gold an affair of wounded *amour propre* rather than of monetary policy.[23] A modern British opinion is less ironic but claims that the views involved were essentially moral and based on 'deep faith in the mechanism of the prewar gold standard'.[24]

The City of London was, of course, interested in restoring its prewar position as a world financial centre, and to a degree it succeeded. German reserves were increasingly held in sterling after stabilization, and after stabilization the Dutch returned balances to London from New York.[25]

British leading opinion was committed to a return to par if possible. The Cunliffe Committee on Currency and Foreign Exchanges After the War, appointed in January 1918, accepted without argument the return to par as an objective. The only open questions were whether it was possible, and if so, when. From a low of $3·40 at the end of 1920, the pound recovered to $4·70 in the spring of 1923 as a result of capital inflows from the Continent fleeing German inflation and French occupation of the

stability of the mark – see Lester V. Chandler, *Benjamin Strong, Central Banker*, The Brookings Institution, Washington, D.C., 1958, p. 335.

22. Sauvy, *Histoire économique de la France entre les deux guerres*, p. 121.

23. M. Perrot, *La Monnaie et l'opinion, en France et en Angleterre, 1924–36*, Colin, Paris, 1955.

24. Moggridge, *The Return to Gold, 1925*, p. 68.

25. See Stephen V. O. Clarke, *Central Bank Cooperation, 1924–31*, Federal Reserve Bank of New York, New York, 1967, pp. 161–3, and Moreau, *Souvenirs d'un gouverneur de la Banque de France*, p. 136.

44

Ruhr. Unemployment rose to 15 per cent. A suggestion that the government might take expansionary measures to correct the unemployment, and the election of the Labour government, which was committed to a capital levy, led to an outflow of funds in the second half of 1923, and depreciation to below $4·30. In February 1924, the Labour government accepted the principles of the Cunliffe Report, and the movement was halted.[26] Expansion did take place, however, and unemployment was reduced without leading to or requiring much depreciation. The Bank of England took advantage of the improvement to press the government to appoint a committee of experts (under the chairmanship first of Sir Austen Chamberlain, and, when he became Foreign Secretary in the Conservative government, of Lord Bradbury), including most of the members of the Cunliffe Committee, to make recommendations on two matters: (a) consolidation of the Treasury note issue which had come into existence during the war with the Bank of England fiduciary issue; and (b) the course to be followed after the expiration of the Gold and Silver (Export Control) Act of 1920 at the end of 1925. The question of the note issue was postponable; some decision to renew or to abandon the gold embargo was not. Abandonment meant going back to gold, at some figure, but presumably par.

The committee held hearings over the summer of 1924. All witnesses except Keynes and McKenna were optimistic about the ability of Britain to restore the pound to par. Calculations of purchasing power parities suggested that British prices were overvalued by about 10 per cent, but most observers, including Keynes, though not Montagu Norman, the Governor of the Bank of England, thought that this discrepancy would be corrected by a rise in United States prices while British levels were held steady. The suggestion had even been advanced in 1923 that Britain should ship an extra $100 million in gold to the United States in payment of war debts to ensure this result, although Norman had countered that the United States could sterilize it. Moggridge characterizes Keynes's testimony as 'ambiguous'.

26. See Robert Z. Aliber, 'Speculation in the Foreign Exchanges: The European Experience, 1919-1926', *Yale Economic Essays*, vol. 2, No. 1 (Spring 1962), pp. 188-90.

Keynes was afraid that removing the gold embargo and appreciating the pound to par would result in Britain not in deflation but in inflation as American prices rose and the United States lost gold to England. Most observers thought that if United States prices did not go up, it would not be impossible to squeeze British prices down another 10 per cent. The committee prepared a draft report in September 1924 saying that there was no practical alternative policy to returning to gold, but suggesting that it might be well to wait until American prices had risen.[27]

At this point, after nine months in office, Britain's first Labour government fell. Snowden was replaced as Chancellor of the Exchequer by Winston Churchill. The general expectation became accepted that sterling would be revalued. Speculation bid the currency up to $4·79$\frac{1}{2}$, within pennies of the $4·86 parity. Norman decided that the time had come. There were a few more opportunities for reversing the course. The Bradbury Committee reported on 5 February and recommended in favour of resumption. On 29 January Churchill circulated a series of questions, largely in the Keynes-McKenna spirit, to Norman at the Bank of England, Lord Bradbury, Otto Niemeyer and Ralph Hawtrey at the Treasury, questioning the desirability of going back to the gold standard, the timing of any return, and whether a better bargain might not be obtained from the United States as a price for a return. Moggridge regards this questioning as partly Churchill's way of coming to a decision, and partly a reaction to worry over Beaverbrook's opposition. Even after he had been satisfied on this score, Churchill asked for Niemeyer's reaction to an article by Keynes in the *Nation* on 'The Return Towards Gold', commenting pointedly: 'I do not know whether France with financial embarrassments is worse off than England with her unemployment.' On 17 March, Churchill gave a dinner party attended by Niemeyer, Bradbury, Keynes, McKenna and Grigg, in which Niemeyer and Bradbury argued for return and Keynes and McKenna against. In Grigg's view the 'ayes' had it.[28] The decision was finally taken on 20 March and announced on 28 April. The Gold Standard Act of 1925 became law on 14 May

27. See Moggridge, *The Return to Gold, 1925, passim.*
28. Grigg, *Prejudice and Judgement*, p. 182.

1925, after operating *de facto* from the date of announcement.

No consideration was given to a return to gold at a different rate. The Bradbury Committee Report states that such a policy needs only to be mentioned to be dismissed.[29] Moggridge quotes an ex-Labour Minister, Tom Johnson, who is said to have remarked after sterling left gold, 'They never told us we could do that.'[30] The perceived choice seems to have been 'Go/No-go' at the prewar parity. Even Keynes accepted the rate. Reddaway blames the accident of the fall of the Labour government in October (over questions of a proposed treaty and loan with the Soviet Union, and the dropping of the prosecution of a Communist journalist) which induced destabilization speculation. This may have affected timing. But the suggestion that a few more months or even years of $4·40 instead of $4·79 would have altered opinion substantially seems unlikely. Keynes and McKenna who were close friends and saw alike on most issues, were heard out but failed to persuade. Keynes was brilliant, but erratic, and his testimony on the issue was 'ambiguous'. Even ten years later at the World Economic Conference, as an American observed, 'John Maynard Keynes was pretty generally regarded as an extremist'.[31] All the small countries wanted stabilization (Sweden, tired of waiting, jumped the gun in March 1924; its central bank governor had been urging resumption). More important was the continuous pressure from the United States, including pressure for speed in returning to gold. Not only Benjamin Strong, the Governor of the Federal Bank of New York, but Secretary Mellon, and a host of other Federal Reserve officials, were unhesitating in informing Norman in December 1924 and January 1925 that the time had come.[32] Strong's views were partly based on world considerations: the need to eliminate the malign effects of disturbed foreign exchange markets on world trade; and partly on two national grounds: the hope (a) of reversing the flow of

29. See W. B. Reddaway, 'Was $4·86 Inevitable in 1925?', *Lloyds Bank Review*, No. 96 (April 1970), p. 23.

30. Moggridge, *The Return to Gold, 1925*, p. 9.

31. James M. Cox, *Journey through My Years*, Simon & Schuster, New York, 1946, p. 367.

32. Moggridge, *The Return to Gold, 1925*, p. 40.

gold to the United States, and (b) of gaining international lending business for New York as a consequence of higher interest rates in London.[33] Under attack from Keynes, Churchill later believed he had made a mistake. At the time he felt he had little choice.

In retrospect, the return to gold at par must be marked up as an inescapable error. Not all critics so regard it. As we have just seen, Reddaway suggests it was an unlucky accident. Youngson and a few other economic historians maintain that the trouble lay elsewhere: 'What wrecked the gold standard was the self-regarding unwisdom of French and American monetary policies.'[34] It was not the pound which was overvalued, but the French franc which was valued too low. The difficulties in British export trades were the consequence not of too high a level for the pound, but of structural changes from the war. This view seems, however, to ignore that contemporary purchasing-power-parity calculations, which suggested that the pound was 10 per cent overvalued, overlooked the need for an adjustment in parity calculations because of the structural setbacks referred to, and included the drastic mistake of thinking that prices and wages were continuously compressible downwards. Overvaluation of the pound was no doubt compounded by undervaluation of the franc, as well as by an ultimate unwillingness to undertake expansive monetary policies in the United States after March 1929 when the stock market started its rise. It was, perhaps, inevitable as an attempt to restore the *status quo ante bellum*. It was none the less an important mistake.

Stabilization of the franc took place gradually over the summer and autumn of 1926 at an undervalued level, good perhaps for France, but disastrous for the international monetary mechanism. But this dictum has also been challenged. Sauvy calls the stabilization an island of reason in a sea of errors, and while reluctant to rewrite history to contemplate what would have happened if

33. Clarke, *Central Bank Cooperation, 1924–31*, p. 72. Strong was also concerned lest the pound deteriorate progressively against the dollar, and provide incentive to the adoption of novel ideas, including especially a weakening of discipline against inflation – see Moggridge, *The Return to Gold, 1925*, p. 41.

34. A. J. Youngson, *The British Economy, 1920–57*, Allen & Unwin, London, 1960, pp. 233–4.

Cleopatra's nose had been longer, is disposed to believe that, at a higher rate, France would have fallen into the world depression earlier.[35] His focus is on the history of France, however, not on that of the system.

At the time, the question was not where to stabilize but whether it was possible to do so at all. Monetary policy in France was in chaos. Reconstruction had been undertaken in the devastated regions with the slogan, *'Le Boche paiera'*. While waiting for reparations, expenditure had been financed with short-term borrowings. No finance minister was able to fund the debt at long term so as to lock creditors in. With most debt in short form, creditors could convert their assets into money in a brief space of time. Any political upset led to capital outflows and depreciation of the franc, inducing Aftalion to devise the 'psychological theory of foreign exchange' which maintained that exchange rates fluctuated with national confidence in the government.

Such confidence was limited. Between the inception of the Dawes Plan in September 1924 and July 1926, there were ten different ministers of finance in almost as many governments. Ministers of finance, and governments generally, would fall when they were unable to get the budget approved by the Chamber of Deputies, and then were refused credits at the Bank of France. From 18 to the dollar and 90 to the pound, the franc depreciated throughout 1925 and on into the spring of 1926. Raoul Péret, Minister of Finance under Briand in the spring of 1926, got his budget through Parliament in April, but the depreciation if anything accelerated. War-debt settlements were made with United States in April, and with Britain, provisionally, in May. From the middle of April to the middle of May, the franc went from 145 to 170 to the pound. On 1 June, Péret appointed a committee of experts to work out a means to halt the haemorrhage. Before the committee report had come out, the Briand cabinet changed finance ministers – from Péret to Caillaux – and changed the governor of the Bank of France from Robineau to Moreau. The franc reached 174. Confidence was still lacking. On 17 July, the Briand government gave way to that of Herriot. The franc went to 220. On 21 July the Herriot government fell. The franc reached

35. Sauvy, *Histoire économique de la France entre les deux guerres*, pp. 96–8.

a low of 243 to the pound (49+ to the dollar, or virtually 2 cents). Citizens of Paris threatened tourists on the streets.

In Herriot's place returned Poincaré, the strong man, who served as his own Minister of Finance. Initially, he reversed the recommendations of the Committee of Experts, published on 3 July, and lowered rather than raised taxes. This won the confidence of the propertied classes. The flow of capital reversed and the franc recovered to 199 to the pound on 25 July, and to 190 on 26 July. At this stage, he adopted the policies of the committee in favour of raising taxes.

From the moment that Poincaré took charge of the government, the French franc was strong and its quotation climbed in the exchange market. As early as 7 August, the Bank of France was authorized to buy foreign exchange with French francs to slow down the rate of appreciation. It was unwilling to undertake such purchases, however, until it received assurance from the Ministry of Finance that any losses it might suffer, from buying sterling at 150 francs to the pound and ultimately selling it at a higher franc rate such as 125, would be made good by the Ministry. Such assurance was forthcoming only at the end of September.[36]

The Bank of France entry into operations to hold down the value of the franc meant to Moreau abandonment of all notion of restoring the currency to its prewar par.[37] Such a hope was a vain one, no doubt, but it had been entertained by Poincaré, who regarded it as a moral question.[38] Even before this had been resolved in favour of a departure from the prewar rate – a long intellectual advance over the British, made possible, no doubt, by the much greater rate of inflation – the question of the eventual rate of stabilization was discussed. There were purchasing-power-parity calculations by Quesnay as early as August,[39] and independently, for Poincaré rather than the Bank of France; and in

36. For the text of the law of authorization of 7 August, and the agreement putting it into effect, see Moreau, *Souvenirs d'un gouverneur de la Banque de France*, pp. 62n. and 105n.

37. ibid., p. 108.

38. ibid., p. vi.

39. ibid., p. 74; Chandler, *Benjamin Strong*, p. 374, records Strong's mistaken belief that the study was by Charles Rist.

November, when the franc was 130, by Rueff.[40] Quesnay's calculation, undertaken to show to Strong, gave a range between 131 and 196, with a preferred zone of 160 to 170 and a best figure of 163 to the pound. Rueff arrived at a range of 100 to 150, from which he deduced a figure of 120, close to the final rate of 124 francs to the pound and 3·92 cents, double the rate of 21 July, but undervalued.

The rate was chosen, however, more by political than by intellectual means. At the end of October, the franc, then between 160 to 170 to the pound, began to rise. Poincaré could not make up his mind. Moreau was conscious of the importance of not too low a rate for the franc so as not to wipe out too much of the fixed-income securities of the middle classes through inflation; on the other hand, he was under pressure from businessmen, especially in the automobile industry, not to let the rate go so high as to put them under deflationary pressure. The Committee of Experts' Report warned of too high a rate which might produce a deflation like that in Britain, ruinous for industry, commerce and agriculture. So far as one can tell from the memoirs, other central banks barely discussed the ultimate rate of stabilization, and when they did, did not all speak with one voice. Strong and Norman were on holiday in France during the mounting of the crisis in the first three weeks of July. When Strong visited Moreau on 20 July, and again in Norman's visit to Moreau on 29 July, the talk was of the need for central banks to remain independent, and the possibility in due course of stabilization loans, but not of the rate. Adolf Miller, of the Board of Governors of the Federal Reserve System, did discuss the rate with Moreau in August; the substance of his view was not recorded. Reginald McKenna suggested that the franc should be allowed to appreciate; Sir Arthur Salter that it should not rise too far.[41] In the final analysis, Poincaré, who vacillated through October, came down on the side of stabiliza-

40. See Jacques Rueff, 'Sur un point d'histoire: le niveau de la stabilisation Poincaré', *Revue d'économie politique*, 69ᵉ année (March–April 1959), pp. 169–78, and Preface to Moreau, *Souvenirs d'un gouverneur de la Banque de France*, p. ix.

41. Moreau, *Souvenirs d'un gouverneur de la Banque de France*, pp. 34 ff., 48 ff., 160 and 170.

tion at 120 francs to the pound, when Léon Jouhaux, the head of the Confédération Générale de Travail, came to protest at rising unemployment in export industries.[42]

Most of the advice given to the French, from without and within, was focused on French problems, not on the impact of the French exchange-rate choice on the system as a whole. Whether one argues that the fault lay in British overvaluation or French undervaluation, or in some division of the blame between the two, there is hardly doubt that the relative overvaluation of the pound and undervaluation of the franc were dangerous for the system. From a national perspective, the French decision was made with care. From the viewpoint of the system as a whole, and with hindsight, it underrated the importance of the large amount of French capital abroad which was unlikely to be re-invested in foreign securities after French losses on Russian bonds, and therefore was likely to return to France. In this circumstance, a moderately undervalued rate to stimulate exports and import-competing industry would have been inappropriate, since it was desirable to have the capital return in part, as it went out of France, in real goods and services, i.e. in the form of an import surplus. A French return flow of capital combined with an export surplus would strain the system, since it would have to be financed by increases in Bank of France reserves.

It is a fair point that the British, rather more than the French, had an interest in underwriting the system, and that the French had much less concern or responsibility. The decision about sterling was therefore more fraught with consequence for the system than that of the franc. The main French error, however, was in thinking only of the impact of the rate chosen on France, and not at all of the system as a whole, given the fact that the British choice had already been made, albeit badly.

42. See Rueff, Preface to ibid., and Charles Rist, 'L'Expérience de 1926 et la franc d'aujourd'hui', in J. Lacour-Gayet et al., Monnaie d'hier et de demain, Éditions SPID, Paris, 1952, p. 66. Rist argues vigorously against Aron, who attributes the world depression in part to the French stabilization rate of 1926, stating that it had more profound causes, its origin was British not French, and that the role of the franc was not only negligible but non-existent (pp. 70–71).

Less importance for the system attaches to the rates at which the Belgian franc, the lira and lev were stabilized, contemporaneously with or subsequent to the franc. In these returns to the gold standard, exchange rates had interest mainly for the country in question, and were widely discussed.[43] Of more significance is the fact that Norman and Moreau found themselves competing for influence among the separate central banks, concerned lest one or the other should take too long a lead in organizing a particular stabilization loan, or should take too large a share in it. Strong, of the Federal Reserve Bank of New York, found himself obliged to mediate between the two, and in the case of the Polish loan, to take the lead to avoid deadlock. Much of subsequent misunderstandings and antipathy grew out of these encounters: Moreau, suspicious, regarded Norman as an imperialist; Norman, impatient, accusing Moreau of introducing political into technical economic and financial matters.[44] It is hard to discern that the French had ambitions of their own beyond resisting British domination, and British gobbling up of all the central-bank allies. Moreover, British designs for the system – the gold-exchange standard, stabilization of exchange rates, restoration of the financial importance (hegemony) of London – could be said to be guided by national considerations rather than or as well as by those of the international monetary system. Norman believed in the dependence of the United Kingdom on the restoration of the world economy, as well as the obverse. For the leader, it is often difficult to distinguish the public from the private good.

The last country to return its currency to par was Japan. It did

43. See Richard H. Meyer, *Bankers' Diplomacy: Monetary Stabilization in the Twenties*, Columbia University Press, New York, 1970, *passim*.

44. One of the most interesting passages in Moreau's memoirs records a report of a visit by Quesnay to London where he saw not only Norman but also Niemeyer, Salter, Strakosch and Kindersley. As reported by Moreau, Quesnay observed that the grand British design was not only to stabilize currencies, even without the support of the Bank of France, but to link up central banks into a cooperative network which could, independent of political considerations, and even of governments, regulate the questions essential for prosperity, viz. monetary security, distribution of credit and movement of prices. Moreau characterizes these views as 'surely doctrinaire, no doubt somewhat utopian, even perhaps Machiavellian, but possible!' See *Souvenirs d'un gouverneur de la Banque de France*, pp. 136–7.

so late. Japan had participated in the inflationary price rise of 1919 to 1921, with prices going from 200 to 320 before falling back to 190 (on the basis of 1913 as 100). It was beginning to stabilize the yen when its problem was compounded by the Tokyo-Yokohama earthquake of 1 September 1923. In March 1924, it let the rate go again under the pressure of easy finance from the circulation of 'earthquake bills'. The depreciation was not severe, and was corrected in 1925 by gold sales. But after *de jure* stabilization of the franc in 1928, Japan was the only major country in the world off gold. Internal and external pressures to stabilize mounted. In particular, exporters and importers grew restive with the slight degree of depreciation, and foreign bankers discussing Japanese financing urged a return to gold (but at a lower parity). Finally, in July 1929, the newly chosen Hamguchi cabinet announced a policy of returning to par. Speculation bid up the rate from a monthly average of 43·88 U.S. cents in June 1929 to 48·96 in December. On 11 January 1930, the yen returned to par. It was very late.[45]

United States lending

It is, of course, an exaggeration to claim that the Dawes loan set in motion foreign lending by the United States. Already, during the war, foreign governments had borrowed in New York and Washington, typically using the facilities of J. P. Morgan & Co. until they were in position to borrow from the United States government. There was a flurry of postwar lending through foreign dollar bonds, which reached sizeable amounts in 1922. Operations in 1924, however, lifted the volume to a new high plateau of more than $900 million a year, from which it rose to above $1,250 million in 1927 and 1928. The increases in loans to Canada and Asia and Oceania were not sensational. Those for Latin America and Europe were. Later, as we shall see, this lending stopped abruptly with awkward consequences.

45. This paragraph draws heavily on a paper by Hugh T. Patrick, 'Some Aspects of the Interwar Economy', prepared for the VIth Seminar of the Conference on Modern Japan: 'Dilemmas of Growth in Prewar Japan', a conference held in Puerto Rico, 2–7 January 1968.

A wide difference existed between the functioning of the New York market for foreign bonds and the London prewar market. This was not entirely for the reason given by Schumpeter, that United States lending offset such disturbances as reparations rather than undertaking new investment which would be transferred to the borrowing countries in real goods and services.[46] Nor was it mainly the high-pressure methods of New York bankers and the wasteful projects in Germany and in Latin America, contrasting with more experienced British bankers, of which so much has been made.[47] More interesting from an economic point of view is the fact that, in Britain, foreign lending and domestic investment were substitutes, except at business-cycle turning points when they responded to interest-rate changes and moved together. In the postwar United States, foreign and domestic lending were positively correlated in response to the cyclical movement of profits and interest rates, except at the turning points. The short-run divergences occurred particularly in the middle of 1928 and the first quarter of 1930.[48]

This profoundly contrasting behaviour may have been linked to the exuberance of the American and the experience of the British investment communities, though it is difficult to see the

46. See J. A. Schumpeter, *Business Cycles, A Theoretical, Historical and Statistical Analysis of the Capitalistic Process*, vol. II, McGraw-Hill, New York and London, 1939, p. 703.

47. See J. W. Beyen, *Money in Maelstrom*, Macmillan, London: Macmillan Co., New York, 1949, p. 45: 'The United States had all the vigour of a new-comer . . . a sales department with a new article.'

48. See Hal B. Lary, *The United States in the World Economy: the International Transactions of the United States during the Interwar Period*, U.S. Government Printing Office, Washington, D.C., 1943, pp. 92 ff.; and Alex K. Cairncross, *Home and Foreign Investment, 1800–1913*, Cambridge University Press, Cambridge, 1953, pp. 187 ff.

Mintz, *Deterioration in the Quality of Foreign Bonds*, p. 11, asserts that United States foreign lending was negatively correlated with the cycle in the 1920s, but her work refers to short cycles, with recessions in 1924 and 1927, rather than to the eight- to nine-year cycles of the 1920s and 1930s. Of relevance to an accelerator model of foreign lending, she observes that Australia, Germany and Italy borrowed chiefly at times when they enjoyed high business activity, whereas Argentina, Brazil and the Netherlands floated most of their loans when they were depressed, Austrian issues were about equal in the two periods, and the results for France were inconclusive (ibid., p. 17).

connection. The difference is more that British lending followed a supply model – in which a fixed supply of investment funds was allocated to domestic and foreign users according to the strength of their respective demands, whereas in the United States the supply of investible funds waxed and waned with the business cycle and was, after 1924, allocated in roughly constant proportions to the two outlets. What makes the economy behave in one way at one time and place and another at another is not, however, self-evident.

In the six years from 1924–9, the United States loaned abroad some $6,400 millions and the United Kingdom $3,300 millions, as Table 1 shows. The patterns and volatility of lending differed.

Table 1. United States and British foreign lending, annually, by regions, 1924–9 (in millions of dollars).

United States	Europe	Asia and Oceania	Africa	Canada and Newfoundland	Latin America	TOTAL*
1924	527	100	—	151	191	969
1925	629	147	—	137	163	1,076
1926	484	38	—	226	377	1,125
1927	577	164	—	237	359	1,337
1928	598	137	—	185	331	1,251
1929	142	58	—	295	176	671
TOTAL	2,957	644	—	1,231	1,597	6,429
United Kingdom						
1924	159	314	66	20	31	590
1925	53	216	72	10	68	419
1926	120	226	32	29	129	536
1927	105	238	136	34	126	639
1928	164	232	80	98	96	670
1929	105	139	51	74	78	447
TOTAL	706	1,365	437	265	528	3,301

*Including a small amount unspecified for the United Kingdom.

SOURCE: League of Nations, *Balances of Payments, 1930*, Geneva, 1932, p. 30.

The dip in British security issues after 1924 was the result of the embargo applied from November 1924 through 1925 and most of

1926. Major declines to Europe and Latin America occurred in United States issues. For Asia and Oceania, largely Australia, the decline from 1928 to 1929 occurred both in Britain and, to a greater proportion, in the United States.

3. The Boom

After recovery to 1925 or 1926, came the boom. It was neither general, uninterrupted nor extensive. Moreover, it contained increasing signs of tension: in the accumulation of inventories of primary products (discussed in Chapter 4); in the rise of security prices to dizzying heights (discussed in Chapter 5); and in the exacerbation of financial and political difficulties. But it was a boom.

The major exceptions were Britain and Japan. Britain shared but little in the expansion, spending virtually all the 1920s in the doldrums. Unemployment was severe throughout the decade, both before, and especially after, the General Strike of 1926, which had resulted from the coal strike which followed the attempt to squeeze prices and wages down further after the stabilization of the pound. Coal, steel, shipbuilding, textiles and housing were depressed. Unemployment was heavily concentrated in Wales, Manchester and the north-east. It is important not to exaggerate. New industries, London and the south-east did well. There was expanding employment and technological progress in motor-cars, chemicals and electrical equipment. The year 1929 showed a sharp spurt in industrial production above 1928. On the whole, however, the 1920s were, except for 1929, a lost decade for the United Kingdom.[1]

1. This is something of an exaggeration. R. S. Sayers makes the point ('The Springs of Technical Progress in Britain, 1919–1939', *Economic Journal*, vol. LX, No. 238 (June 1950), pp. 275–91) that while coal, steel, textiles and shipbuilding were deeply depressed, chemicals, automobiles and electricity flourished as Britain applied German and American innovations. The result was an impressive rise in real productivity. I. Svennilson calculates that real

On the other side of the world, Japan suffered relative depression, growing at only half the speed it achieved in the preceding and following decades, as government and financial authorities held credit tight in an effort to improve the value of the yen. A major cause was the Tokyo-Yokohama earthquake of 1 September 1923, which required a large programme of reconstruction and credit expansion, and depreciated the yen. A banking crisis in 1927 cut short a threatened new expansion of credit. A three-week moratorium was necessary in April and May; many small banks failed, and some large ones were merged. But the Japanese economy was not tightly bound to the rest of the world; its troubles had no repercussions.

In addition to exceptions, there were interruptions. The United States experienced a 'recession' in 1927 when the industrial production index based on 1923–5 fell from 111 in May to 99 in November. In retrospect, this episode is thought to lack the characteristics of a normal business cycle and to reflect primarily the decision of Henry Ford to close down automobile production for six months to permit the changeover from the Model T, on which production had been concentrated for years since before the war, to the Model A in an effort to compete more effectively with Chevrolet. This recession was not without importance in contributing to the decision to lower interest rates in the United States to help to resolve a European financial impasse.

The other interruption, which occurred in Germany, was interesting largely because it resembled 1928–9 in everything but causation and outcome. The capital inflow of 1924 and early 1925 was highly stimulating to German investment. The Stinnes firm failed in June 1925, and a great increase in unemployment took place in the winter of 1925–6. A swing from 2,700 million R M of investment in 1925 to disinvestment of 2,500 million R M in 1926 was only partly offset by the decline in the current-account deficit in the balance of payments by 2,500 million R M. The response to lower interest rates was a renewed capital inflow,

---

income rose from 82 in 1921 to 105 in 1929, or 28 per cent in eight years (*Growth and Stagnation in the European Economy*, United Nations, Geneva, 1954, Table A.1, p. 233). But 1929 was lower in real income per head than 1919 (ibid.), and 1921 was particularly depressed.

investment picking up again, and with it national income. The inventory swing from 1926–7 was from −2,500 million to + 4,100 million RM, for a total of 6,600 million, offset to the extent of 3,300 million RM by an increase in the current-account deficit. The origin of the trouble was internal, and the interruption was fleeting. In 1928 and 1929, the autonomous change took place abroad in the halt of the capital inflow. Instead of a decline in inventory investment leading to a reduction in interest rates, a rise in interest rates produced the decline in investment. The current account in the balance of payments improved sharply in 1926 and 1929 along with the reduction in capital inflow. In 1930 and 1931, it kept on improving as domestic investment and the capital inflow continued to shrink.[2]

The boom was pronounced in the United States, in Australia and Canada, in France and Italy. In the less developed countries, there were signs of trouble in the accumulation of stocks and the beginnings of weakness in raw-material prices. Even in the United States there were the problems already referred to: a collapse of the Florida land boom in 1925, with bank failures set in train; a decline starts in housing, which reached 950,000 in 1925 and then declined until May 1927 before recovering briefly between then and April 1928.

In the United States, the boom was built around the automobile; not only the manufacture of vehicles, but tyres, other components, roads, petrol stations, oil refineries, garages, suburbs. The combustion engine spread into haulage with the use of trucks, and on to the farm, where tractors replaced horses. Electrical appliances, unknown at the start of the decade, were commonplace by 1929:

2. For a breakdown of investment and its financial counterpart, see Rolf E. Lüke, *Von der Stabilisierung zur Krise*, Polygraphischer, Zürich, 1958, p. 217. My colleague, Peter Temin, takes sharp exception to the view that the halt of the capital inflow precipitated the decline in 1928–9, but much of his argument is based on the demonstration that the decline in investment in 1926 led to the reduction of the capital inflow, rather than the other way around. In 1925 and 1926, interest rates were falling, whereas in 1928 and 1929 they were going up. This should indicate that the domestic fall in investment led in the earlier period, but the halt in capital imports in the later. See his 'The Beginning of the Depression in Germany', *Economic History Review*, vol. XXIV, No. 2 (May 1971), pp. 240–48.

radios, refrigerators, vacuum cleaners. Another innovation was in motion pictures, with talkies introduced in 1926. The sale of more expensive items was assisted by the introduction during this period of hire purchase, or instalment credit as it is known in the United States. By 1925, the volume of instalment paper outstanding was $1,375 million, and by 1929, $3,000 million.

While impressive, the boom was not frenzied, except perhaps in stock-market speculation. Pressure on real resources was moderate. Unemployment was 3·1 per cent in 1929. In January 1929, wages were only 5 per cent above January 1925. Commodity prices fell almost 5 per cent from 1926 to 1929, rising 5 per cent in farm products and falling almost 8 per cent in other commodities. Unless one concentrated on the stock market – and even there there are questions, as will appear – the boom was not spectacular.

The relevance of these remarks is that there is an important school of thought which believes that whatever goes up must come down, and that it cannot come down unless it has gone up. 'It is agreed that to prevent the depression, the only effective method is to prevent a boom.'[3] 'A condition of recovery is the gold standard to preserve interlocal equilibrium and avoid the development of booms.'[4] 'A satisfactory theory of the boom explains the depression. In the crisis what has been sown during the boom has to be reaped.'[5]

Friedman and Schwartz are explicit in separating out the stock market in the United States from business expansion. 'Far from being an inflationary decade, the twenties were the reverse.' 'Federal Reserve policy was not restrictive enough to halt the bull market yet too restrictive to foster vigorous business expansion.' They are particularly concerned to dismiss the 1920s as a period of marked inflation and expansion because the stock of money failed to rise – 'a phenomenon not matched by any

3. Lionel Robbins, *The Great Depression*, Macmillan, London, 1934, p. 171.
4. ibid., p. 172.
5. Wilhelm Roepke, *Crises and Cycles*, William Hodge, London, n.d. (but the Preface to this book, translated from the German, is dated 1936), p. 119.

previous or subsequent expansion'.[6] This goes too far in the other direction to deny the reality of the boom. Industrial production in 1929 reached a level of 75 per cent above 1913 in the United States, contrasted with 10 per cent for Germany and 9 per cent for Britain, 52 per cent for Belgium and $39\frac{1}{2}$ per cent for France. If comparison is made with 1924 rather than 1913, however, Germany does better than any of the other industrial countries.

Fed by the undervaluation of the franc, the French boom not only did well compared with 1913 or 1924, but endured. In the first place, industrial production reached its peak in the first half of 1930, rather than in 1929, and did not slow down until the latter half of 1931. Secondly, the records reached in 1929 lasted until well after the Second World War. This tells more about the depression in France than about the boom. But there is no gainsaying an increase in output which took the annual index of production up from 110 in 1927 (down from 126 in 1926) to 139·5 in 1929. The French budget ran large surpluses, the government debt to the Bank of France was paid off, security prices doubled after currency stabilization. Late in 1929, the French Minister of Finance, Henri Chéron, announced that he had accumulated a surplus of 17,000 million francs in the Treasury, compared to only one million in July 1926. This had contributed to the surplus in the balance of payments of the previous years. Its rapid expenditure, upon publication of its existence, helped to maintain French domestic prosperity into 1930, but turned the balance of payments around.[7]

6. Milton Friedman and Anna Jacobson Schwartz, *A Monetary History of the United States, 1867–1960*, Princeton University Press, Princeton, 1963, pp. 298–9.

7. A. Sauvy, *Histoire économique de la France entre les deux guerres*, vol. I: *1918–31*, Fayard, Paris, 1965, pp. 105–6. Note the similarity to the Juliusturm, accumulated by the Germans from the French indemnity in 1871, and the Schäffer surplus in the same country after 1951; see Frederick G. Reuss, *Fiscal Policy for Growth without Inflation: the German Experiment*, Johns Hopkins Press, Baltimore, 1963, pp. 157–8.

The gold-exchange standard

In 1922, the League of Nations assembled a conference of financial experts at Genoa to worry about the supply of gold. The increase of the world price level during the war both enlarged the demand for gold in central bank reserves and threatened to cut the supply as a result of rising costs pressing against a fixed price. The experts recommended that national monetary authorities should explicitly adopt the substitution of foreign exchange for gold in reserve holdings. Many central banks had, in fact, held reserves in claims on London. The recommendation was that this practice be institutionalized.

But the experts did not recommend that any particular central bank should hold foreign exchange, or which foreign exchange should be held. Moreover, foreign exchange is both an asset and a liability, and where there are alternative assets, such as gold or other currencies, it is a sensitive liability. In domestic monetary theory, a distinction is made between outside money – an asset which is no one's liability, such as gold, or a liability which no one expects to be paid off, such as locally held government debt. In the international economy, gold was the only outside money, and it was relatively scarce. In addition, together with gold, the dollar was an alternative to sterling.

Sterling in the hands of the British Commonwealth was perhaps outside money: like domestic government debt, no one expected it to be paid off. But sterling in other hands, and especially in those of continental bankers who contemplated moving out of sterling into dollars or gold, was clearly inside money – an unstable component of the total.

Part of the problem for a central bank with liabilities to foreign holders arose from market conditions. There were various reasons why an asset holder would want to hold foreign assets rather than gold, and one foreign exchange rather than another. These reasons include safety, trading requirements, convenience, tradition, loyalty and hope of speculative gain. In addition to these reasons, however, there is also the return. Other things being equal, asset holders kept their funds where they could earn the highest yield.

This meant that a country which wanted to discourage foreigners from withdrawing their funds and converting them to domestic currency or gold had to maintain competitive interest rates.

Foreign central banks are moved by most of the considerations which affect private asset holders, plus several more. A central bank is presumably not a profit-making institution and can disregard fine calculations to maximize earnings, even though it needs income to operate. Its responsibility for the safety of its assets is a grave one, since it acts for the country as a whole. But the central bank may choose to move from gold to foreign exchange, or *vice versa*, or from one currency to another, as a matter of economic policy, affecting the interest-differential between its market and foreign markets, or a particular foreign market. Or it may do so for the purely political reasons of assisting a foreign country in its policies, or bringing pressure to bear upon it.

Germany had originally accumulated sterling as the counterpart of the British share of the Dawes loan. Schacht and Norman worked together closely in the issuance of the loan and in getting the Golddiskonto bank established, and Schacht had every interest in assisting in the stabilization of the pound at par, to the limited extent the Reichsbank then counted, since a rise in the pound increased the value of the bank's reserve holdings. When, towards the end of 1926, there was an excessive inflow of foreign capital into Germany, however, he faced a dilemma. He was unwilling to see the inflow of capital continue, but equally reluctant to repel it by lowering domestic interest rates, which would have contributed to domestic expansion. Accordingly, he chose to convert sterling to gold to tighten interest rates abroad. This would keep the capital in London.

The Bank of England was as unwilling to raise the interest rate as the Reichsbank was unwilling to lower it. British unemployment was widespread; still tighter money would have produced resistance from the Treasury and political unrest. Accordingly, the Bank of England allowed the gold to leave without responding in the traditional manner. German power over the London market was not substantial. But the episode suggested that the period of effective functioning of the gold standard was coming to an end.

French accumulation of sterling

The stabilization of the franc at 124+ to the pound and 25+ to the dollar (3·92 cents) raised a more serious problem. The under-valued rate both stimulated the current account in the balance of payments, subsidizing exports and import-competing production in France, and encouraged inward capital movements. Much of the capital inflow was the repatriation of French capital which had been exported in 1925 and early 1926 when the franc depreciated. Some was doubtless foreign capital buying francs in hopes of a further appreciation in the future. The Bank of France bought foreign exchange to hold down the rate of exchange, carrying it on its balance sheet under 'Miscellaneous Assets', since the regulations made no provisions for holding foreign exchange. Purchases started off slowly in November 1926, and proceeded steadily in the early months of 1927. At the end of April, the Bank of France paid back a loan from the Bank of England which convinced the market that the only direction the franc could go was up. There was no longer use in keeping French funds abroad, and foreign capitalists who thought the rate might appreciate placed their bets. The Bank of France's holdings of foreign exchange went from £5,300,000 in November 1926 to £20 million at the end of February, £60 million at the end of April, and £160 million at the end of May.[8]

This accumulation of sterling put Moreau in a strong position, and Norman in a weak one. As an opening gambit, the Bank of France began to convert sterling into gold. A conference in Paris at the end of May brought confrontation between two viewpoints, Norman asking the French to declare the franc legally stabilized, to discourage those speculating on a rise in its value; and the French, like Schacht earlier, asking the British to raise interest rates as a means of slowing down the capital inflow into France. The French were unwilling to stabilize; there were banking interests like Rothschild who hoped for a still higher rate, based

8. See Lester V. Chandler, *Benjamin Strong, Central Banker*, The Brookings Institution, Washington, D.C., 1958, p. 371, and Stephen V. O. Clarke, *Central Bank Cooperation, 1924–31*, Federal Reserve Bank of New York, New York, 1967, p. 111.

not on considerations of international stability but on domestic interests. By the same token, Norman was unable to raise interest rates; a storm would break out if he tried it, he said, with its centre presumably Churchill at the Exchequer.

There were threats of further conversions of sterling into gold, although the French were unwilling to push so hard as to force Britain back off gold. On the other side, the British threatened to present for the collection of the whole war debt, since the French had not ratified the Churchill–Caillaux war-debt agreement of 1926, even though they were paying on schedule.

A compromise was reached, involving New York. The French agreed to hold a certain amount of sterling representing what it was estimated would be needed to pay off foreign bull speculators in francs when they at last became discouraged and unwound their positions. This amount was given as £70 million to £80 million. Of this, £30 million would be converted immediately to gold, with the Federal Reserve Bank of New York furnishing £12 million in gold from its London stock against sterling. To complete the deal, the Bank of France altered its support prices in the exchange market to discriminate in buying against sterling and in favour of dollars.[9]

This agreement relieved the immediate situation. An attempt to build wider and stronger means of cooperation was sought at a conference held between Norman, Strong and Schacht, with Rist representing Moreau, in early July 1927 at the home of the United States Secretary of the Treasury, Ogden Mills, on Long Island. The purpose was to see whether the pressure on Germany and Britain could be relieved by lowering rates in the United States, rather than by raising them in Europe; to explore the relationship, if any, that existed between monetary policies in general and slipping commodity prices world-wide; and to deal with the Bank of France's large and growing accumulation of sterling and dollars. There is no complete account of this conference, which lasted, or at least was intended to last, for eight days, but only a short paragraph in Moreau's diary. This summarized the decisions of the Federal Reserve Bank of New York to lower its interest rate to help London and Berlin (but not Paris,

9. See Clarke, *Central Bank Cooperation, 1924–31*, pp. 119–20 and 167.

Moreau records); to make gold available to Continental Europe from New York at the same price as gold in London in an effort to spare London's stock; and to buy the Bank of France's sterling with dollars.[10]

The famous 1927 action of the Federal Reserve System in lowering interest rates can wait briefly. First, it is worth noticing the device that was hit upon by the Bank of France to undertake domestic open-market operations in a contracting direction without inducing a flow of foreign capital to Paris. From a domestic viewpoint, gold was as awkward as sterling. Forward contracts to buy sterling, however, were not. Accordingly, from August 1927, after the inflow of capital into France had subsided, the Bank of France operated in its money market by selling sterling to the market against forward cover rather than selling franc securities. The forward purchase of sterling (sale of francs) could be adjusted to make it attractive for the Paris money market to hold sterling spot against a forward sale. Private funds were thus subtracted from the Paris market and added to the British. The policy was initiated not just before *de jure* stabilization in June 1928, as Ragnar Nurkse states,[11] but in August 1927. In May 1928, these forward purchase contracts of the Bank of France amounted to $440 million, and by June 1928 almost $600 million.[12]

Total claims of the Bank of France on the gold of the rest of the world, represented by its total exchange, spot and forward, amounted to $1,450 million in May 1928, and somewhat less a month later at the time of stabilization. This gave it tremendous power over the markets where it held claims. The fact that, as at June 1928, a third to half of this amount consisted of forward claims, unbeknown to the British authorities, lent still greater instability to the system. The British were aware of the likelihood

10. Émile Moreau, *Souvenirs d'un gouverneur de la Banque de France*, Génin, Paris, 1954, p. 372. In the last item, Moreau was probably referring to a decision by the Bank of England to buy French sterling with dollars to the amount of $25 million.

11. League of Nations (Ragnar Nurkse), *International Currency Experience, Lessons of the Interwar Period*, League of Nations, Princeton, N.J., 1944, p. 36.

12. See Lester V. Chandler, *Benjamin Strong, Central Banker*, p. 417; Clarke, *Central Bank Cooperation, 1924–31*, pp. 121–2.

that Bank of France official claims might be converted into gold – an eventuality which it was important to guard against. Privately held sterling was doubtless regarded as different. To the extent that such sterling is held against a forward sale to an official body, however, it presents an identical risk of conversion as official sterling.[13] There is no indication that the British knew the size of the problem they laboured under as a result of awareness of the French forward operations. Nervous as they were, they were not nervous enough.

All this time the Bank of France and the Bank of England quarrelled with each other about the unimportant issue of which would take leadership in the stabilization programme of the lesser currencies of Europe. Governor Strong of the Federal Reserve Bank of New York was called in to blunt the dispute. He sympathized with Moreau to the extent that he thought Norman's intrigues and interest in financial leadership petty. But he found Moreau threatening.[14] Moreau was Strong's friend, but Norman was his intimate. He would have preferred not to take sides. More and more, together with Schacht and Moreau, but not Norman, he regarded the gold-exchange standard rationalized at Genoa as an uncertain basis for the world economy.

13. For a modern distinction between private and official foreign exchange holdings, which similarly fails to distinguish between outright private dollars and those held under official forward contracts, see Review Committee for Balance of Payments Statistics, Report to the Budget Bureau, *The Balance of Payments Statistics of the United States, A Review and Appraisal* (E. M. Bernstein Report), U.S. Government Printing Office, Washington, D.C., 1965.

14. See Chandler, *Benjamin Strong, Central Banker*, p. 421. Some years later, Moreau wrote an article in the *Revue des Deux Mondes* revealing that he had been conscious of his capacity to push Britain off the gold standard as early as May 1927. This is extensively quoted in Sir Henry Clay, *Lord Norman*, Macmillan, London, pp. 228–32. For an explicit statement in Moreau's diary, see the entry for 6 February 1928, recording Moreau's discussion of the imperialism of the Bank of England with Poincaré: 'We have powerful means of pressure on the Bank of England. Would it not be useful to have a serious conversation with M. Norman, with a view to dividing Europe into two zones of financial influence which would be attributed respectively to France and to Britain?' – *Souvenirs d'un gouverneur de la Banque de France*, p. 489.

Easy money in the United States and the stock market

The Long Island conference of early July 1927 set in motion a decision of the Federal Reserve System to reduce its interest rates. This was not done solely for the purpose of assisting the British in attracting capital and halting the loss of gold. It was not a 'dilemma situation', in which domestic considerations pushed in one direction, international in another. The 1927 recession was in the minds of the Federal Reserve authorities, and slipping world commodity prices. Beginning in July 1927 and stretching to September, the Federal Reserve System bought $200 million in open-market purchases and lowered its discount rate over the system by half a percentage point, with $3\frac{1}{2}$ per cent as the rate for the Federal Reserve Bank of New York.

How significant this action was in stimulating the rise in the stock market which began in the spring of 1928 is debatable. Galbraith dismisses it out of hand.[15] Friedman and Schwartz are inclined to think it may have contributed to the rise of the stock market, but that the Federal Reserve System's error occurred later in directing policy partly to the stock market and partly to the level of business, so that conflict was bound to arise between the two objectives of monetary policy. They believe that the authorities should have ignored the stock market, as they had ignored the Florida land boom, and concentrated on the level of business, which would have supported a more expansionary policy from 1927 through to 1929. But either objective would have been better than both. The trouble came from stalking two targets with one weapon.[16]

15. J. K. Galbraith, *The Great Crash, 1929*, Houghton Mifflin, Boston: Hamish Hamilton, London, 1955, p. 16.

16. Friedman and Schwartz, *A Monetary History of the United States, 1867–1960*, pp. 291 ff. Jørgen Pedersen agrees with the Friedman and Schwartz position but for a different reason. He believes the market was not unduly high. Differently from them, moreover, he blames the Federal Reserve System for the crash, and believes that the crash was important for the subsequent depression. See 'Some Notes on the Economic Policy of the United States during the Period 1919–1932', in Hugo Hegeland, ed., *Money, Growth and Methodology*, In Honor of Johan Åkerman, Lund Social Science Studies, Lund, 1961, pp. 482 ff.

To lay all the blame for the 1928–9 stock-market rise and the subsequent crash at the door of the 1927 action is excessive, but to dismiss the easier monetary policy as irrelevant also goes too far. That monetary policy was reversed in the spring of 1928 without restraining the market does not settle the issue in favour of there being no connection. A touch of the whip may be enough to cause nervous and excitable horses to run away and later to resist powerful hauling on the reins. Nervousness and excitability in this case are more important than the character or extent of the stimulus. The market had been working up to a speculative climax since 1924. Three million share days had been reached twice in 1925 and three times in the spring of 1926. Four million shares were traded on 1 March 1928. Brokers' loans rose 24 per cent in the second half of 1927, to $4,400 millions. New issues boomed.

Nor is it reasonable to ask that the Federal Reserve should have ignored security markets, which have an effect on business conditions, albeit an indirect one. If there was no dilemma as between the international monetary economy and domestic business, that between business and domestic financial markets was painful. Herbert Hoover warned against stock-market speculation from his position as Secretary of Commerce, just as Schacht preached against German borrowing. But President Coolidge was not stirred.[17] And there was no way to forecast in mid 1927 how nervous and excitable the stock market would become.

The halt in foreign lending

Foreign long-term lending kept pace with the New York stock market through the first half of 1928. Domestic corporate bonds had turned down in mid 1927 in favour of corporate stocks, but foreign bonds reached new peaks in the fourth quarter of 1927 and the first half of 1928. The collapse occurred after June 1928,

17. *The Memoirs of Herbert Hoover*, vol. III: *The Great Depression, 1929–1941*, Macmillan Co., New York: Hollis & Carter, London, 1952, pp. 5–13. Hoover was supported by Adolph Miller of the Board of Governors of the Federal Reserve System in opposing Strong's help for the international position. He called Strong 'a mental annex to Europe' (p. 8).

especially for German, other European, and Asian and Oceanian issues, as Table 2 shows. Canadian borrowing dropped sharply in the third quarter of 1928, but recovered. New issues for Latin America held up for a year until the third quarter of 1929. But the change after June 1928 is unmistakable.

Table 2.   New capital issues for foreign account in the United States, quarterly, 1928–30: nominal values, excluding refunding (in millions of dollars).

1928	Capital exporting countries*	Germany	Other	North America Total	Latin America	Asia and Oceania	Total
I	13·2	46·7	109·5	179·4	40·5	86·4	15·6	312·1
II	32·0	153·8	94·2	280·0	74·8	74·3	100·6	529·7
III	16·1	14·2	19·5	49·8	6·8	81·9	0·4	118·9
IV	11·7	62·4	24·6	93·7	63·4	88·4	19·9	270·4
1929							
I	42·9	21·0	16·4	80·4	56·8	73·4	53·7	264·3
II	3·9	—	3·3	7·2	114·1	70·3	2·0	193·6
III	14·0	—	8·7	21·7	28·8	29·8	0·4	79·7
IV	24·2	8·5	—	32·7	96·1	2·5	2·3	133·7
1930							
I	—	43·3	26·6	69·9	42·9	39·3	11·5	269·3†
II	—	113·5	14·5	128·0	83·7	143·0	50·3	429·6†
III	—	10·0	25·0	35·0	49·0	16·1	—	100·1
IV	—	—	—	—	105·7	0·6	—	106·3

   * Belgium, Czechoslovakia, France, the Netherlands, Sweden, Switzerland and the United Kingdom.
   † Including 'international issues', not specified in the preceding columns, amounting to $105·7 million and $24·6 million respectively during the first and second quarters.

SOURCE: League of Nations (Bertil Ohlin), *The Course and Phases of the World Economic Depression*, Geneva, 1931, pp. 320–21.

A somewhat parallel change took place in trade in outstanding securities, especially United States securities representing mainly equities traded on the New York Stock Exchange. Instead, however, of an outflow which halted, there was a small outflow in 1927 which gave way to a sizeable inflow in 1928 and 1929. The figures are shown in Table 3, together with the annual data for 1927–9 on United States trade in outstanding foreign securities, as opposed to the new issues of Table 2. These last show a somewhat, but not wholly, different pattern.[18]

Table 3.   Transactions in outstanding securities between the United States and foreign countries, 1927–9 (in millions of dollars).

	Domestic securities			Foreign securities		
	Purchases from foreigners	Sales to foreigners	Net purchases (−) or sales (+)	Purchases from foreigners	Sales to foreigners	Net purchases (−) or sales (+)
1927	624	594	−30	143	336	+193
1928	490	973	+483	483	389	−94
1929	917	1,295	+378	307	412	+105

SOURCE: Hal B. Lary, *The United States and the World Economy, the International Transactions of the United States during the Interwar Period*, U.S. Government Printing Office, Washington, D.C., 1943, p. 107.

In a thesis at Yale, Heywood Fleisig has attempted to break down these data on trade in outstanding securities within calendar years so as to form an estimate of the total change in capital flow from the eighteen months before 30 June 1928, to the fifteen months which followed to the end of September 1929. The object of this exercise, of course, is to form an impression of the size of the convulsive change in the long-term capital flow which occurred at the end of June 1928.

The movement in new issues can be estimated directly, and the change in direct investment is small and readily gauged. The problem comes in estimating the change in the flow through outstanding securities. The breakdown of trade in outstanding securities within the calendar years 1928 and 1929 is undertaken

18. J. W. Beyen points out that the Netherlands floated a number of loans in New York because of the low rates of interest, but was not interested in the foreign exchange. When New York rates rose, and the bonds cheapened, they were repatriated rapidly, within a year of issue – *Money in a Maelstrom*, Macmillan Co., New York, 1949; Macmillan, London, 1951, p. 13.

on a variety of assumptions. The first is a straight proportion of the annual figures within quarters. The second assumes that American and European investors sell each other's securities when the New York stock market is steady or declining, but buy when prices in that market are rising. The third assumes that when the New York stock market is steady or declining, Europeans sell United States securities while Americans buy European securities, capital flowing out on both accounts, whereas when New York stock prices are rising, there is an opposite combined capital inflow. Fleisig also makes assumptions about the size of the response to these price changes, as well as about the direction. The total net movement for the three years is unchanged. Varying the assumptions about what happens in the first two and three quarters thereafter gives one not only the swing figure between the eighteen months to June 1928 and the fifteen months thereafter, but an implicit capital movement for the last three months of 1929, as shown in Table 4.

Table 4. *Change in capital flows from the United States in outstanding securities, by particular periods, 1927–9, under various assumptions (in millions of dollars; U.S. purchases −; sales +).*

	Assumption 1 (proration)	Assumption 2 (opposing flows)	Assumption 3 (parallel flows)
1 January 1927 to 30 June 1928	+350	−50	−800
1 July 1928 to 30 September 1929	+500	+1350	+3050
(change)	(+150)	(+1400)	(+3850)
Implicit 1 October 1929 to 31 December 1929	+200	−250	−1200
THREE-YEAR TOTAL	+1050	+1050	+1050

SOURCE: Heywood W. Fleisig, 'Long-Term Capital Flows and the Great Depression: the Role of the United States, 1927–1933', doctoral dissertation, Yale University, 1970, Table 1, p. 33 (figures rounded).

No one of the assumptions has evident validity as a dominant rationalization of actual behaviour. They are good mainly to churn out numbers. A comparison of the figures in Table 4 and gross purchases and sales in Table 3, however, makes the results produced by Assumption 3 impossible. The implicit outflow of capital for the last three months of 1929 is equal to total gross purchases of U.S. and foreign securities from foreigners for the whole year of 1929. Moreover, in the nature of security transactions, the normal practice, even in rapidly moving markets, is for foreigners to buy and sell, with net sales or purchases as a rule less than 20 per cent of the gross movement in the same direction. The straight proration of Assumption 1 understates the change in the capital inflow after June 1928, but Assumption 2 probably overstates it by a considerable amount. As an educated guess, I am inclined to suggest inflows of $200 million in the first eighteen months, $900 in the next fifteen, for a swing of $700 million, and an implicit outflow of $50 million in the last three months of 1929.

On this showing, there was a swing of something in the order of $2,000 millions in lending by the United States between the eighteen months from 1 January 1927 to 30 June 1928, and from 1 July 1928 to 30 September 1929, $1,275 million in new foreign securities, minus $100 million in direct investment, plus, perhaps, $700 million in outstanding securities. This was a substantial amount.

What was it that hit United States foreign lending in June 1928? The short answer is the stock market. Investors were diverted into stocks; financial intermediaries, who were not permitted to buy stocks, loaned funds on the call market. Interest rates rose sharply beginning in the spring of 1928 as the Federal Reserve System sold off the additions to its open-market portfolio of the summer of 1927, and more, and raised the rediscount rate three times. Turnover rose on the New York Stock Exchange. Call-money loans went from $4,400 million at the end of 1927 to $5,275 million at mid 1928 and $6,400 million at the end of the year. Banks withdrew to an extent from the market, but nonbanks took their place and more. Railroads and industrial companies as well as financial houses turned from real investment to call loans which were safe, liquid (it was thought) and high-yielding.

An ancient dispute going back to the 1920s concerns whether the stock-market boom absorbs money.[19] We shall encounter later the question whether the stock-market crash hurt business. The question here is whether the boom also hurt it by diverting money from normal business transactions. It is evident that the stock-market boom can stimulate business by making investment financing easier – as appears to have been the case of foreign direct investment – by raising dividends and wealth to increase household spending, and by lifting business and household expectations. The negative possibilities are largely the impact on monetary policy, evidenced in the pressure of the Federal Reserve System in the first half of 1928 to tighten credit, and in the diversion of money from business and household spending to stock-market speculation. The last two factors work together to tighten credit conditions in the industrial and commercial sectors.

An *a priori* objection to the view that the stock market absorbs credit is that for each individual or company that buys a security and uses money for the purpose, there is another who sells it and acquires money. The stock market therefore leaves the volume of money unchanged. Like so many *a priori* arguments, this is irrefutable on its own terms, but of doubtful empirical relevance. If the money supply is divided between the financial circulation on the one hand and the transaction circulation on the other (to use an expression of Keynes denoting money used for expenditure against goods and services), a stock-market boom can draw funds from the transactions to the financial circulation. New security issues, of course, produce a movement in the opposite direction. Intense interest in the stock market, however, is likely to enlarge the amount of funds held ready for opportunities to speculate, and to shrink those which normally turn over in the production, distribution and consumption of goods. The boom may not reduce the supply of money in general, and hence escape

19. This discussion has benefited from attendance at a seminar by George D. Green: 'Speculation on Speculation: The Economic Impact of the Stock Market Boom and Crash of 1929', dinner meeting of the Friends of Economic and Business History, Harvard Faculty Club, 12 May 1970.

detection, but does it reduce that available to sustain income flows?[20]

The debate is generally put in the context of a closed economy. In an open economy, with financial connections with other markets there is little doubt that a stock-market boom can absorb funds from abroad. This may be positive, as when foreigners buy United States securities on balance: money is reduced abroad in the financial or transactions circulation, and increased in the United States in the financial circulation. The symmetry found in the *a priori* argument does not apply here. If the stock-market boom cuts off foreign lending, the analysis is slightly more complex. A foreign economy had presumably counted on a flow of monies from the U.S. financial circulation to the transaction circulation abroad. This is now stopped, so that there is a relative shrinkage of the foreign transactions circulation, with expansion of the United States financial circulation.

What applies to international transactions, moreover, equally fits interregional movements in the United States. A stock-market boom may, as the *a priori* reasoning insists, leave the total money supply unchanged, but divert funds from the country to the city.

While expectations, increases in wealth and easy credit in the boom stimulate spending and prosperity, the absorption of funds from abroad, from the country and from the transactions circulation locally applies contractive pressure to the system.

20. Temin, with many others, insists that financial investment in the stock market cannot absorb funds: '. . . What did the people who sold the American stocks do with the money they were paid? If they did not send it abroad, they must have spent it abroad or held it as idle balances. And if they did increase domestic spending or idle balances, it is on this that the explanation for the fall in capital exports should center, not the stock market' – *Economic History Review*, art. cit., p. 242. In the present analysis, increased stock-market speculation, and call-money lending to support it, increase idle balances, but the increase in idle balances is an induced phenomenon brought about by stock-market speculation, not an autonomous event.

The World Economic Conference of 1927

The 1920s saw both an increase in tariffs throughout the world and pressures, largely unsuccessful, to reduce them. The tariffs had been applied after the war to protect the new industries which had grown up when trade was cut off; or, for instance, to protect new countries carved out of the Austro-Hungarian Empire. International conferences at Brussels in 1920, Portorose in 1921 and Genoa in 1922 strongly recommended against the imposition of higher tariffs, but to little avail. There was no escape from the Fordney-McCumber tariff in the United States in 1922 or the McKenna duties in Britain of 1916, rationalized in the Safeguarding of Industries Act 1921. Tariff increases were particularly substantial in the outlying portions of the British Commonwealth, which at the Imperial Conferences of 1923 and 1926 urged Britain to consider preferential duties favouring dominion goods. The fall of the Baldwin government, which led to Britain's first Labour administration in December 1923, had been over an attempt by the Conservatives to abandon the tradition of free trade.

The League of Nations was disturbed by this upward trend in tariffs and undertook to hold a World Economic Conference in Geneva in 1927 so as to negotiate a tariff truce. The effort was largely a European one, and the issue was not critical. Foreign lending lubricated international trade more than tariffs restricted it. But tariffs were a potentially disturbing element in the system, and especially the prospect of abandonment of most-favoured-nation treatment and the spread of preferences. One achievement of the conference was a convention to abolish prohibitions of imports, but this was covered with reservations by one and another country and failed to secure enough ratifications to come into force. The other was a tariff truce, looking to ultimate reductions. This succeeded. In his presidential campaign in the summer of 1928, however, Herbert Hoover promised to raise tariffs in the United States to assist farmers struggling with falling prices. Following his inauguration in March 1929, he called a special session of the Congress to make good his promise. Hearings before the House Ways and Means Committee began in the last days of the Coolidge régime, starting on 7 January 1929. Notice of the hearings did not restrict the contemplated tariff increases to agricultural products. The process thus started was to result, fifteen months later, in the Smoot-Hawley Tariff Act, which became law in June 1930.

There was little force behind the 1927 movement to reduce tariffs. Britain was in two minds on the subject: Labour supported lower tariffs, but the Conservative government was tempted by Empire preference while the Liberals were ineffectual. Its high-tariff tradition left the Continent uninterested. Indeed, as wheat prices went off after 1926, Germany reimposed the duties she had been forbidden to levy prior to the Dawes Plan; Mussolini opened war in the Battle for Wheat in July 1925; and the French imposed tariffs and milling quotas, requiring large admixtures of domestic with imported wheat by millers. The subject of wheat arose in the World Economic Conference of 1927, but nothing was done about it. Not only was the United States not a member of the League of Nations; it was governed by Republicans with a high-tariff tradition. There was no leadership. There was no action.

The Young Plan

In June 1928, the Agent-General for Reparations, S. Parker Gilbert, suggested in his regular report that the time had come to replace the Dawes Plan with a settlement of the reparations question. No single reason underlay this proposal. Gilbert was worried that reparations had been paid largely by borrowing, though it is doubtful whether he foresaw any imminent decline in loans. Germany was discontented with an arrangement which imposed restrictions on her sovereignty, such as the occupation of the Rhineland and the surveillance of her budget by the Reparations Agency. There was still no total sum fixed. The French wanted the Dawes obligation to be commercialized. It was generally recognized that the annuity of 2,500 million gold marks was too onerous for the German economy, despite its recovery. A decision was reached in September 1928 to convoke a new committee of experts to meet in Paris in February 1929 and to prepare a 'final and definitive settlement' for recommendation to governments.

The neutral chairman was Owen D. Young from the United States, which took no part in the conference but kept in touch with Young and instructed him to keep war debts out of the discussion. In this he failed, and reparation payments were made subject to reduction by eight twelfths of any net relief on war debts obtained by the creditors. Schacht represented Germany. His negotiating offer on 16 April 1929 was regarded as an ultimatum. In it he seemed to demand the return of German colonies and the Polish Corridor – or, as he later claimed, merely stated that, without the colonies and the Corridor, Germany would be unable to pay reparations.[21]

The French were furious and the conference was in crisis. In subsequent accounts, Schacht accused the French of deliberately attacking the German currency by statements to the press and instructing French banks to withdraw their deposits from Germany, and he drew a sombre conclusion: 'This French attack . . . upon German currency . . . was the seed of that ever-growing lack of confidence which today [1931] hangs over the entire world'.[22] The statement that the French deliberately attacked the mark by withdrawals of French private funds is repeated in the Reichsbank *Annual Report* for 1929 and receives apparent confirmation by Pierre Quesnay from two disparate sources. The files of Owen D. Young record a remark of Quesnay to Fred Bate, Secretary to the Young Committee, on 18 April, that $200 million would be withdrawn from Germany by noon the next day.[23] Shepherd

21. See Hjalmar Schacht, *The End of Reparations*, Jonathan Cape, London: Jonathan Cape and Harrison Smith, New York, 1931, pp. 66, 73–5 and 139, Chapter 17 (pp. 231 ff.); and Hjalmar Schacht, *Confessions of 'The Old Wizard'*, Houghton Mifflin, Boston, 1956, p. 224 (see Bibliography for details of British publication). For Schacht's fixation on lost colonies, see also Hjalmar Schacht, *The Stabilization of the Mark*, Allen & Unwin, London, 1927, p. 245 and esp. p. 246, where he notes, 'Colonial activities have an educative and moral significance . . . a moral effort for any people. They imply self-training and discipline.' Ten years later, he was still harping on the same theme: see Hjalmar Schacht, 'Germany's Colonial Demands', *Foreign Affairs*, vol. xv, No. 2 (January 1937), pp. 223–34.

22. Schacht, *The End of Reparations*, p. 91.

23. Clarke, *Central Bank Cooperation*, p. 165.

Morgan, of the Reparations Agency Staff, another American, reports that when he asked Quesnay what the French withdrawals from Germany meant, he received the reply, '*C'est la guerre*.'[24] But the story is not wholly credible.

Simpson, who is very favourable towards Schacht in a recent biography, does not mention it, neither do other persons who were present, such as Leith-Ross.[25] *The Economist* notes the rumour of a 'deliberate attack', but states that it 'is doubted for there is no evidence of any large withdrawal of short-term money by either Paris or London banks'.[26] The figure alleged to have come from Quesnay is likewise unbelievable. The $200 million is roughly the total amount of gold lost by the Reichsbank from the beginning of the year to 23 April 1929: 745 million RM. It lost another 251 million RM, in the following week, which included the near-panic day of 26 April. But the French made no long-term loans to Germany.[27] The only figure for the short-term loans is 700 million RM for June 1931 – much later, and consistent with a short-term claim of $200 million in 1929. Schacht asserts that he stopped the withdrawal by threatening Parker Gilbert that if the French withdrew their balances, Germany would cease paying reparations, and that Gilbert succeeded in inducing the French to halt the action.[28] That there were withdrawals from Germany was clear, but this may have been as a result only of concern that the

24. Lüke, *Von der Stabilisierung zur Krise*, pp. 171–2.

25. Amos E. Simpson, *Hjalmar Schacht in Perspective*, Mouton, The Hague, 1969, Chapter II, 'The Young Plan and After', pp. 28 ff.; Sir Frederick Leith-Ross, *Money Talks, Fifty Years of International Finance*, Hutchinson, London, 1968, Chapter X, 'The General Strike and the Revision of Reparations', esp. p. 119. Leith-Ross mentions the 'tantrums and exhibitionism of Dr Schacht'. Another participant who makes no reference to the episode in his memoirs is Dr Paul Schmidt, later Hitler's interpreter, who was present as second German interpreter, ranked by a man from the Ministry of Finance. Schmidt claims that Moreau received exact instructions from Poincaré, and states that the only man who lost his temper ('*Choleriker*') was Émile Francqui, the Belgian delegate. See Paul Schmidt, *Statist auf diplomatischen Bühne, 1923–45*, Athenaeum-Verlag, Bonn, 1949, pp. 166–7.

26. *The Economist*, vol. CVIII, No. 4471 (4 May 1929), p. 966.

27. League of Nations, *Balance of Payments, 1930, Including an Analysis of Capital Movements in 1931*, Geneva, 1932, p. 92.

28. Schacht, *Confessions of 'The Old Wizard'*, p. 222.

Reparations Conference was breaking down. What actually happened is in some doubt. That central-bank cooperation between France and Germany had broken down is not.

The excitement subsided and the Reichsmark gained strength in the exchange market, though it did not recover its gold. Schacht signed the experts' report in June, though he confessed to some misgivings. If he signed because of German financial weakness, as is alleged, the French threat, if there were one, would have been successful in the short run, but at a cost to the system.[29]

The details of the settlement are of limited relevance to the depression. Politically, it differed sharply from the Dawes Plan in that it was not to be imposed on Germany but to be freely accepted by her. The Reparations Agency would be withdrawn from surveillance of German finances, French occupation troops from the Ruhr. In economic terms, compromise was reached between a German offer of 1,650 million gold marks a year for thirty-seven years and an Allied demand for 2,300 million gold marks for fifty-nine. It was agreed that the reparations would start at the lower figure and rise towards the higher. The annual payment was divided into an unconditional and a conditional amount, the latter of which could be postponed in the event of transfer difficulties. A bank was established to monitor the payments from the outside and assist in effecting transfer. A $300 million Young Plan loan, divided two thirds among the creditors and one third available to Germany, started the system off.

The Young Plan is possibly connected with a run on another currency, the pound. The experts' report was debated by the Allied Powers at a conference at The Hague in August 1929, and was finally agreed, in January 1930, at a second Hague conference after expert committees had resolved some loose ends. It took effect from 7 April 1930. The central issue at the First Hague Conference had been the unwillingness of Philip Snowden, the Labour Chancellor of the Exchequer, to accept the experts' recommendation on the division of reparations. The British policy of collecting in reparations and war debts what it paid out in war-debt service had not been fully carried out; striking an attitude

29. Edward W. Bennett, *Germany and the Diplomacy of the Financial Crisis, 1931,* Harvard University Press, 1962, p. 7.

he thought would be popular in Britain, Snowden insisted upon a new division which would raise the British share. The Prime Minister, Ramsay MacDonald, and the Foreign Office thought it absurd to raise an international conflict and threaten to break up the conference over 80 per cent of £2,500,000.[30] In the course of the debates, Snowden called an argument by Chéron, the French Minister of Finance, 'ridiculous and grotesque', an expression strong in English but still stronger in French.[31] This led to difficulty. Shortly thereafter, Quesnay, in the company of two other experts, Pirelli from Italy and Francqui from Belgium, waited on Leith-Ross and stated that the French government viewed Snowden's attempt to change the division of the Young Plan as inadmissible. If he did not change his demand, he went on, the French government would convert its sterling into gold and transfer it to Paris. As he tells the story, Leith-Ross rang for a messenger and had the men shown out without a reply.[32] But there are those who think that the French with £240 million, as Leith-Ross put the figure, actually did withdraw some in gold in September. Most opinion holds that the serious British gold losses of August and that month, which amounted to $45 million, were the result of capital flows to New York after the Federal Reserve discount rate was finally raised. On the other showing, the words 'ridiculous and grotesque' led to French conversions in London and forced the Bank of England to put up its discount rate. This, rather than the failure of the Hatry companies, triggered off the rise in the Bank of England discount rate and the collapse of the New York Stock Market. But we are getting ahead of our story. We must now look away from Europe and the United States to world commodity markets.

30. P. J. Grigg, *Prejudice and Judgement*, Jonathan Cape, London, 1948, p. 228.

31. Schmidt, who was present at The Hague as a German interpreter, claims that '*ridicule et grotesque*' is an inexact translation of 'ridiculous and grotesque'. The latter expression could be used in the House of Commons; the former would not be accepted in the Chamber of Deputies. See Schmidt, *Statist auf diplomatischen Bühne, 1923–45*, p. 178.

32. Leith-Ross, *Money Talks*, p. 124.

4. The Agricultural Depression

An independent depression in agriculture?

After the New York stock-market crash in October 1929, the collapse in industrial production and the financial crisis of 1931 led to a deep depression in agriculture and more generally in industrial production. The loss of real income in agriculture was broadly as acute as in industry, although output was sustained and prices declined rather than the other way round. Before the crash, however, it is an open question whether an independent depression in agriculture helped to cause the stock-market crash, the decline in industrial output and the banking collapse. Observers such as Sir Arthur Salter have claimed that there was a business cycle, an agricultural depression and a financial crisis – largely independent of each other.[1] This follows the school which ascribed the Great Depression to a series of historical accidents. In his State of the Union message of 2 December 1930, President Hoover attributed the origin of the depression to some extent to factors within the borders of the United States, particularly speculation, but also pointed to other deep-seated causes, chiefly worldwide, especially overproduction in 'wheat, rubber, coffee, sugar, silver, zinc and to some extent cotton'.[2] Later he narrowed the blame to Europe, and overproduction by cartels artificially increasing prices: 'European statesmen did not have the courage

1. Sir Arthur Salter, *Recovery, the Second Effort*, Bell, London: Century, New York, 1932, pp. 32 and 37.
2. Department of State, *Foreign Relations of the United States, 1930*, vol. I, U.S. Government Printing Office, Washington, D.C., 1945, p. vii.

to meet these issues.'[3] But a usual view is that the depression started where it started: in speculation in the United States, as Europeans thought, or in structural changes arising from the First World War, as was widely believed, and that the depression in agriculture was a consequence not a cause.

The extent of the depression in agriculture before October 1929 raises awkward questions of timing. A loss of farm income worldwide may have occurred but without implications for industrial production or financial conditions, and have been on its way to being overcome when it encountered an industrial depression or a financial bind. Or, contrariwise, agriculture may seem to have been bearing up, with income and output sustained, but only by making commitments to fortune so as to render it extraordinarily vulnerable to a mild setback outside the sector. As in every aspect of the story of the depression, moreover, one must make clear why certain difficulties of, say, overproduction do not correct themselves through the pricing mechanism, rather than lead to cumulative reductions in prices, value of sales and income for primary producers.

In the account that follows, considerable importance is given to interconnections among the agricultural, industrial and financial sectors, both in originating and spreading the depression and in making it so difficult to overcome. In particular, it rejects the view of modern Keynesian thought that price changes of one set of producers are unimportant to macroeconomic behaviour since losses of this group are offset by gains to its customers. The conventional wisdom was, in this judgement, correct in the importance it attached to raising primary-product prices, though wrong in the way it went about it. The attempt by individual countries to raise agriculture prices by quotas and tariffs for imported goods, or subsidies and exchange depreciation for exports, could not help being mutually frustrating and making matters worse. Any good that might arise from the efforts of one country to cut back supply to the level of existing demand (at existing prices) was likely to be reaped by other producers. International agreement to raise prices in concert eluded success because of the difficulty,

3. *The Memoirs of Herbert Hoover*, vol. III: *The Great Depression, 1929–1941*, Macmillan Co., New York: Hollis & Carter, London, 1952, pp. 61–2.

without strong leadership (and sacrifices by the leader), to arrive at a workable solution which would not reward violators. It was to prove impossible to raise agricultural prices by themselves. The answer was to increase world spending to provide enough lubrication for the system and make resource reallocation possible.

Agriculture and the business cycle

Up to the business cycle of 1857, or perhaps 1866, the harvest was the measure of business conditions. A bumper crop lowered the price of bread, and hence industrial wages, and simultaneously provided an outlet for industrial produce by enlarging farm income. Crop failure, on the other hand, led to depression. Differences existed from situation to situation, depending upon particular conditions in land tenure and whether the economy was open for foreign trade. The system of land tenure affected the distribution of income between landlord and farmer, and hence the character of farm spending. More rather than less foreign trade dampened the movement of prices resulting from changes in yield, and hence stabilized wages but destabilized farm income.

Some time after the middle of the nineteenth century, however, business cycles appeared to exist largely independent of farm income, and to be related to financial conditions or the state of industrial inventories, expenditure for plant and equipment, or population movements. There was a tendency to forget agriculture altogether. When an economist laid stress on structural dislocation, as Ingvar Svennilson did, for example, it had to do with excessive investment or failure to readapt in industry.[4]

Outside Western Europe, however, agriculture was of importance. Farming accounted for a quarter of total employment in the United States in 1929, and farm exports for 28 per cent of farm income. Regions of recent settlement, including the Domin-

4. See his *Growth and Stagnation in the European Economy*, Economic Commission for Europe, United Nations, Geneva, 1954. Erik Lundberg, his fellow-countryman, dismisses structural factors in coal-mining, ship-building, and textiles after the First World War, on the ground that they existed again after the Second World War, but proved unimportant under the impact of sustained demand. See his *Instability and Economic Growth*, Yale University Press, New Haven, 1968, p. 33.

ions, Argentina and Uruguay, had higher percentages on both scores. Almost two fifths of world trade was in agricultural products, and another fifth in mineral raw materials.

The failure of the price system in farm products, moreover, is readily explained. In part, it resulted from the restoration of production in Europe under circumstances where production elsewhere had expanded to fill wartime gaps. In part it was the usual failure of the price system in products with a long period of gestation between new investment, in response to price increases, and ultimate output, as in tree crops.

Once overproduction gets under way, government policy in producing areas enters the picture. As prices slip, exports may be subsidized, or stockpiles accumulated, or, in a few cases, exports (and occasionally production) restricted. For agricultural production as a whole, Timoshenko suggests that stocks are a better index of oversupply than prices, because of government attempts to maintain price by purchases.[5] An index of world agricultural prices and stocks based on 1923–5 as 100, shows prices declining gradually from the end of 1925 to a level of about 70 from July to October 1929, while stockpiles increased by about 75 per cent. Thereafter, as finance for holding stocks became scarce, the pace of price declines increased, in December 1932 falling to 24·4 per cent of the base year, while stocks rose another 50 or so per cent to 260.[6] The annual price declines for 1930, 1931 and 1932 were 40, 28 and 12 per cent respectively.

Commodity problems

The leading agricultural commodities in 1929 world trade are set forth in Table 5, which covers all items of more than $250 million. The list is arbitrary, since the total array from which it is drawn separates some items, e.g. wheat and wheat flour, or corn and lard,

5. Vladimir P. Timoshenko, *World Agriculture and the Depression*, University of Michigan School of Business Administration, Ann Arbor, 1953 (Michigan Business Studies, vol. v, No. 5), p. 25.

6. ibid., Table 10, pp. 122–3. The indexes cover (with weights) cotton (9), wheat (6), sugar (6), rubber (3), silk (2), coffee (2) and tea (1). The figures for stocks exclude those on the farm, and in consequence represent an understatement.

or wool and wool, carded and combed, and combines others. It is evident at a glance that the commodity problems are by no means

Table 5.   Value of world agricultural exports, 1929, and percentage each is of total.

	Value (in millions of dollars)	Percent of total
Raw cotton and linters	1,400	11·3
Wheat	825	6·6
Sugar, including glucose	725	5·8
Wool	700	5·5
Coffee	575	4·5
Silk	550	4·4
Rubber	425	3·4
Butter	400	3·3
Rice	400	3·3
Tobacco, raw and waste	350	2·8
Corn	250	2·0
Enumerated items	6,600	49·9
TOTAL	12,500	100·0

SOURCE: Henry C. Taylor and Ann Dewess Taylor, *World Trade in Agricultural Products*, Macmillan Co., New York, 1943, Table 2, pp. 10–12.

all European. Of the enumerated list, only wheat, sugar, silk and butter are produced in any quantity in Europe.

Figure 2 shows world production prices and stocks for cotton, wheat, sugar, silk and rubber from the list in Table 5, plus tea and tin, and a general index of all commodities, taken from the League of Nations study of instability. Note that 1929 = 100, which means that the curves all intersect then without any implication that this is an equilibrium year. From the fact that stocks are rapidly rising, and prices rapidly falling, it will be evident that 1929 was not stable.

Figure 3 groups three commodities from Timoshenko for a shorter period, ending in 1932, and with a different base, 1923–5: coffee and wool, not covered in the League chart, and rubber, which is repeated to assist comparison.

87

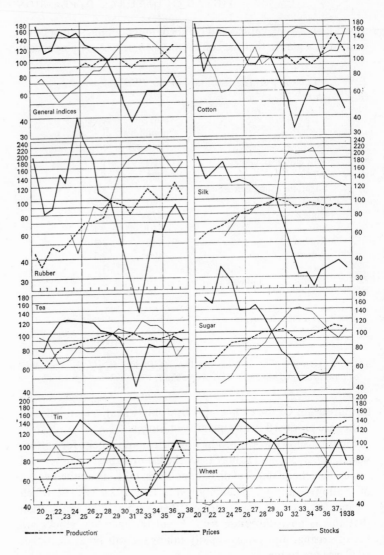

Figure 2. World production, prices and stocks of primary commodities, 1920–38 (1929 = 100).

SOURCE: League of Nations, *Economic Instability in the Postwar World*, Geneva, 1945, p. 85.

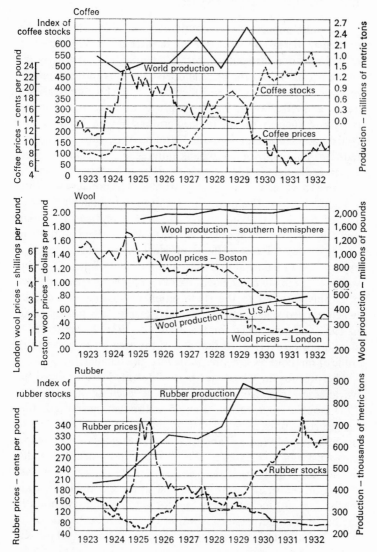

Figure 3. World production, prices and stocks of coffee, wool and rubber, 1923–32.

SOURCE: V. P. Timoshenko, *World Agriculture and the Depression*, School of Business Administration Studies, University of Michigan, Ann Arbor, vol. v, No. 5, 1953, pp. 20 and 21.

89

The most important commodity by value – cotton – shows no particular increase in stocks or fall in price until 1929. An attack of boll weevil in the south-eastern United States in the early part of the decade raised the price and gave impetus to the expansion of cotton production by new methods of machine cultivation in Texas and Oklahoma, and by more traditional means in new countries, such as Brazil, India, Peru and Egypt. Production in Alabama, Georgia and South Carolina was, however, greatly reduced. This contributed to bank failures in the Atlanta Federal Reserve district in 1929, prior to the stock-market crash, but cotton as a whole was not in great trouble. The pressure was local.

None the less, the position of cotton was important to the United States. Testifying to the House Committee on Banking and Currency in the spring of 1926, Governor Benjamin Strong of the Federal Reserve Bank of New York said: 'Our chief exports are agricultural products, and the chief of them is cotton, which goes mostly to England.' And then, in a remark which was ostensibly directed to the stabilization of sterling in 1925, but which carried overtones of Federal Reserve easy-money policy in 1927 and prescience for the events of 1931, he went on, 'It should not be overlooked that one of the greatest menaces to the trade of this country is depreciating foreign exchange.'[7]

The position in wheat was very different. Price declined and world stocks rose from 1925, with some levelling of stocks after 1929 though a precipitous fall in price. Production showed only a limited rise. Acreage outside Europe had expanded greatly during the First World War, as Table 6 shows. It was aided by immigration into Australia and Canada, and by the reduced need for fodder for horses. Within the United States total, moreover, there was a shift from the small farms of the east to the Great Plains, where mechanization, including tractors for seeding and combines for the harvest, could produce wheat at 60 cents a bushel as against $1 in the east.[8] In Europe, acreage came back, but not all the way.

7. Lester V. Chandler, *Benjamin Strong, Central Banker*, The Brookings Institution, Washington, D.C., 1958, p. 267.

8. J. A. Schumpeter, *Business Cycles, A Theoretical, Historical and Statistical Analysis of the Capitalistic Process*, McGraw-Hill, New York and London, 1939, p. 739.

*Table 6.   Wheat acreage, selected countries and world, 1909–14,
compared with 1924–9 (in millions of acres).*

	1909–14	1924–9
Overseas exporters	87·51	117·37
of which Argentina	16·05	19·94
Australia	7·60	11·97
Canada	9·95	22·57
United States	53·91	62·99
Europe	187·13	183·13
of which European exporters	95·31	89·42
ex-European exporters	37·27	41·70
European importers	50·48	47·39
ex-European importers	4·07	4·62
TOTAL	274·64	300·50

SOURCE: Wilfred Malenbaum, *The World Wheat Economy, 1885–1939*,
Harvard University Press, Cambridge, Mass., 1953, pp. 236–7.

In the United States and Canada, attempts were made to support the price of wheat on a national basis. The United States had the Federal Farm Board, which bought and stockpiled. The comparable organization in Canada was the Wheat Pool, operating out of Winnipeg. The McNary-Haugen Bill, which would have subsidized U.S. exports to maintain the domestic price, was vetoed. Australia and Argentina lacked the financial capacity to hold up the price for their farmers, and even if they had been able to borrow abroad could hardly have held wheat for long through the lack of storage facilities. They were thus obliged to export. As the Continental markets outside Britain closed down one by one, they sold where they could and drove prices downwards.

The capacity to finance wheat in storage was not an unmixed blessing. It lead to the temptation to speculate, which was not always rewarded. In the autumn of 1928, Canada already had a large amount of wheat in storage, but with a record crop and a world shortage of hard wheat, which usually commanded a premium over the ordinary wheats of other major exporters, it decided to hold back exports. This was expensive for the economy and for the balance of payments. It was necessary to dump some

91

securities in the New York market and to withdraw funds from the call-money market. In January 1929, the gold drain led to an informal embargo on gold exports, but short-term capital inflows prevented the Canadian dollar from depreciating. Also in January, the prospect of damage to winter wheat from storms in the Soviet Union and the United States led to more holding back of exports. But European buyers went on strike against the high premiums of hard over other wheats and switched sources of supply. Black Tuesday on the Winnipeg Wheat Exchange in early May drove the price down. Lower prices failed to repair the decline in exports. Compounding their mistake and relying on mediocre 1928–9 crops in Argentina and Australia, the Wheat Pool and private grade interests continued restraint in selling the 1929 wheat crop. This policy proved disastrous, leading to loss of wheat exports, weakness in the Canadian dollar, tight money and widespread losses. The shortage of hard wheat produced a spread of 42 per cent in July 1929, compared to a normal one of 10 cents on a bushel of wheat priced at $1·25. When Canada was forced to sell for lack of storage space towards the end of the year, however, the spread returned to normal in a matter of months.[9]

At this time, there was little to be said for the Australian response of a 'Grow More Wheat Campaign' undertaken after the collapse of prices of wheat and wool in mid. 1929. A Labour government headed by Scullin replaced the Nationalist–Country party coalition in the autumn of 1929 and raised wheat acreage by 22 per cent in 1930. With little or no capacity to store, it had to be exported and contributed further to the reduction of the world price.

Various attempts were made to tackle the wheat problem on an international basis, but with no results until much later. Wheat came in for discussion at the World Economic Conference in 1927, but no resolutions were reached. Following the precipitous fall in price in 1929, twenty international conferences seriously

9. See Edward Marcus, *Canada and the International Business Cycle, 1927–39*, Bookman Associates, New York, 1954, pp. 12, pp. 53–6; Vernon W. Malach, *International Cycles and Canada's Balance of Payments, 1921–33*, University of Toronto Press, Toronto, 1954, p. 29.

addressed themselves to the question between 1930 and 1933, two being devoted to imperial preference, seven being limited to the producers of Eastern Europe, and eleven being general. Only in 1933, and then aided by a drought in North America, did it prove possible to reach agreement in principle among the major overseas producers. This was embodied in the International Wheat Agreement, but it did not extend to detailed acreage reductions.[10]

A further element in the world wheat market was the Soviet Union. Grain exports had made up 36 per cent of Russian exports in 1913 and somewhat less in the middle 1920s. Soviet policy was directed at changing from grain to industrial exports. Difficulties in breaking into markets for finished goods and in obtaining credit for needed imports of capital equipment led to a decision in 1927 and 1928 to force wheat exports. The first year was hurt by poor crops; the second by difficulties in getting peasants to deliver their surpluses to the foreign-trade organization. In 1930, a bumper crop made it possible to expand exports from 100,000 metric tons in 1929 by twenty-three times to 2,290,000 tons in 1930. But prices were falling, and the value of exports increased only ten times from $15 million to $150 million. As prices continued to fall in 1931, compulsory and widespread collectivization was combined with rationing in cities and areas which normally had grain deficits. Exports doubled to 5,220,000 metric tons, but the value of exports failed to rise. Untold millions of peasants starved to death as exports were forced on the world in the face of surpluses elsewhere. Campaigns were launched against Soviet imports in many countries – the United States, Canada, France, Belgium, the Netherlands and Eastern Europe – but not in Germany or the United Kingdom. The Soviet Union has many times been accused of seeking to undermine the capitalistic system by dumping goods on it at low prices.[11] In this case, as in

10. Malenbaum, *The World Wheat Economy*, Chapter XI, 'Solution by International Agreement'.

11. In his State of the Union message of 2 December 1930, President Hoover blamed the 'methods' by which Russia sold her 'increasing agricultural exports to European markets' for contributing to the prolonging and deepening of the depression. But this was still 1930, and the worst was yet to come.

practically all others, the country was acting in what it regarded as its own best interests, but clumsily and at great sacrifice to its people.[12]

The pattern in sugar was broadly similar to that in wheat, though applying to a different set of countries. Rapid expansion after the war, especially in Cuba and Java, was followed by a comeback in European production. To the expected recovery of Continental Europe were added new policies in Britain: imperial preference for cane beginning in 1919 and subsidy to domestic beet-sugar producers after 1 October 1924. So rapid was the European recovery, that by the mid 1920s Czechoslovakia was unable to find markets for her traditional exports.[13] Hardest hit in the depression was Java. During the 1920s, it had benefited from the development by Dutch agronomists of new seeds which increased production. But it lacked a sheltered market. Protection cut off its market in India, where a white-sugar process, which did not use bone char and was therefore not offensive to Hindu sensitivities, was put into production in 1930. This forced Javanese exports down from three million tons in 1928–9 to one sixth of that amount three years later. The fall in prices produced trouble everywhere. Riots broke out in Cuba as early as 1928, not waiting for the actual depression, which was to stimulate fifty revolutions in Latin America.[14] Attempts at international agreement were undertaken consistently after 1927, but none was reached until the ('Chadbourne') International Sugar Agreement of May 1931, which halted the rise in stocks, and ultimately cut them back, but without stabilizing or raising the price.

Rubber and coffee follow a broadly similar pattern of rising stocks and falling prices starting before 1929, except for the addition of two factors: (a) very high prices early in the decade, which, because of the period of gestation, stimulated output with long

12. See Michael R. Dohan, 'Soviet Foreign Trade – the NEP Economic and Soviet Industrialization Strategy', doctoral dissertation, Massachusetts Institute of Technology, September 1969, esp. pp. 560 ff.

13. Vladimir P. Timoshenko and Boris C. Swerling, *The World's Sugar, Progress and Policy*, Stanford University Press, Stanford, 1957, p. 19.

14. Robert H. Ferrell, *American Diplomacy in the Great Depression: Hoover-Stimson Foreign Policy, 1929–1933*, Yale University Press, New Haven, 1957, p. 222.

delays, and (b) valorization schemes. That in coffee was formal. In rubber, the Stevenson Plan of 1923–4 in British Malaya and Ceylon raised the price of rubber to the highest level of the commodities charted, from which it fell to the lowest. The Netherlands East Indies, which did not restrict output, earned vast profits and expanded planting.

Rubber and coffee are alike in that new plantings take a long time to yield output, and this gives rise to a cobweb cycle, in which today's rise in price stays high for an extended period. This is moderated somewhat in rubber by native production, produced from existing trees, in which tapping varies with price. Bumper crops in coffee in 1927 and 1929 would have driven the price down much sooner, had it not been for the valorization programme. Undertaken by the Brazilian government in 1917 and 1921, it was partly responsible for the rapid extension of planting in the mid 1920s. In 1924 the federal government abandoned the attempt to maintain the price, but the provincial government of São Paulo took over. This managed to hold the price to September 1929, through one bumper crop when stocks climbed from three million bags to thirteen million, and a short crop when they fell to 10·3 million. The second bumper crop of 1929–30 added another ten million bags to stocks, financed with difficulty by a São Paulo loan in London of £100 million By the end of 1929, the price had fallen in half.

Wool showed the same pattern as wheat, with a few changes in the countries concerned. Sheep numbers grew everywhere during the 1920s, and the average fleece rose 16 per cent in weight in Australia, which had by far the largest flock. Prices declined gently after 1924–5, and then, after a sharp break in August 1929, much more precipitously. From the behaviour of an index of woollen-using industrial activity in six major countries, Ronald Walker argues that the fall in the wool price was the consequence not of expanded supply, nor of substitution for wool by other fibres, but primarily of demand for textiles as a whole. This is put forward only as a 'fair conclusion' as opposed to a self-evident one.[15] But it is notable that when Germany stopped borrowing,

15. E. Ronald Walker, *Australia in the World Depression*, P. S. King, London, 1933, p. 92.

the volume of its wool imports between 1928 and 1929 dropped 19 per cent.[16] Seventy-seven per cent of Australian production was exported, and accounted for more than 42 per cent of total exports and 14 per cent of national income. With the break in wool and wheat prices coming in August and June 1929, prior to the stock-market crash, Australia was well into the depression before most of the rest of the world.

One of the worst-hit commodities, though it is not included in the list, was lard. Corn is used to fatten hogs on the farm more than it is sold as feed, and hogs are slaughtered for pork and lard. Denmark, Canada and New Zealand slaughter their pigs at an early age and at a light weight to obtain lean bacon. American farmers, with excellent land for growing corn, feed animals to much greater weights so as to produce fat pork and lard. The United States produced some 2,500 million pounds of lard in 1929, and exported one third of it. The two largest markets were Germany and Cuba, with 26 per cent and 10 per cent of exports respectively. Income in both was affected early in the depression: Germany by the halt in foreign lending, Cuba by the decline in the price of sugar. American farmers believed that the decline in the price of hogs was intimately bound up with the collapse of the United States export market for lard and pork (a much smaller proportion of total output). Tariff increases abroad were attributed in turn to retaliation against the Smoot-Hawley Tariff Act of June 1930, although balance-of-payments difficulties and the desire to protect their own farmers are sufficient explanation for the German and Cuban actions. After the droughts of 1934 and 1936, the United States found it necessary to import corn from Argentina, and the export market in lard was never regained. In the early days of the depression, however, the decline in the prices of corn, hogs and lard spread bank failures from the wheat country of the Minnesota, Kansas City and St Louis Federal Reserve districts to the Chicago district covering rural Iowa and Illinois.

16. ibid., p. 91. With 23 per cent of her wool exports, Germany was the leading Argentine market in 1929, even after the decline. See Carlos F. Díaz Alejandro, *Essays on the Economic History of the Argentine Republic*, Yale University Press, New Haven, 1970, p. 21.

Falling farm prices and tight money

Falling farm prices, the halt to foreign loans and protective tariffs all interacted. To begin with, farm debt was serious. Total farm mortgages in the United States had risen from $3,300 million in 1910 to $6,700 million in 1920 and $9,400 million in 1925. In some states as much as 85 per cent of farms were mortgaged. In Canada, in 1931, more than one third of wholly owned farms had mortgages averaging 40 per cent of their value. In Germany, landowners had paid off their debt in the inflation, but had contracted new ones, with the largest farms mortgaged for half their value.

What was true of the farm sector within industrial countries applied equally to agricultural countries. The gross debt service of six major agricultural exporters – Argentina, Australia, Canada, India, New Zealand and the Union of South Africa – rose from $725 million in 1923 to $900 million in 1928. Brazil and the Netherlands East Indies accounted for debt service of $300 million annually in 1928–9, and Poland, Romania, Hungary and Yugoslavia for $200 million more. For all twelve countries, the total of interest and principal due was $1,400 million with only small gross receipts, and $100 million for Canada, as an offset.[17] A halt in lending to Germany cut down the market for their primary products. A halt in lending to the countries themselves put them under pressure which led to drawing on overseas balances, sales of gold and, in a number of cases, to exchange depreciation pushing the burden of adjustment on to other countries. When the international economy works well, declines in exports are matched by increased borrowing. When borrowing halts at the same time that exports fall, adjustment in national economies labours under a double handicap.

The position can be illustrated with the well-documented case of Australia.[18] From 1923 to 1928, the external debt of Australia rose

17. Timoshenko, *World Agriculture and the Depression*, pp. 55–6.

18. In these paragraphs, I have benefited not only from E. Ronald Walker, *Australia in the World Depression*, and Sir Douglas Copland, *Australia in the World Crisis, 1929–1933*, Cambridge University Press, Cambridge: Macmillan Co., New York, 1934, but also from two draft chapters of an Australian economic history, not completed, by Mrs Helen Hughes.

from £420 million to £570 million, or an average increase of £30 million annually. This was regarded by some as an 'orgy of foreign borrowing'. Others considered it as merely 'excessive'. Debt service rose from 16·2 per cent of exports to 19·2 per cent. Part of the difficulty lay in the method of borrowing. Commonwealth and Provincial governments would run overdrafts with London banks and pay them off by floating bond issues when either the sums became large enough to warrant it or the banks extending the overdrafts became restless. In 1927, a shortage of London funds led briefly to financial stringency in Australia, partly to be attributed to the rapid development at home of hire purchase. A British economic mission visited the dominion and attributed the difficulties to departures from traditional English *laissez faire*, and especially to government ownership of the railways and central bank, the arbitration system for setting wages, and the tariff, which had laid 'an excessive and possibly even a dangerous load upon the unsheltered primary industries'. Shortly thereafter the Australians appointed their own commission, headed by J. B. Brigden and including Copland and Giblin. This defended the tariff as enabling Australia to support a higher population than it could otherwise, but expressed concern over the rising burden of overseas debt, referring both to its amount and higher interest cost.

In 1929, the situation became more difficult. In January, a London loan was subscribed to the extent of only 16 per cent and had to be taken up by the underwriters. In April, the London market refused to issue a loan. London banks pressed for payments on overdrafts. Slowly and reluctantly the Australian banks were obliged to restrict advances, putting pressure on the local economy. By May unemployment was rising rapidly. By November, it affected 13 per cent of trade union members. (This was to rise to 30 per cent in the second quarter of 1932.) From £24 million in 1928, London funds of the Commonwealth Bank sank to £16 million by June 1929 and to under £8 million by September. The trading banks were asked to exchange their gold for notes in November; in December 1929 the exchange of gold against notes became compulsory for banks and public. Australian currency began to depreciate, a process euphemistically termed developing

98

a premium on sterling. The Commonwealth Bank rationed sterling to the trading banks, and the trading banks in turn rationed their customers. Outside the trading banks, a market developed in which sterling was traded at a premium. The premium started at 1 per cent in December 1929, went to 2 per cent in January 1930, and officially to $6\frac{1}{4}$ per cent (higher in many dealings) in March 1930. The rate further rose to a 9 per cent premium in November 1930, and then broke wide open. The Bank of New South Wales withdrew from the bank cartel in January 1931 to trade at the market. The premium rose to 18 per cent, then 25 per cent, and finally reached $30\frac{1}{4}$ per cent in March 1931, when it was frozen by the Commonwealth Bank. When the pound sterling went off gold in September 1931, however, the Australians held sterling at the $30\frac{1}{4}$ per cent premium (28 per cent depreciation of the Australian pound) to obtain the additional benefit of the decline in the pound. While Australian export prices in gold went to the 30 per cent range of 1928, and sterling prices to the 40s, prices in Australian currency were in the 50 per cent range, and sometimes the 60s, as Figure 4 shows.

There was almost no support for exchange depreciation. Bankers felt that sterling exchange parity 'had almost a mystical force'. Scullin, the new Labour Prime Minister in Australia, sought help in London early in 1930, but received only a new British economic mission, headed by Sir Otto Niemeyer, which advised deflation and clinging to sterling parity. The Labour Treasurer, G. G. Theodore, was practically the only heretic who wanted a policy of expansionary central bank credit for government spending, with exchange depreciation to hold the balance of payments in check. A group of Australian economists, however, including Giblin, Dyason and Copland, in June 1930 drew up a programme for deflation and equal sacrifice. This provided for the exchange rate to find its own level, but largely as a substitute for tariffs, which distorted efficiency. This was ultimately accepted as government policy, and early in 1931 it resulted in a 10 per cent wage cut as a part of the equality of sacrifice.

The combination of reduced exports and the impossibility of borrowing led to losses of reserves and exchange depreciation, shifting the burden of adjustment to others. This was the case not

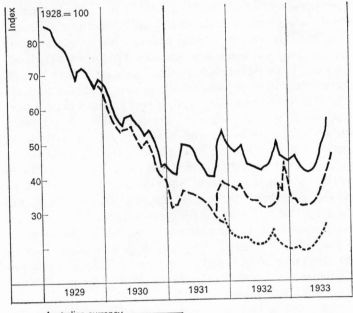

Figure 4. Australian export prices in Australian currency, sterling and gold, 1929–33 (1928 = 100).

SOURCE: Douglas Copland, *Australia in the World Crisis, 1929–1933*, Cambridge University Press, Cambridge: Macmillan Co., New York, 1934, p. 30.

only in Argentina and Australia, but also in the two countries closely associated with them – Uruguay and New Zealand respectively – and beyond these pairs, and prior to 1931, in Brazil, Bolivia, Venezuela and Spain. Canada, Chile and the Eastern European countries, not to mention the grain-producing areas of the United States and the Soviet Union, bore the strain without submitting to exchange depreciation. The first group shifted rather than avoided its losses, and the gold standard began its disintegration on the periphery of the world economy.[19]

19. William Adams Brown, Jr, *The International Gold Standard Reinterpreted, 1914–1934*, National Bureau of Economic Research, New York, 1940, vol. II, p. 902.

Gold losses

It is difficult in the statistics for this period to form a view of what happens to gold and foreign-exchange reserves together. The gold figures have been compiled by the Federal Reserve Board for year-ends to 1927, and monthly since 30 June 1928, when the Bank of France's new statement was issued. Data on gold holdings do not tell unambiguously what the state is of a country's balance of payments, since it may have been gaining or losing foreign exchange. Typically, however, a primary-producing country will allow its foreign-exchange holdings to rise and fall, calling on gold only when its foreign exchange is dangerously low. To the extent that this is the case, gold losses are a signal of considerable distress.

Latin America and the Far East lost gold throughout the whole depression, as the Federal Reserve Bulletin data on movements indicate. These are shown in Table 7.

Table 7. Gold movements of Latin America and the Far East, 1929–32 (in millions of dollars, net exports (−)).

	Latin America	Far East
1929	−178·5	−28
1930	−183	−12
1931	−190	−179
1932	−13	−28

SOURCE: *Federal Reserve Bulletin*, July 1931, p. 394, for original data, and subsequent issues.

It is notable, however, that the wheat countries lost gold well before those specializing in other commodities. The Australian example, not covered in the table, has already been cited. Canadian gold movements are affected by the complex financial relations between that country and the United States, and so perhaps do not signify. Its gold losses were heavy in the six months to June 1928, and again in the first nine months of 1929, before the stock-market crash. The substantial Latin American loss in the table is attributable almost entirely to Argentina. That country had gained

101

gold during the course of borrowing to June 1928, but lost it precipitously thereafter. During 1929, it lost a total of $173·3 million, 64 per cent of it before the crash, i.e. by the end of September. Hungary, the largest of the European wheat exporters, lost one fifth of its small gold stock – $7 million – again in 1929 before the crash. Australian gold losses were recorded in the last three months of the year; their independence of the stock-market crash is attested by the earlier decline in London funds of the Commonwealth bank referred to above.

Java, the sugar country, lost gold prior to September. (Cuba at that time had no central bank, and the U.S. dollar circulated in the country side by side with the peso.) The coffee countries held on to their gold until the first six months of 1930, and so did Japan with its silk.

Something of the same pattern may be detected in the redistribution of reserves among the several Federal Reserve districts within the United States, although the data are by no means unambiguous. Between the end of 1928 and the last week in September 1929, New York gained reserves together with a number of other districts, and the western agricultural districts – St Louis, Minneapolis and Dallas – all lost. After the effects of the crash had subsided, moreover, and pressure was again on the agricultural regions, New York once more gained, while the heavy losers percentagewise were Chicago, St Louis, Minneapolis, Dallas and, irrelevant for this view, Boston.

Like Australia, Argentina was finally unable to prevent exchange depreciation. The rate slipped slightly from 97 U.S. cents plus to the peso in the first half of 1928, to 95½ cents at the end of the year, where it held to November 1929; in December 1929, together with Uruguay, it abandoned the gold standard, the first of a long line of abandonments. The average exchange rate for the month came to 93 cents, then 85 cents by March 1930 and 75 cents by December 1930. Pressure on the price of corn in the United States was substantial through third markets in which the two countries competed for exports, even though the Smoot-Hawley tariff of 25 cents kept Argentine corn out of American markets.

Theory suggests that exchange depreciation raises the price of exports in local currency, or lowers the price in foreign currency, or a little of both. What happens depends on the elasticities. For a small country which has no impact on world prices, so that the demand for its products is infinitely elastic at the going price, the total impact will be felt in rising prices in local currency. For the major exporter of a commodity in inelastic demand, price abroad will fall. Typically, it makes a considerable difference whether the world is prosperous and able to take additional exports readily, or depressed, with any one price decline matched by others.

In the 1930s, the depreciation of the peso failed to raise prices in Argentina but depressed them in gold, i.e. in dollars and sterling. A 6 per cent depreciation of the Australian pound and a 20 per cent depreciation of the Argentine peso were not responsible for the total fall in the price of wheat by 50 per cent and more between December 1929 and a year later. The Australian pound especially can be exonerated, for it held steady at a 6 per cent premium on sterling from April 1930 to October while the price of Australian wheat in London was falling from 40s. a quarter to less than 30s. Moreover, in 1930, gold prices of other commodities fell as fast as or faster than the Australian-Argentine commodities of wheat, wool and hides. It is even possible that the strong correlation between depreciation of the peso and weakness of wheat prices in Winnipeg, Chicago and Liverpool runs from the price of wheat to the peso rather than the other way. And yet the depreciations created real difficulty. A detailed study of the relation suggested to Marcus that the causation ran from depreciation to decline in the world wheat price, rather than the other way round.[20] In 1930, the Argentine peso made the pace; from December 1930 to March 1931, when the price of wheat fell from 57 cents U.S. to 41 cents, it was the Australian pound.

Copland insists that Australia did not indulge in competitive currency depreciation, since gold export prices fell 50 per cent in 1930 when the depreciation was limited, and suggests that gold prices were being deflated independently. For 1931 and 1932, when Australian gold export prices fell another 35 per cent, he concedes that the case is more serious, but is unwilling to accept the con-

20. Marcus, *Canada and the International Business Cycle, 1927–39*, p. 91.

clusion that depreciation caused the decline in gold prices, which were, again, the result of international deflation.[21] But this is the essence. Begin with deflation, and then let one country depreciate – Argentina. This drives the deflation further. Then another – Australia: more international deflation. With inelastic demands, a small surplus added to currency depreciation by successive countries drives the deflationary pressure on.

Agricultural prices and the depression

There is no doubt that the primary-producing countries were having difficulties prior to October 1929, with falling prices, rising stocks, inability to sustain borrowing and the necessity to maintain debt service. For the world, however, the question is why these lower prices, for example, did not lead to higher real incomes in the industrial sector, and hence to more spending and prosperity; or why the halt in lending to this sector did not lead to more loans and higher investment in other areas. Many economists argue that deflation in one sector cannot spread because the losses of primary producers are offset by the gains of the rest of the world: '. . . as a matter of principle, an amount of purchasing power exactly equal to the loss in agricultural countries would be devoted by consumers in industrial countries to purchasing industrial goods previously exported to agricultural countries'.[22]

The question is in the same class as those which ask whether the stock-market boom can cut spending, or whether the effects of depreciation are not symmetrical, with deflation in the appreciating country matched by expansion in the country whose currency depreciates. The view taken here is that symmetry may obtain in the scholar's study, but that it is hard to find in the real world. The reason is partly money illusion, which hides the fact of the

21. Copland, *Australia in the World Crisis, 1929–33*, pp. 103 ff., and esp. 107. Díaz Alejandro, *Essays on the Economic History of the Argentine Republic*, p. 102n., states that Argentine policies – depreciation *cum* import duties – were 'to some extent of the beggar-thy-neighbour type'.

22. Hans Neisser, *Some International Aspects of the Business Cycle*, University of Pennsylvania Press, Philadelphia, 1936, p. 31.

gain in purchasing power from the consumer countries facing lower prices; and partly the dynamics of deflation, which produce an immediate response in the country of falling prices, and a slow one, often overtaken by spreading deflation, in the country with improved terms of trade, i.e. lower import prices. The consuming countries might ultimately have realized that their real incomes had increased and permitted them to expand spending. But the process is time-consuming. Meanwhile the primary producers cannot wait. They spring into action with tariffs, quotas and exchange depreciation.

Even the consuming countries do not find the improved terms of trade welcome in all respects. To defend the import-competing sector – typically the farmer, who in addition to serving as a romantic and idealized type often has political power – the consuming countries impose quotas and tariffs and resist cheap imports. Deflation gets the edge over expansion through increased real income owing to lower prices at a constant money income.

Exchange depreciation compounds the difficulty. In most cases it was an involuntary rather than a positive act of expansion. That fact did not make the world impact symmetrical. Some theorists claim that using depreciation to correct overvaluation is inflationary for the world, whereas depreciation which achieves undervaluation is deflationary.[23] The distinction is less interesting than differences in the setting, as between a world of inflation and a world poised on the edge of deflation. Under the latter condition, any exchange depreciation is deflationary. The pressure on agricultural prices weakens the position of banks and insurance companies loaded with mortgages. The deflation spreads.

Structural deflation

In the period following the Second World War, a model of structural inflation was developed to explain persistent inflation in less developed countries. Starting with a small excess of demand over productive capacity, a country can find itself on a course of con-

23. Milton Gilbert, *Currency Depreciation*, University of Pennsylvania Press, Philadelphia, 1939, p. 157; see also Gottfried Haberler, *Prosperity and Depression*, League of Nations, Geneva, 1937, p. 334.

tinuous inflation as the various sectors try to pass on to the others the burden of the shortfall. Workers raise wages, industrialists prices, farmers hold back supplies. Rising prices turn the balance of payments adverse, leading to exchange depreciation, a rise in the cost of living as foreign-goods prices mount, and a new attempt by workers to raise wages. Monetarists maintain that the process would be halted once monetary authorities refused to permit expansion of the money supply, so that, say, industrialists could not obtain the credit to pay higher wages, or consumers credit to pay higher industrial prices. The structuralist answer is that the alternative to a small credit expansion at each point where the issue arises is a large collapse, possibly economic, possibly political, and there is no firm ground which the monetary authorities can occupy to take their stand.

From 1925 to 1929, a process of what might by analogy be called structural deflation occurred in the world primary-product economy. Instead of excess demand, there was excess supply. A few countries tried to meet the situation by absorbing the excess supply in stockpiles. Without an adjustment in production, this only stored up trouble. Other countries, one by one, found it necessary to evade the consequences of the excess supply by keeping it out of the domestic market, or selling the crop for what it could bring, perhaps cushioning the consequences at home by depreciation, which forced prices down abroad. The excess supply imposed a kind of structural deflation on the system.

Deflation spreads from commodity to commodity, on the farm and from the farm to the city. T. W. Schultz was quoted in 1934 as stating:

> When foreign markets for cotton, wheat, lard and tobacco disappear, it is only a matter of time until the prices of butter, beef, mutton and eggs are dragged down. American farming is still dominated by the export group . . . Nor is the city outside of its influence . . . [24]

No mechanism is specified for the spread of deflation from export to domestic crops, though presumably what Schultz had in

24. *International Economic Relations*, Report of the Commission of Inquiry into National Policy in International Economic Relations, University of Minnesota Press, Minneapolis, 1934, p. 215 (quoted by C. E. Hearts, President, Iowa Farm Bureau Federation).

mind was supply shifts out of one line into the other. For the impact of farm depression on urban unemployment, Schultz set out the familiar purchasing-power argument, without specifying why the city did not gain from improvements in its terms of trade.

The monetarists will argue that this deflation is monetary in character, and that had the countries of the world prevented shrinkage in their money supplies, the deflationary spiral could have been halted. Albert Hahn wrote in 1931: 'Just as in inflation, it first seems that individual prices are going up, so in deflation one speaks of separate price declines of copper, rubber, agricultural products, automobiles, instead of a rise in the value of money'.[25] We may agree that this was so after the stock-market crash. The rise in agricultural stocks and the slippage of prices after 1925 make it clear, however, that there were structural factors at work. The abundance of credit up to the middle of 1928 helped to paper over the structural cracks while excluding the monetary explanation to that stage. The world might have evaded the consequences of raw-material overproduction had it escaped monetary deflation. Surpluses and deflation provided the fateful mixture.

25. Quoted by the author in L. Albert Hahn, *Fünfzig Jahre zwischen Inflation und Deflation*, J. C. B. Mohr (Paul Siebeck), Tübingen, 1963, p. 84.

5. The 1929 Stock-Market Crash

The market

To the extent that the depression was ushered in by the stock-market crash, it was that of New York. Canadian prices went higher from 1926, and declined further from their peaks. They were the tail of the dog. European security markets had for the most part turned down earlier: Germany as far back as 1927, the United Kingdom in mid 1928, France in February 1929. The Vienna stock market, which had led the parade in the crisis of 1873, was quiet, waiting for 1931. The action was in New York. It had its effect world-wide, but not through parallel movements in security prices.

At the time, the rise of the New York stock market seemed spectacular. The Dow-Jones industrial average went from a low of 191 in early 1928 to a high of 300 in December and a peak of 381 in September 1929, or double in two years. Two sharp setbacks occurred, in December 1928 and March 1929. In October 1929 these tended to lull speculators into thinking that the market was merely undergoing another adjustment. Daily turnover increased at the peaks from four million shares in March 1928 and 6·9 million in November 1928 to 8·2 million in March 1929. The average number of shares traded daily in 1929 was 4,277,000; with only 1,100 million shares listed, this was an annual turnover of 119 per cent for outstanding shares, as contrasted with 13 per cent in 1962.[1] Profits were substantial, and while price–earnings ratios rose from a conservative 10 or 12 to 20, and higher for the

1. Robert Sobel, *The Great Bull Market: Wall Street in the 1920s*, W. W. Norton, New York, 1968, p. 123. Sobel comments that turnover reached 160 per cent in 1907 and a record 319 per cent in 1901.

market's favourites, this was in anticipation of continued increases in earnings and dividends. The market has been described as an orgy of speculation, a mania, a bubble, and other terms denoting a loss of contact with reality. There was, to be sure, the normal quota of frauds, such as Insull; speculators in high places like Charles Mitchell and Albert Wiggins at the head of the two' largest New York banks, the National City and the Chase; foolish predictions of continued price increases, prosperity, new eras and the like, about which it is easy to be ironic. The fact is that the Dow-Jones industrial peak of 381 for 1929 is not out of line, after allowance for the change in the value of money, with the same index at close to 1,000 in 1968 and not much ahead of 750 in 1970. The danger posed by the market was not inherent in the level of prices and turnover so much as in the precarious credit mechanism which supported it, and the pressure which it exerted on credit throughout the United States and the world.

If, with the advantage of hindsight, the market no longer looks as if it was at dizzying heights, it seemed so to contemporary observers. Hoover had been warning against the use of credit in the market since 1925, although he was unable to persuade Calvin Coolidge to speak out against stock-market speculation. Coolidge in fact insisted in March 1929, as he left office, that United States prosperity was absolutely sound and that stocks were cheap at current prices. Hoover claimed that Adolph Miller, an idiosyncratic member of the Board of Governors of the Federal Reserve System, supported his views of the danger inherent in the market, and that the board took action when Hoover became President.[2] This is not entirely accurate. Governor Roy Young, Chairman of the Federal Reserve Board, spoke out against excessive speculation in February 1929, and stated that unless the banks curbed their brokers' loans, which were feeding the speculation, the Federal Reserve would take action. But in March the Board of Governors turned down a recommendation by George Harrison, President of the Federal Reserve Bank of New York (in Benjamin Strong's place after his death in October 1928), for an increase in the discount rate from 5 to 6 per cent. It was too

2. *The Memoirs of Herbert Hoover*, vol. III: *The Great Depression, 1929–1941*, Macmillan Co., New York: Hollis & Carter, London, 1952, p. 13.

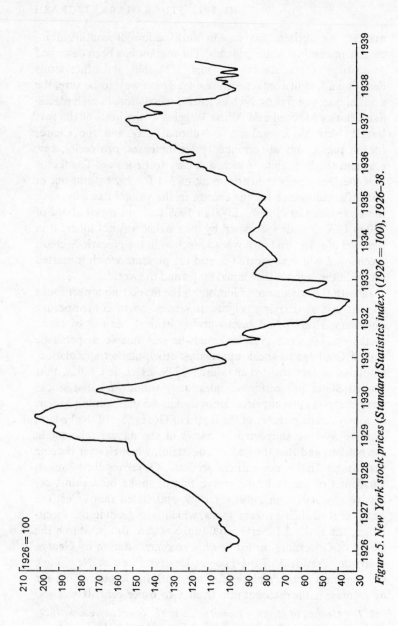

Figure 5. New York stock prices (Standard Statistics index) (1926 = 100), 1926–38.

	1926	1927	1928	1929	1930	1931	1932	1933	1934	1935	1936	1937	1938
Jan.	102	106	137	193	149	103	54	46	84	81	114	148	100
Feb.	102	108	135	192	156	110	53	43	88	80	120	154	99
Mar.	96	109	141	196	167	112	54	42	85	75	124	154	96
Apr.	93	110	150	193	171	100	42	49	88	79	124	144	86
May	93	113	155	193	160	81	38	65	80	86	118	138	86
Jun.	97	114	148	191	143	87	34	77	81	88	119	134	92
Jul.	100	117	148	203	140	90	36	84	80	92	128	142	106
Aug.	103	112	153	210	139	89	52	79	77	95	131	144	103
Sep.	104	129	162	216	139	76	56	81	76	98	133	124	104
Oct.	102	128	166	194	118	65	48	76	76	100	141	105	114
Nov.	103	131	179	145	109	68	45	77	80	110	146	96	114
Dec.	105	136	178	147	102	54	45	79	80	110	144	95	112

Source: League of Nations, *Statistical Yearbook*, to 1934, 1935-8, Standard Statistics (1934-6 index converted to 1926 base).

soon after the completion of the Treasury's financing at 4½ per cent. The New York bank was concerned that market rates had risen above the rediscount rate, and that the banks were only too comfortable with $1,000 million of borrowed Federal funds. On the other hand, it hesitated to raise interest rates for fear of the pressure this would place on the gold reserves of European central banks.

The agony of the dilemma is apparent in the exchange between Harrison in New York and his chairman of the board, Owen D. Young, at the Young Plan talks in Paris. Young insisted on the need for the Federal Reserve Bank to take prompt and effective control of the market, not only for prestige but also to curb the call-money rate, which dominated the world's monetary position and menaced the reserves of central banks recently returned to the gold standard.[3] In a separate telegram, he suggested that Harrison should go over the head of the board in Washington and take the case to President Hoover or to the Secretary of the Treasury, Andrew Mellon. In reply, C. M. Woolley, secretary of the New York bank, informed Young that the board had rejected a rate increase, that the bank would possibly tackle Hoover and Mellon, but that if this did not help, it might consider lowering the discount rate to repel foreign funds attracted to the call-money market.[4] The present position was exquisitely painful. A higher rate to break the stock market, or a lower rate to repulse the attraction of call money – one or the other might furnish relief.

Governor Roy Young was followed in public utterance to talk down the stock market by Paul M. Warburg, one of the fathers of the Federal Reserve System, and the leader of Kuhn, Loeb & Co. The signals reminded Warburg of the panic of 1907. Stock prices were too high, forced up by a colossal volume of loans and an orgy of speculation to a level unrelated to prospective increases in plant, property or earning power. The market paused, regrouped and moved higher. Bankers, barbers, bootblacks and professors talked the market up. The Federal Reserve Bank of New York was

3. Federal Reserve Bank of New York files, Owen D. Young (Paris) to Harrison, 12 March 1929.

4. ibid., C. M. Woolley to Young (Paris), 15 March 1929.

finally permitted to raise its discount rate to 6 per cent on 9 August. The market paid it no attention. On 1 September, the Stock Exchange added more seats, awarding a quarter seat to each member in its own stock split. The price of a seat hit an all-time high of $625,000, up more than four-fold over the $150,000 level of 1926. With the help of a sizeable expansion in brokers' loans at 10 per cent, the market inched up another notch. In Figure 5, the Standard Statistics index of industrial shares hit 216 for a monthly average at its peak above a base of 1926 as 100.

The credit squeeze

As the market rose, the pressure on the international financial system mounted. If the New York Federal Reserve Bank had not been allowed to raise the discount rate since July 1928, or to sell off its open-market portfolio, it could still apply pressure to commercial banks in the city to restrain their loans and those for their banking correspondents to the call-loan market after the end of the year, as Table 8 shows. Their place was taken by others.

Table 8.   Brokers' loans by source, 1927–9 (in millions of dollars).

Date	New York banks	Banks outside New York	Others	TOTAL
31 Dec. 1927	1,550	1,050	1,830	4,430
30 June 1928	1,080	960	2,860	4,900
31 Dec. 1928	1,640	915	3,885	6,440
30 June 1929	1,360	665	5,045	7,070
4 Oct. 1929	1,095	790	6,640	8,525
31 Dec. 1929	1,200	460	2,450	4,110

SOURCE: Federal Reserve System, *Banking and Monetary Statistics*, Washington, D.C., 1943, p. 494.

The vast bulk of brokers' loans by others came from United States firms. Some considerable amount came from abroad, together with foreign purchases of U.S. stocks. The data are inadequately detailed to trace the extent of the movement. Breakdowns are available only for year-ends which are not turning points, and then fail to give adequate coverage.[5] But there is universal agreement that the New York stock market, nervousness over the Young Plan in April and May 1929, plus French gold conversions, put great pressure on the system. How much was owing to each one of the three forces is impossible to say. Italy raised its discount rate first in January, Britain a full percentage point in February. Then Italy again and the Netherlands in March. Tension in Paris over the Young Plan in April and May led to discount rate increases in Central Europe, especially in Germany, Austria and Hungary. In July, the rate was increased at the National Bank of Belgium. The pressure from New York was persistent and continuous. In the first half of 1929, the United States gained $210 million in gold and France $182 million.

The pressure was particularly acute on London. With New York rates high, various borrowers – from Germany, Hungary, Denmark and Italy – were seeking sterling loans when they really wanted dollars.[6] Norman expressed concern about the scramble for gold. Bank of England reserves reached a high for the year of $791 million at the end of May, following the Young Plan crisis, but declined steadily thereafter, and precipitously in July. Norman raised with Harrison the possibility of long-term financing by European central banks in New York, either with the Federal Reserve system or in the market. Discussions were undertaken, carried some distance, but finally abandoned, apparently when the new Labour government in Britain decided to deal with the gold losses by raising the fiduciary issue and releasing gold behind the Bank of England's note liabilities.[7] Norman recorded in his diary that, 'Nearly half the time was taken up by bank rate and international interest rates.' The Labour Chancellor, Snowden, was opposed to an increase in the discount rate on the

5. Lary notes that foreign monies loaned to brokers via overseas banks through their American agencies are recorded as a deposit inflow and a brokers' loan of a New York bank – see Hal B. Lary, *The United States in the World Economy*, U.S. Government Printing Office, Washington, D.C., 1943, p. 114, n. 31. Three such agencies were responsible for $115 million of such loans at the end of 1928 and $53 million at the end of 1929.

6. Sir Henry Clay, *Lord Norman*, Macmillan, London, 1957, p. 251.

7. Stephen V. O. Clarke, *Central Bank Cooperation, 1924–31*, Federal Reserve Bank of New York, 1967, pp. 162–4.

ground that this would hurt business and not help the balance of payments, merely leading to still higher rates elsewhere. The Governor promised he would not raise bank rates for fun, but only if it were essential.[8] It proved to be.

On 9 August, the Federal Reserve Bank of New York moved again. The booming stock market called for higher interest rates; faint signs of weakness in the economy suggested the opposite course. In a telegram sent to the principal European central banks, President Harrison explained that the rediscount rate was being raised from 5 to 6 per cent, but that the bank hoped to buy bills later to ease the market, presumably after the stock-market rise had been halted. 'While our domestic situation calls for such a policy, we of course have in mind the need of the European economy also for lower interest rates in New York.'[9]

The New York stock market took no notice of the instruction. The pressure on London continued. Norman was looking for an excuse to raise the Bank of England rediscount rate. On 20 September, one day after a new high in the New York market – one which proved to be the interwar peak on the *New York Times* index – the occasion presented itself. The Hatry empire collapsed in London. This was a series of companies, investment trusts and operating units with interests in photographic supplies, cameras, slot machines and small-loan companies, controlled by one Clarence Hatry. Caught up in the speculative fever, Hatry was having difficulty borrowing £8 million to buy United Steel and use it as a base for a wider *coup* in British steel. He tried to use fraudulent collateral from his various companies, was caught out and went into bankruptcy. Stock-exchange dealings in the Hatry securities were suspended, and the financier and several of his associates arrested. In the unsettlement, the Bank of England rate was raised from 5½ to 6½ per cent on 26 September.

Apart from the Frankfurt Insurance Company in August, and unlike other crashes, it was the only warning.[10]

8. Clay, *Lord Norman*, pp. 297–8.

9. Federal Reserve Bank of New York files, Harrison cable to principal European central banks, 10 August 1929.

10. Alexander Dana Noyes, *The Market Place, Reminiscences of a Financial Editor*, Little Brown, Boston, 1938, p. 326.

The pressure spread to Scandinavia, and Sweden, Denmark and Norway put up their rates. By the end of September, the Bank of England gold stock was down to $640 million, a decline of almost 20 per cent in four months. On 5 August, Norman had told the Committee of the Treasury that unless there was a change, especially in France and the United States, some part of Europe, including the United Kingdom, might be forced off the gold standard.[11] In these circumstances the New York stock-market crash came as great relief, and Norman expressed surprise that they had not been forced off gold.[12]

Business decline

All this time, business was slipping. The National Bureau of Economic Research puts the reference-cycle peaks as April for Germany, June for the United States and July for Britain. Production in Belgium hit a peak in March and declined by 7 per cent to the end of the year. In Canada, various depressing influences took over after the spring of 1929 and produced a decline in business activity.[13] In South Africa the downturn came in the second quarter.[14] Everywhere except France money was tight, consumption had levelled off, new capacity was coming on the market for which there was no evident demand, inventories were piling up. Only in France was production rising.

Conditions were at their worst in Germany. There had been a lockout in the Rhenish-Westphalian steel industry in November and the early days of December 1928, which depressed output and the indexes. Next followed a period of intense cold from December to March 1929, with the average temperature in Berlin the lowest since the start of record-keeping early in the nineteenth century. Much tighter money, owing to the withdrawals of April-May, had eased somewhat with the return flow after the settlement of the Young Plan, but by the summer of 1929 the existence of

11. Clay, *Lord Norman*, p. 252.

12. ibid., p. 254.

13. Edward Marcus, *Canada and the International Business Cycle, 1927–39*, Bookman Associates, New York, 1954, p. 13.

14. J. C. DuPlessis, *Economic Fluctuations in South Africa, 1910–1949*, Bureau of Economic Research, Stellenbosch, n.d. (1950 or 1951), p. 50.

depression was unmistakable.[15] Inventories rose prior to the stock-market crash. Unemployment at 1·9 million persons was larger than the 1·6 million unemployed in the United States, although the population was, at sixty-four million, only half of the American 122 million.[16] The Frankfurt Insurance Company provided a spectacular failure in August. By the autumn, the numbers of business failures and protested bills were rising sharply.

The slowdowns in the United States have been ascribed to a variety of causes, which to some extent converge, but show wide variation in emphasis and some contradiction. The decline in housing was attributable partly to the reduced family formation, which in turn resulted from the stoppage of immigration in the early 1920s and a variety of cultural consequences of the war. In part, it was the result of a scarcity of financing. The over-expansion of fixed investment was a function of the stock-market boom, and of easy credit for business investment, or of the too high profits, relative to wages, which raised the demand for new plant. Under-consumption is the counterpart of over-investment, arising from diversion of income into the stock market or from a lag of wages behind profits. The result was a temporary exhaustion of investment opportunities, the piling up of inventories and uncertainty.

Business was in trouble long before the crash. In March, a Federal Reserve official noted that building contracts awarded were decreasing rapidly, 'always a precursor of a general decline'.[17] March was also the peak of automobile production, which fell from 622,000 in that month to 416,000 in September, at the height of the stock market. The industrial-production index fell after June, and the decline in industrial production, prices and personal income from August to October was at annual rates of 20, $7\frac{1}{2}$ and 5 per cent.[18] These last indications of malaise were not

15. Carl T. Schmidt, *German Business Cycles, 1924–1933*, National Bureau of Economic Research, New York, 1934, p. 50.

16. Karl E. Born, *Die deutsche Bankenkrise, 1931, Finanzen und Politik*, R. Piper, Munich, 1967, pp. 33 and 38.

17. Federal Reserve Bank of New York files, C. M. Woolley to Young (Paris), 15 March 1929.

18. Milton Friedman and Anna Jacobson Schwartz, *A Monetary History of the United States, 1867–1960*, Princeton University Press, Princeton, 1963, p. 306.

apparent before the market collapse. On this showing, the stock-market rise may have contributed to a weakening of the business position, but the crash was less a cause of the depression than a signal of the need to pause and regroup.[19]

The stock-market crash

September 1929 marked the peak of the market, on average, as well as for a day on 19 September (on the *New York Times* index). It started slipping on 3 October, declined throughout the week of 14 October, and gave way to panic on 'Black Thursday', 24 October. An attempt was made by the leading bankers to organize a pool to stop the collapse; Richard Whitney went from post to post on the floor of the exchange, placing bids for a syndicate. But the following week saw a further slipping on Monday and a new panic on Tuesday, 29 October, 'Black Tuesday', with 16,400,000 shares traded, a record that stood for almost forty years. Some recovery took place to the end of the month, and then lows for the year were reached on 13 November. The Dow-Jones industrial average had fallen to 198 from 381 on 3 September. It ended the year at 250.

Two weeks before the 23 October drop, brokers' loans for 'others' declined by $120 million, largely because of withdrawals by foreigners.[20] If this was the trigger, was it the last link in a chain which led from Snowden's characterization of Chéron's argument as 'grotesque and ridiculous' via Bank of France gold conversions and the Bank of England increase in the discount rate; or in a less political and more commercial linkage which ran from the August increase in the bank rate in New York, to pressure on London, which resulted in the Hatry bankruptcy, which raised interest rates there and drew funds back from New York? Whichever it was, once the panic had set in, 'others' contributed to it by withdrawing their brokers' loans. Some companies became worried that the fall in prices might lead to closing of the

19. Sir William Arthur Lewis, *Economic Survey, 1919–1939*, Allen & Unwin, London, 1949; Blakiston, Philadelphia, 1950, pp. 53–5.
20. Friedman and Schwartz, *A Monetary History of the United States, 1867–1960*, p. 305n.

Stock Exchange and freezing their assets which had earlier seemed so liquid.[21]

New York financiers tried to support stock-market prices, not only by direct purchase but by holding back on margin calls and taking over loans called by outsiders. In October alone, the New York banks took over $1,000 million of these loans.[22] In their efforts to stop the panic, New York banks were assisted by the Federal Reserve Bank of New York, which violated its standing orders from the Open-Market Committee, which limited operations to $25 million a week and bought $160 million worth of securities in the week ended 30 October, and $370 million in all to the end of November. These actions were later ratified by the Board of Governors, but Harrison's action in exceeding his authority was the basis for later recrimination and dispute between the New York and Washington authorities. Together with the open-market expansion, the rediscount rate was lowered to 5 per cent on 1 November and to $4\frac{1}{2}$ per cent on 15 November. Liquidation of foreign balances and loans in New York continued: $450 million was withdrawn from 31 October 1929 (after the crash, but the nearest reporting date) to the end of the first quarter of 1930, and another $100 million was bought from private hands by foreign central banks.[23] Half the withdrawals were for the account of the United Kingdom.

Did the stock-market crash produce effects of its own? On 29 October, Governors Hamlin and James of the Federal Reserve System feared it would bring on a real business depression, although the other members of the board did not think it would.[24] More than forty years later, the majority opinion receives strong analytical support:

The stock market crash in 1929 was a momentous event, but it did not produce the Great Depression and it was not a major factor in the Depression's severity. A sharp but not unprecedented contraction was converted into a catastrophe by bad monetary policy . . .

21. Noyes, *The Market Place*, p. 333.
22. Sobel, *The Great Bull Market*, p. 149.
23. Lary, *The United States in the World Economy*, pp. 117 and 119.
24. Elmus R. Wicker, *Federal Reserve Monetary Policy, 1917–1933*, Random House, New York, 1966, p. 147.

119

Whatever happens in a stock market, it cannot lead to a great depression unless it produces or is accompanied by a monetary collapse.[25]

Friedman does not have in mind Harrison's effort to soften the tension in the New York money market during the autumn of 1929. In his view, such discounting in a period of panic is unimportant. What is important is to maintain the money supply over time. This is an issue which must be postponed until later, however. There was no decline in the United States money supply until October or December 1930, during which time the depression may or may not have been great, but it was certainly deepening rapidly.

The first impact of the crash on the international monetary scene was to relieve it. The Bank of England lowered its discount rates three times between 29 October and the end of the year; the Netherlands and Norway twice; Austria, Belgium, Denmark, Germany, Hungary and Sweden once. An exception to this easing tendency was Canada, where the U.S. dollar went to a sharp premium. Margin calls from Canadian speculators in the New York market produced a higher demand for U.S. dollars than the supply emanating from money withdrawn from the brokers' loan market.[26] Considerable deflation was communicated to Canada and Belgium through the decline in the stock market, with some in other countries, as Figure 6 shows. The December average was down 33 per cent from the peak for the United States, Canada and Belgium, 16 per cent for Germany and Austria, but showed little or no change for the other European countries. Any immediate deflationary impact was felt through other means.

That a rising stock market can hurt business through tightening credit was suggested in Chapter 3, even though firms selling equities may raise capital more easily, and it should follow that a falling stock market can help it by financial ease. The effect through reducing the incentive to issue securities is likely to outweigh the gain through lower interest rates. But the economy does not always behave symmetrically, and a difference may be made if the stock-market decline takes place in a shorter compass than the

25. Milton Friedman in *Newsweek*, 25 May 1970, p. 78.

26. Marcus, *Canada and the International Business Cycle, 1927–39*, pp. 64 and 69.

rise. There may well be no aid for business in lower interest rates overtaken by faster and more powerful forces of deflation.

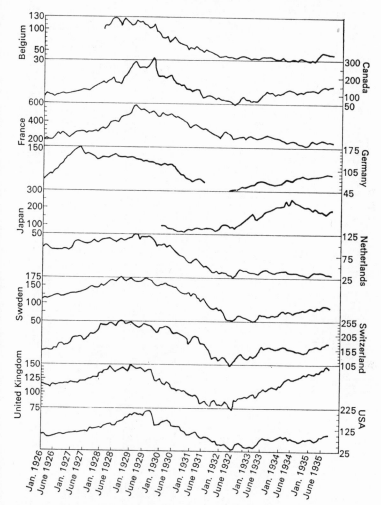

Figure 6. Share prices in selected markets, monthly, 1926–35.

SOURCE: League of Nations, *Statistical Yearbook*, various issues.

121

	Belgium	Canada	France	Germany	Japan	Nether-lands	Sweden	Switz-erland	United Kingdom	United States
Base	Jan. 1928 =100	1924 =100	1913 =100	1924–6 =100	Jan. 1930 =100	1921–5 =100	Dec. 31 1924 =100	nominal =100	1924 =100	1926 =100
1926										
Jan.		92	205	72		95	111	154	**116**	102
Feb.		99	210	79		97	113	158	114	102
Mar.		94	200	83		96	112	160	113	96
Apr.		93	200	92		93	114	158	111	93
May		91	205	91		91	117	158	113	93
Jun.		93	223	97		91	121	169	115	97
Jul.		96	259	106		91	124	169	113	100
Aug.		101	246	117		91	124	176	114	103
Sep.		106	263	120		91	122	177	116	104
Oct.		104	253	132		92	123	173	116	102
Nov.		106	234	140		92	124	175	117	103
Dec.		107	222	139		91	125	175	116	105
1927										
Jan.		109	244	158		94	127	185	120	106
Feb.		114	249	169		104	127	197	119	108
Mar.		117	270	163		105	127	198	119	109
Apr.		121	288	175		104	130	198	119	110
May		125	279	168		103	134	200	122	113
Jun.		122	269	152		102	136	190	122	114
Jul.		121	279	158		102	139	193	122	117
Aug.		131	275	155		103	146	198	124	112
Sep.		146	281	148		107	149	211	126	129
Oct.		155	283	143		112	146	210	131	128
Nov.		158	271	128		110	146	213	131	131
Dec.		162	305	136		109	146	223	131	136
1928										
Jan.	100	173	333	143		111	155	243	137	137
Feb.	110	168	320	138		115	150	242	136	135
Mar.	108	172	362	136		116	154	242	141	141
Apr.	121	177	408	143		118	158	247	143	150
May	127	184	413	147		117	163	249	148	155
Jun.	129	170	414	148		111	163	244	143	148
Jul.	121	170	396	144		109	161	240	139	148
Aug.	108	167	444	143		113	170	250	140	153
Sep.	126	185	458	143		115	176	256	143	162
Oct.	120	201	459	141		112	170	255	146	166
Nov.	115	229	476	140		113	168	251	143	179
Dec.	111	237	498	142		115	170	253	139	178
1929										
Jan.	112	286	579	139		120	172	254	149	193
Feb.	121	293	585	134		125	167	249	148	192
Mar.	118	266	564	133		125	165	239	143	196
Apr.	119	269	541	133		116	164	231	143	193
May	111	269	546	128		121	165	236	144	193
Jun.	109	264	524	131		121	169	246	141	191
Jul.	104	271	500	129		121	173	243	138	203
Aug.	107	294	506	127		122	171	242	142	210
Sep.	112	316	526	125		118	167	239	144	216
Oct.	98	255	496	116		113	162	221	135	194
Nov.	92	209	465	112		98	155	212	121	145
Dec.	79	210	469	107		100	154	215	121	147
1930										
Jan.	79	209	501	113	100	100	157	232	**124**	149
Feb.	80	206	487	113	99	101	157	233	119	156
Mar.	70	210	485	111	90	98	160	236	116	167
Apr.	77	221	495	114	79	100	155	234	120	171
May	80	196	474	114	79	94	153	223	119	160
Jun.	75	165	448	109	68	85	148	209	112	143
Jul.	70	162	454	102	65	82	147	211	112	140
Aug.	66	153	436	95	66	76	137	212	106	134
Sep.	64	160	428	93	60	75	134	209	110	139
Oct.	62	129	395	87	57	73	129	202	103	118

122

	Belgium	Canada	France	Germany	Japan	Nether-lands	Sweden	Switz-erland	United Kingdom	United States
	Jan. 1928	1924	1913	1924–6	Jan. 1930	1921–5	Dec. 31 1924	nominal	1924	1926
Base	=100	=100	=100	=100	=100	=100	=100	=100	=100	=100
Nov.	53	129	378	83	65	67	129	195	105	109
Dec.	57	120	349	78	69	60	132	178	99	102
1931										
Jan.	55	125	366	72	69	60	123	188	96	103
Feb.	61	129	369	77	74	67	130	204	94	110
Mar.	56	128	359	83	80	69	129	207	96	112
Apr.	53	107	343	84	79	64	120	200	94	100
May	46	89	318	74	77	56	110	180	80	89
Jun.	54	91	326	67	82	50	120	181	82	87
Jul.	49	95	309		86	51	108	169	86	90
Aug.	45	94	300		81	45	99	157	82	89
Sep.	40	79	264		78	37	85	123	78	76
Oct.	39	74	245		65	37	82	129	87	65
Nov.	35	87	239		68	39	86	132	92	68
Dec.	36	74	217		78	35	79	117	81	54
1932										
Jan.	38	74	253		97	37	83	124	82	54
Feb.	39	71	294		99	37	78	131	81	53
Mar.	37	72	272		97	36	56	129	86	54
Apr.	34	58	253	45	89	28	52	116	83	42
May	31	51	225	46	90	27	51	103	77	38
Jun.	32	49	229	46	86	25	51	106	73	34
Jul.	34	57	235	46	92	28	58	121	88	36
Aug.	41	70	243	49	96	35	66	131	86	52
Sep.	41	74	245	56	106	39	66	138	90	56
Oct.	38	63	231	54	109	37	63	131	90	48
Nov.	34	63	235	55	126	37	61	127	92	45
Dec.	37	58	247	59	157	35	57	126	91	45
1933										
Jan.	35	61	239	61	169	35	54	135	95	46
Feb.	33	58	229	61	152	33	50	129	96	43
Mar.	31	59	215	67	149	32	52	133	92	42
Apr.	34	70	218	71	157	31	59	140	93	49
May	37	89	238	72	160	35	66	155	96	65
Jun.	38	107	251	70	166	39	65	166	101	77
Jul.	38	122	253	69	174	40	65	158	108	84
Aug.	38	117	251	65	174	39	63	160	106	79
Sep.	35	119	241	61	193	36	64	160	110	81
Oct.	33	104	233	60	206	34	65	158	115	76
Nov.	33	113	225	62	211	34	64	156	114	77
Dec.	32	111	224	65	210	37	65	156	113	79
1934										
Jan.	37	119	212	68	215	39	72	160	118	84
Feb.	32	124	210	72	215	39	76	162	116	88
Mar.	30	129	194	75	237	39	71	162	122	85
Apr.	30	133	200	73	223	38	76	159	124	88
May	32	128	201	72	229	36	74	157	127	80
Jun.	32	126	194	75	253	34	71	157	124	81
Jul.	30	117	185	77	236	34	73	155	124	80
Aug.	34	120	179	79	232	33	74	153	125	77
Sep.	33	119	170	82	220	33	76	152	127	76
Oct.	31	122	164	81	214	32	82	148	128	76
Nov.	30	125	158	78	197	29	80	148	132	80
Dec.	29	126	163	78	202	28	83	152	131	80
1935										
Jan.	31	130	198	81	192	30	86	160	137	81
Feb.	29	129	188	83	186	34	84	160	133	80
Mar.	38	126	185	85	193	34	80	164	130	75
Apr.	44	131	190	87	178	34	83	167	138	79
May	48	144	215	88	178	34	86	160	137	86
Jun.	46	145	207	91	163	33	90	170	141	88
Jul.	44	144	188	92	162	32	90	171	141	92
Aug.	42	146	191	93	172	32	87	174	148	95
Sep.	43	147	185	90	187	30	85	172	141	98

123

The onset of the depression

The foreign capitalists and United States out-of-town banks and corporations who withdrew call money from the New York market caused large losses to individual investors. These cut their spending. Firms which had counted on ready access to the New York stock and bond markets joined in the race for liquidity, and cut their spending. Production fell sharply, and inventories were run off. The liquidity panic extended to mortgages, which were normally financed at that time in the United States on unamortized three-year obligations, so that a third came due annually. House-owners seldom had the cash to pay them off. Where a mortgage holder wanted the money and a house-owner had difficulty in getting a new loan elsewhere – which was the frequent case – foreclosure was undertaken. The price of housing and new building dropped sharply.[27]

The speed of the drop was impressive. Industrial production fell from 110 in October (on a seasonally adjusted basis) to 105 in November and 100 in December – the fastest drop in the index since 1920. Much of this was the result of the behaviour of automobiles, which fell from 440,000 units in August to 319,000 in October, 169,500 in November and 92,500 in December. Model changes came at the end of the year in the 1920s, but the low point was normally November, not December.

More impressive than industrial production was the decline in commodity prices and in imports. Hoover claims that the decline in farm prices did not come until January 1930, as a result of the support operations of the Farm Board.[28] It is true that the averages show a fall of only 3 to 5 cents on wheat from September to December, following a decline of 14 cents in the first half of November, and cotton only 5 per cent. But corn was off 14 cents from October to December, from 92 cents in September, and foreign products like coffee, cocoa, rubber, silk, hides and tin were badly hit. The worst was coffee, which fell from $23\frac{1}{2}$ cents

27. See William F. Butler, 'Is Another Great Depression Possible?', unpublished memorandum, Chase Manhattan Bank, 28 April 1969, p. 5.

28. *Memoirs of Herbert Hoover*, vol. III, p. 50.

on the average in September to 15½ cents in December under the combined impact of the large crop and the liquidity squeeze. The sluggish overall price index of the Bureau of Labour Statistics dropped from 140 in September to 135 in November and December, starting a decline which was to continue for three years.

What is surprising is the speed with which imports fell. The value of United States imports declined from $396 million in September – somewhat above the $360 million average of the three previous months – to $307 million in December – a decline of more than 20 per cent, or one sixth, depending upon which base is chosen. *A priori*, one would expect price declines and cancellations to be reflected in imports with a lag. Imports presumably are ordered, shipped and do not enter the statistics until they are received – a process of some months. In commodities such as cocoa, coffee, rubber, silk and tin, however, actively traded on the New York commodity market, commodities sent on consignment might be recorded in the trade returns at current prices. There may have been sizeable cancellations of import orders when the market fell. The decline in German imports, shown in Figure 7 with imports of the United States, did not take place until the first quarter of 1930. The result of the rapid decline in imports into the United States was an export surplus of more than $100 million each in the four months from October 1929 to January 1930 until the decline in exports caught up.

Deflation then moved from the decline in stock markets to production cuts and inventory runoffs in one sequence, and from stock prices to commodity prices to the reduced value of imports in another. Both were fast. The connection between the stock market and commodity markets was partly psychological and undoubtedly at the outset partly through the credit machinery as banks and firms struggled to become liquid. By the end of the year, credit markets were easing rapidly and this source of pressure was over. It was too late. The positive-feedback mechanism, cutting imports from less developed countries which cut imports from the developed, was well under way and gathering force. On the rise, the stock market cut off capital movements to the developing countries; in decline, it produced a liquidity crisis which led to rapid reduction in these countries' exports. The

125

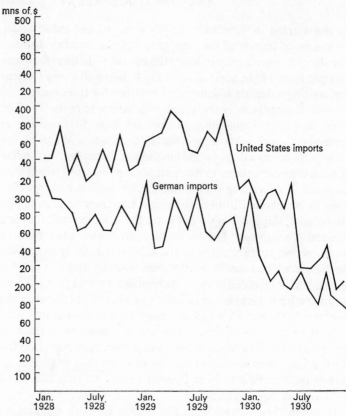

Figure 7. United States and German merchandise imports, monthly, 1928–30 (in millions of dollars).

SOURCE: League of Nations, *Statistical Yearbook*, various issues.

	United States			Germany		
	1928	1929	1930	1928	1929	1930
January	341	359	317	321	312	311
February	342	364	283	298	243	236
March	379	371	304	295	244	199
April	327	396	306	281	299	212
May	348	381	282	260	271	198
June	317	350	320	266	258	195
July	323	347	218	283	305	217
August	353	373	217	260	257	190
September	325	357	227	261	248	176
October	368	396	245	290	364	236
November	328	332	197	271	277	175
December	334	307	201	264	240	163

Source: League of Nations, *Monthly Bulletin of Statistics.*

126

process fed back to the United States. By the turn of the year, United States exports had turned sharply downward.

The other connections between the stock market and business conditions through credit availability for business, and wealth and income effects on owners of securities, doubtless came into operation in 1930. None of them can have had time to work in 1929, except perhaps in the anticipation of businessmen. Such of them that were expansive were overwhelmed by the cumulative forces of deflation already under way.

In the light of the sudden collapse of business, commodity prices and imports at the end of 1929, it is difficult to maintain that the stock market was a superficial phenomenon, a signal or a triggering, rather than part of the deflationary mechanism. One should not be dogmatic about it, but it is hard to avoid the conclusion that there is something to the conventional wisdom which characterized the crash as the start of a process. The crash led to a scramble for liquidity on the part of both lenders to the call market and of owners of stocks. In the process, orders were cancelled and loans called. The action of the Federal Reserve in buying securities in the open market and lowering the rediscount rate in New York brought credit markets quickly into good order. By this time, however, the deflation had been communicated to fragile commodity markets and durable-goods industries. The stock-market crash is less interesting for the irony it permits the historian, bemused by the foibles of greedy men, than for starting a process which took on a dynamic of its own.

6. The Slide to the Abyss

Revival in early 1930

The New York stock market levelled off in the first few months of 1930, as Figure 5 (pp. 110–11) indicates, and so did a variety of other indicators, including industrial production, imports and employment. Employment actually picked up from the December level. Prices continued to decline in a number of commodities – cocoa, coffee, rubber, hides, silks, copper, tin – during the first quarter, but less precipitously than in the closing three months of 1929. On 1 May President Hoover stated that the United States was not through its difficulties, but that he was convinced that the country had passed the worst. Correct on the first score, he could hardly have been more wrong on the second.

International lending revived, both for the less developed countries and for Europe, largely Germany. Total United States, British, Dutch and Swiss foreign issues amounted to $1,700 million for the year 1930 as a whole, compared with $1,300 million in 1929 and $2,100 million in 1928. The largest amount was issued in the second quarter, when loans totalled $727 million, compared to the record figure of $750 million in the second quarter of 1928.[1] Of this, $300 million represented the Young loan, issued in June; £100 million was borrowed by São Paulo in London to finance the coffee surplus, swollen by the 1929 bumper crop. In March, faced with budgetary difficulties over aid to agriculture and unemployment relief, the German government borrowed $125 million from Kreuger and Toll, the Swedish match monopoly, which the latter discounted with Lee, Higginson

1. Lionel Robbins, *The Great Depression*, Macmillan, London, 1934, p. 72.

128

& Co. in the United States. Other borrowers in New York were from Latin America, Australia and Japan; in Britain, from the Dominions. For a time, it looked as though the international capital market were functioning again after its diversion of a year and a half. It was needed. The halt during the stock-market boom had postponed many security offerings, some of which were still wanted, despite a lower level of capacity utilization. Writing in October 1929 of Germany's recovery, James W. Angell expected that a large part of the foreign issues held up by the Paris Conference (on the Young Plan in April–May 1929) would be offered in the United States in the autumn and winter of 1929. He went on to conclude that though it sometimes reflects weakness, borrowing in the case of Germany represented the building up of the country's strength from which were flowing rich returns.[2]

The Young loan provided a sharp contrast to the Dawes loan of 1924. Rather than being oversubscribed ten times and leading to a wave of foreign lending, the United States tranche, $100 million of the total, went to a discount shortly after issuance. Moreover, while the United States was reducing interest rates, capital was leaving for France. The French capital market showed interest in the capital issue for the Bank for International Settlements in May, and for the Young loan. Tranches of both were oversubscribed. The momentum could not be sustained. Mobilizing the Young monies strained the market, diverting it from foreign lending and attracting short-term funds to Paris from New York and London. At the end of July, Harrison of the New York bank cabled to Moreau that he was concerned about losses of gold to France, not for the United States, but in the broad aspects of the whole problem. In particular, he hoped for more foreign loans from France. The Bank of France replied through Moret, who was to be Moreau's successor upon the latter's resignation in September. Moret asserted that France did not want the gold inflow, which he believed to be largely seasonal. There were difficulties in the way of expanding foreign lending, especially the depression, which discouraged demand, and the

2. James W. Angell, *The Recovery of Germany*, Yale University Press (originally published October 1929), enlarged and revised edition, March 1932, p. 359.

need to dispose of certain prior issues, such as the failure of Vienna to settle her prewar debts.[3]

On one view of the depression, the continued revival of international long-term lending was vital. Those who blamed the depression on the preceding boom or inflation were typically not moved to make lending easy. They thought it necessary to put the system through the wringer, to liquidate the mistakes of the past and eliminate dead wood. Their ranks included such economists as Robbins and Hayek, and, in the United States government, the Secretary of the Treasury, Andrew Mellon. Opposing them were many differing schools of thought, ranging from monetarists, market stabilizers and interventionists to planners, all of whom thought it useful, however, to bolster rather than liquidate markets. The issue is fundamental. In a stabilized world, a recession in one part of the world economy is balanced by expanded lending by the depressed country. This finances balance-of-payments deficits of other countries, and enables investment to be maintained. Britain operated such a mechanism in the years before 1914; it was unable to do so after 1929. The United States cut its spending on the products of the rest of the world. But neither it nor France proved able or willing to maintain the system with loans.[4]

It is not entirely clear why this was so. The 1924 and 1927 mini-depressions in the United States had been cushioned by U.S. and British lending. A start was made in the first months of 1930. Neisser and Modigliani suggest that no other country than Britain had the apparatus to undertake compensatory lending. The explanation may fit France. In the United States, the market mechanism existed, though it may have suffered from the decline in foreign lending in the year-and-a-half layoff, and to some extent had been discredited by excesses. But the machinery started up well enough. Why did it come to a stop?

One reason was that potential borrowers had lost their credit-

3. Federal Reserve Bank of New York correspondence, Harrison cable to Moreau, 31 July 1930; Moret cable to Harrison, 2 August 1930.

4. Hans Neisser and Franco Modigliani, *National Incomes and International Trade, A Quantitative Analysis*, University of Illinois Press, Urbana, 1953, pp. 131–4.

worthiness. Default, currency depreciation, political *coups*, but especially falling prices made most countries unattractive risks for loans. There were no borrowers except governments in need of foreign exchange or seeking to fill budget deficits. Fleisig notes in a table that, while United States portfolio lending to the 'periphery' rose between 1929 and 1930 (from $71 million to $225 million for Latin America, and from $17 million to $77 million for Asia, Oceania and Africa), direct investment declined. In 1929, United States firms invested $205 million in businesses in Latin America, in 1930 only $41 million; the comparable figures for Asia, Oceania and Africa are $65 million and $14 million respectively.[5] In 1930, the London market was closed to issues for foreign governments. Sometime after March 1930, prices started down again. The timing differed from commodity to commodity, but there was by June no mistaking the direction and extent of the movement. Profit opportunities were shrinking rapidly. The depression had passed a point of no return from which it was impossible to recover by loans for ordinary business purposes.

Tariffs

The conference to settle the details of the tariff truce, proposed in 1929 as a holding action while the tariff reductions agreed in principle at the World Economic Conference of 1927 were worked out, finally convened in February 1930. The time was not propitious. The Smoot-Hawley Tariff Bill had passed the House of Representatives in May 1929 and was under intensive study in the Senate. Neither the United States nor the Dominions, which were planning tariff increases, attended the 'Preliminary Conference with a View to Concerted Economic Action'; of the twenty-seven countries which did attend, only eleven signed the final convention not to raise tariffs before April 1931. The limit for ratification, 1 November 1930, saw the list reduced to seven: Britain, the four Scandinavian countries, Belgium and Switzerland.

5. Heywood W. Fleisig, 'The United States and the World Periphery During the Early Years of the Great Depression', forthcoming in Herman van der Wee, ed., *The Great Depression Revisited*, Nyhoff, The Hague, 1972.

While other countries had raised tariffs before the Smoot-Hawley Bill became law, the course of the legislation through Congress had been followed with close attention, and the chances of a presidential veto carefully weighed. There were thirty-four or thirty-eight formal foreign governmental protests. Some of the retaliation is said by Jones to have anticipated the enactment of the legislation, but it is difficult to disengage reason from excuse.[6] France and Italy raised tariffs on motor-cars in March 1929. India put up its tariff on piece goods in February 1929. A new and general tariff increase took place in Australia in April 1930, on top of a series of special increases in November and December 1929. But the passage of the Smoot-Hawley tariff through the Senate in March 1930, its emergence from Committee in April, final passage, and signing into law on 17 June 1930 let loose a wave of retaliation. Jones discusses in detail the reactions of Spain, concerned about the tariffs on grapes, oranges, cork and onions, which passed the Wais tariff of 22 July 1930; of Switzerland, which objected to increased duties on watches, embroideries and shoes, and undertook a boycott of U.S. exports; of Canada, reacting to tariffs on many food products, logs and timber, which changed governments in August 1930 and then raised tariffs three times through the Ottawa Agreement of August 1932; and of Italy, which objected to tariffs on hats and bonnets of straw, wool-felt hats and olive oil, and took reprisals against United States (and French) automobiles on 30 June 1930. New tariffs were also enacted by Cuba, Mexico, France, Australia and New Zealand.

In his 1932 presidential election campaign, Roosevelt attacked the tariff as a cause of the depression in a speech at Sioux City, Iowa, on 29 September 1932, accusing the 'Grundy tariff', as he called it after the Senator from Pennsylvania who had played a leading role in its passage, of having forced other countries off gold by preventing them from paying their debts in goods. This was the standard accusation that the United States had failed to act like a creditor nation. Roosevelt went on to claim that when they ran out of gold, foreign countries sent more goods, which

6. Joseph M. Jones, Jr, *Tariff Retaliation, Repercussions of the Smoot-Hawley Bill*, University of Pennsylvania Press, Philadelphia, 1934, *passim*.

meant that tariffs had the effect of lowering prices, rather than the usual one of raising them. Hoover's reply to these charges was evasive. He accused the Democrats of threatening to lower tariffs and weaken the position of American agriculture. As he signed the Bill, he remarked that no tariff Act was perfect. In his *Memoirs*, he emphasizes that the tariff had nothing to do with the depression, having been enacted nine months after the stock-market crash – a thin argument in the light of the year and a half it had been in the process of passage.[7] In general, he dismisses the issue as unimportant.

The importance of the 1930 tariff to war debts and reparations is clearly overrated. Unlike the 1,028 American economists who urged President Hoover to veto the Bill, most economists are not disposed today to use balance-of-payments arguments for or against tariffs. While tariffs have macroeconomic effects on income and payments, which will cumulate if tariffs pile up through mutual retaliation, the main impact of a single tariff increase is felt in resource allocation and income distribution. Moreover, while the macroeconomic effect on trade abroad is adverse, it is offset to some degree by the favourable domestic macroeconomic effect on income. The decline in imports at the old level of income is partly undone by the increase in income from the spending diverted from abroad to home products. Lewis asserts that it was not a mistake to raise tariffs in 1930, though they should have been lowered in 1933.[8]

The failure was in leadership. Hoover can perhaps be forgiven for thinking of agricultural tariffs in the 1928 presidential campaign. Tariffs were, as Schumpeter put it, 'the household remedy' of the Republican party. The error was in treating it as a sovereign remedy, given to all who asked.[9] Democrats had to share the blame with Republicans, since the latter, together with the White

7. *The Memoirs of Herbert Hoover*, vol. III: *The Great Depression, 1929–1941*, Macmillan Co., New York: Hollis & Carter, London, 1952, p. 291.

8. Sir William Arthur Lewis, *Economic Survey, 1919–1939*, Allen & Unwin, London, 1949; Blakiston, Philadelphia, 1950, pp. 60–61.

9. E. E. Schattschneider, *Politics, Pressures and Tariffs: A Study of Free Private Enterprise in Pressure Politics as Shown by the 1929–30 Revision of the Tariff*, Prentice-Hall, New York, 1935, pp. 283–4.

House, lost control of the Bill. Schattschneider concludes his classic study of the passage of the legislation: 'To manage pressure is to govern; to let pressures run wild is to abdicate.'[10] Hoover and the United States abdicated. The signing of the Bill was 'a turning point in world history',[11] not for technical economic reasons, but because it made clear that in the world economy there was no one in charge.

If cultural identification of an economic instrument and a political party led to higher tariffs in the United States, it held them back in Britain. Unemployment had risen from 1,204,000 men in March 1929 to 1,700,000 a year later. The Labour government, which had taken office in July 1929, was committed to free trade. An economic advisory council, appointed by MacDonald in January 1930, set up a task force under Keynes's direction to provide a diagnosis of the underlying economic position and to recommend remedies. The secretary, Hubert Henderson, wrote progress reports on the depression and thought its cause was high interest rates, and that it could be cured by cheap money. Keynes and G. D. H. Cole, the intellectuals on the subcommittee, favoured stimulation of home investment, tariffs and controls on imports, and subsidies for exports, in contrast to the business view of their colleagues that the difficulties were the result of high taxation and wages, social services, trade union restriction and the prospect of more to follow under the Labour government.[12] The Conservative opposition greeted Keynes's espousal of tariffs, their pet remedy, with pleasure, but MacDonald, and Snowden in particular, were pleased with neither conclusion. When the House of Commons met in October 1930, the King's Speech put forth the grave concern of the government, but offered no programme. Labour backbenchers complained that it offered no Socialism;

10. ibid, p. 293.

11. Sir Arthur Salter, *Recovery, The Second Effort*, Bell, London: Century, New York, 1932, pp. 172–3.

12. Robert Skidelsky, *Politicians and the Slump, The Labour Government of 1929–1931*, Macmillan, London, 1967, pp. 141–5. Keynes's conversion to import tariffs and export subsidies did not, however, become known until an article of his was published in *The Nation and Athenaeum* on 7 March 1931; this is reprinted in J. M. Keynes, *Essays in Persuasion*, Macmillan, London, 1931; Harcourt Brace, New York, 1932, pp. 271–80.

the leading Liberal, Lloyd George, no public works; the Tories, no protection.[13]

At the Imperial Conference of October 1930, Bennett, the Canadian Prime Minister, whose country had enacted an emergency tariff against 125 classes of American products the month before, came down hard in favour of a Canada- and Empire-first policy. The British government was unwilling to cooperate. Together with the Dutch, the British proposed to the second International Conference with a View to Concerted Economic Action in November that other members of the conference should reduce their tariffs by 25 per cent, especially on textiles and iron and steel, as a *quid pro quo* for the British and the Dutch remaining committed to free trade. The answers received the following spring were noncommittal. British leadership in commercial policy was undermined intellectually at home and in practice in the Empire, and was ineffective in Europe.

When Great Britain ceased to provide world leadership in the field of trade restraints, it did so with a vengeance. When the Netherlands, Belgium and Luxemburg initialled an agreement at Ouchy for mutual tariff concessions of 5 per cent a year for ten years, in violation of their most-favoured-nation commitments, but to defend their exchange parities against the pressure exerted by external depreciation, the United States, a bitter opponent of trade discrimination, reserved its rights. Britain demanded reciprocity, even though her negotiators were on their way to Ottawa to work out the scheme for Empire preference. This torpedoed the Ouchy Convention.

U.S. monetary policy

In November 1929, President Hoover decided to lower taxes and to ask firms not to reduce wages but to maintain investment. Niveau comments, 'Keynes could not have done better.'[14] No element in the implied policies was developed far or for long. The

13. P. J. Grigg, *Prejudice and Judgement*, Jonathan Cape, London, 1948, pp. 243–5.

14. Maurice Niveau, *Histoire des faits économiques contemporains*, 2ᵉᵐᵉ édition, Presses Universitaires de France, Paris, 1969, p. 231.

major tool of anti-cyclical policy was cheap money. Elsewhere, and especially in Germany, the authorities embraced budget-balancing to maintain business confidence.

The New York rediscount rate, which had been reduced twice in November, was lowered four more times, in $\frac{1}{2}$ per cent steps, in February, March, May and June. This brought the rate on 20 June to $2\frac{1}{2}$ per cent compared with 6 per cent in August 1929. It was to fall to $1\frac{1}{2}$ per cent in May 1931. Bank indebtedness to the Federal Reserve System declined from $1,000 million in June 1929 to slightly under $200 million a year later as a consequence of the open-market operations following the crash, the return of currency from circulation and gold inflows from the Far East and Latin America, largely Brazil. The New York bank asked the board to reduce the rate from $3\frac{1}{2}$ to 3 per cent in April rather than in May. This was unanimously disapproved. In June, Harrison asked the Open-Market Committee to undertake more vigorous purchases of government securities. He was voted down by four to one. Later in the summer he was urged by other officials in the Federal Reserve Bank of New York to go back and push for more open-market operations. He was sceptical. On the whole, the Federal Reserve Bank of New York, and the board in Washington, expected to accomplish through rate reductions what should have been done by open-market operations.[15] In July 1930, Harrison, in a long letter favouring expansion, argued in terms of credit conditions and made no reference to the stock of money.[16]

Friedman and Schwartz argue that, between January and October 1930, the Federal Reserve System should have undertaken massive open-market operations.[17] This conclusion is based on an analysis which states that credit conditions are unimportant compared to the stock of money. The interest rate may be low in historic perspective, but high relative to investment opportunities, so that it fails to encourage loans. What counts is money supply.

15. Elmus R. Wicker, *Federal Reserve Monetary Policy, 1917–1933*, Random House, New York, 1966, pp. 150–53.

16. Milton Friedman and Anna Jacobson Schwartz, *A Monetary History of the United States, 1867–1960*, Princeton University Press, Princeton, 1963, p. 370.

17. ibid., p. 392.

But by this criterion and their interpretation of the statistics, there was no occasion for a different money policy until October 1930,[18] when, under the impact of bank failures, money started to decline in Missouri, Indiana, Illinois, Iowa, Arkansas and North Carolina, not to mention Kentucky and Tennessee. Money by any of the measures developed in their book did not decline significantly until March 1931.[19] By the first measure, the decline in money was from $26,300 million in March 1930 to $25,000 million in September, or 5 per cent, with no real change between September 1930 and March 1931. With hindsight, it is possible to argue that the purchase of $1,000 million in open-market operations in the spring of 1930 would have helped, and a monetarist would find some support for this position in the Friedman and Schwartz figures. But not much. The decline in velocity was 13 per cent between 1929 and 1930, contrasting with normal falls of 4 to 5 per cent in previous depressions. Commodity prices went inexorably down from about May 1930. Schumpeter put it that the first half of 1930 was satisfactory in the United States, but the second half altogether different: 'People felt the ground give way beneath their feet.'[20] There is no evident mechanism by which firms and financial intermediaries exchanging government bonds for money could have stopped it. There was no panic until the failure of the Bank

18. ibid., p. 309.

19. Friedman and Schwartz state that the stock of money started to decline in October 1930, after having gone sideways. This is difficult to accept on their own figures:

	Currency held by public and demand deposits	Currency and commercial bank deposits	Currency, commercial bank deposits, mutual and post savings deposits
	(in millions of dollars)		
August 1929	26,471	46,278	55,303
September 1930	25,042	45,080	54,502
March 1931	24,758	43,882	53,839
December 1931	21,894	37,339	47,913

SOURCE: ibid., basic tables, pp. 712–13.

20. Joseph A. Schumpeter, *Business Cycles, A Theoretical, Historical and Statistical Analysis of the Capitalistic Process*, McGraw-Hill, New York and London, 1939, vol. II, p. 911.

of the United States in December. Prices kept going down. The inefficacy of monetary policy at this stage – which is not to say that it was not badly handled later – is illustrated by the fact that yields on bonds which had been moving in concert went separate ways. That on government and corporate Aaa bonds declined; Baa bonds issued by firms of less certain financial standing went from under 6 to over 9 per cent.[21] It was not sufficient to make money abundant and cheap; one also had to improve credit-worthiness by reversing the outlook.

German political difficulties

When Germany restricted long-term borrowing abroad in the late 1920s, it failed to limit short-term. It is not clear why. Beyen suggests that the dangers were not faced inside Germany, even by Schacht, adding, 'It would not have been the first nor the last time . . . that consciousness was being "repressed".'[22] By the end of 1930, short-term credits to Germany had reached 14,500 million to 15,000 million RM, compared with 10,800 million RM of long-term loans.[23] The consequence was that Germany was sensitive to political developments, not only in the international situation, as recounted in connection with the Paris meeting on the Young Plan in April 1929, but to domestic events. It lacked only an Aftalion to develop a psychological theory of foreign exchange; the major difference with France in 1924 to 1926 was that Germany was subject to the outflow of foreign funds, France to domestic.[24]

21. Friedman and Schwartz, *A Monetary History of the United States, 1867–1960*, Chart 35, p. 454.

22. J. W. Beyen, *Money in a Maelstrom*, Macmillan Co., New York, 1949; Macmillan, London, 1951, p. 45.

23. Rudolf Stucken, *Deutsche Geld- und Kreditpolitik, 1914 bis 1963*, J. C. B. Mohr (Paul Siebeck), Tübingen, 1964, p. 71n. These figures are from an investigation of 1933 which produced a higher result for the end of July than the Layton-Wiggins figures usually cited, i.e. 13,100 million RM, instead of 8,000 million RM.

24. Dietmar Keese, 'Die volkswirtschaftlichen Gesamtgrössen für das Deutsche Reich in den Jahren 1925–36', in *Die Staats- und Wirtschaftskrise des Deutschen Reiches, 1929–1933*, Ernst Klett, Stuttgart, 1967, pp. 70 ff., argues from balance-of-payments data that the outflow of domestic capital

A crisis occurred in March 1930 because of unemployment. When provision for unemployment insurance had been made in 1927, it was contemplated that it might be necessary to support as many as 800,000 unemployed at one time. By early 1930, the numbers were 1·9 million. The Unemployment Insurance Fund, being in deficit, had to be made up by the German government, which thereby suffered a budget deficit. The Socialist party proposed raising contributions to the fund by a 4 per cent levy largely on government officials, whose contracts provided protection from unemployment. In the clash within the governmental coalition between the Socialists and the German People's party representing the government workers, Brüning sought to mediate. When the Müller government fell, Brüning took over in a new coalition which included no Socialists and proceeded to deflate. Deflation was called for by German obligations under the Young Plan, by the fear of inflation, which persisted from 1923, and by the notion that profits could be restored by pushing wages down as far as prices had fallen. The budget had to be balanced: old taxes were raised on incomes, turnover and beer, and new ones imposed on unmarried persons, warehouses and mineral water. Expenditures were reduced.[25]

The deflationary policy was followed for two fateful years, though its inadequacy should have been immediately clear. In March 1930, 537,000 fewer were employed than in March 1929, compared with a December-to-December difference, 1928 to 1929, of 176,000. With Brüning's taking of office, the number rose to 1,432,000 in April, and in August, after his first decrees, to two million. After Brüning's further deflationary steps of December 1930, the difference between March 1931 and March 1929 employment reached 2·8 million.[26]

---

was more important than foreign withdrawals. The case relies on associating the substantial 'Errors and Omissions' item with domestic capital flight, whereas Keese acknowledges that much of it reflects the failure of foreigners to renew trade credits.

25. These paragraphs rely heavily on Karl Erich Born, *Die deutsche Bankenkrise, 1931, Finanzen und Politik*, R. Piper, Munich, 1967.

26. Keese, in *Die Staats- und Wirtschaftskrise des Deutschen Reiches, 1929–1933*, p. 39.

One group in Germany did not share in the sacrifices: agriculture, especially the large-scale agriculture of eastern Germany. This class received protection, cheap credit and special consideration in the form of *Osthilfe*, help for the East. Under the Dawes Plan, certain taxes had been levied on German industry to pay reparations. When the Young Plan superseded the Dawes arrangements, the tax was not abandoned but diverted to *Osthilfe* as interest and tax reductions for 13,000 large landowners. In the depth of the depression, it amounted to 170 million RM. It was perhaps inconsequential in comparison with import restrictions, which raised German agricultural prices 2,000 million RM above the level of world prices in 1932. The incidence was clearer.

The process of raising revenue and cutting expenditure was political, and while Brüning governed by decree, under Article 48 of the Weimar Constitution he had to submit the programme to the Reichstag. On 18 June 1930 the Reichstag voted to abrogate his decrees. Brüning's reply was to dissolve the Reichstag and call for new elections on 14 September two years before they were required. It proved disastrous.

The September elections showed marked gains, from twelve to 107 seats for the National Socialists, but also gains on the opposite wing for the Communists from fifty-four to seventy-seven seats. Brüning's Centre party recorded a small advance, but the other members of the coalition lost heavily. The Socialists remained the largest party with 145 seats; the coalition had only 171. Two immediate consequences followed, both serious: first a withdrawal of foreign funds, and secondly a decision by Brüning, who chose to continue in office, to develop a more nationalistic policy as a means of governing.[27] This consisted primarily of opposition to reparations, but later came to include naval rearmament and a proposed Austro-German customs union. The attack on reparations was muted briefly during the loan negotiations. It was raised by Schacht, out of office, who undertook a tour of

27. Heinrich Brüning, *Memoiren, 1918–1934*, Deutsche Verlags-Anstalt, Stuttgart, 1970, p. 199, where veiled suggestions over the necessity for a revision of reparations calmed the cooperating parties and were clearly understood in the United States and the United Kingdom without arousing a negative reaction at the moment (October 1930).

the United States to speak against the Young Plan. But it aroused strenuous opposition in France, whose newspapers threatened withdrawal of French credits to Germany; and a milder reaction from Britain in the form of a note, dated 10 December 1930, which challenged Germany's interpretation of its obligations.[28] The withdrawal of foreign funds forced the Germans to organize a new credit of $125 million from a syndicate headed by Lee, Higginson & Co. This was completed on 11 October.

German commercial banks had about 18,000 million RM of deposits in June 1930, up from a monthly average of less than half that amount in 1926. By 1929, 38 per cent was of foreign origin. The ratio of own capital to deposits was 1:10 as opposed to the earlier level of 1:7 and British practice of 1:3. Liquidity ratios had fallen from a prewar level of 7·3 per cent to 3·8 per cent in 1929; secondary reserves had equally shrunk from 49 to 37 per cent.[29] Certain assets short-term in form were long-term in fact, whereas a considerable but unknown portion of the bankers' acceptances, ostensibly owed abroad on the basis of bills of lading for goods moving in international trade, were actually finance bills with nothing behind them but the credit of the drawing banks.[30]

Deposits in German commercial banks declined by 330 million RM in August, by 225 million in September and by 720 million in October, a total of 1,280 million RM. The Reichsbank lost 1,000 million RM in gold. The position was stabilized by the loan at the end of the year. It remained weak. Nor did the banks aid it by buying up their own shares, which were falling on the securities market. The banks were to be obliged to write off large security losses at the end of the year. Meanwhile the Darmstädter u. Nationalbank (Danatbank) bought up 28 million of its out-

28. Edward W. Bennett, *Germany and the Diplomacy of the Financial Crisis, 1931*, Harvard University Press, Cambridge, Mass., 1962, pp. 22 and 26.

29. Born, *Die deutsche Bankenkrise, 1931*, pp. 19–22.

30. Beyen, *Money in a Maelstrom*, p. 82. Beyen notes that one German company claimed that the foreign banks knew the collateral was non-existent. In a class in money and banking which I took at Columbia in 1933, Ralph W. Robey recounted the story of a New York banker adding up the amounts of a number of bills drawn upon his bank by a German correspondent, with the result that a series of odd sums added to a round amount in the millions.

standing 60 million RM of capital (to the summer of 1931); the Commerz u. Privatbank, 37 million out of 75 million RM, the Deutschebank u. Diskontogesellschaft, 35 million out of 285 million RM. This reduced their liquidity and lowered their capital to deposit ratios.[31] Money rates which had eased with the relaxation of credit in the United States in the first half of the year, tightened in the second. One-month money, for example, which had declined from 8·78 per cent in December 1929 to 4·43 per cent in August, was back to 7·24 per cent at the end of the year. The strain was mounting, politically, financially and economically.

Commodity prices

Lewis states that the failure of the recovery of the first half of 1930 to hold up was the result of the continued decline in commodity prices.[32] The point is at variance with Lewis's other remark about prices, which is that they do not matter because one sector's loss is another's gain.[33] Fleisig offers the suggestion that if the transfer is from poor to rich, total spending will contract as the gainers save a larger portion of the transfer than the losers dissave.[34] This is a small and academic point. The essential truth is found in the conventional wisdom that price declines are deflationary in so far as they 'check confidence, provoke bank failures, encourage hoarding and in various ways discourage investment'.[35]

Table 9 shows the pattern of price decline for a number of significant commodities by monthly averages for the end of each quarter from June 1929 to the end of 1930. There is no single profile, although in most cases the drop from September to December 1929 was sharp, together with that from March to June 1930 or June to September. Coffee, cotton, rubber and wheat fell more than 50 per cent between September 1929 and December 1930, with disastrous consequences for the exports, income and central-bank reserves of Brazil, Colombia, the Netherlands East

31. Born, *Die deutsche Bankenkrise, 1931*, pp. 60–61.
32. Lewis, *Economic Survey, 1919–1939*, p. 55.
33. ibid., p. 46.
34. Fleisig, doctoral dissertation, p. 35.
35. Lewis, *Economic Survey, 1919–1939*, p. 56.

Table 9. Prices of specified commodities (selected months, 1929–30).

	cocoa	coffee	copper	corn	cotton	hides	lead	rubber	silk	sugar	tin	wheat	wool	zinc
	¢ per lb	¢ per lb	£ per long ton	¢ per bu	¢ per lb	¢ per lb	¢ per lb	¢ per lb	$ per lb	¢ per lb	¢ per lb	$ per bu	¢ per lb	¢ per lb
1929														
June	10·51	23½	74·3		18·04	16·8	6·80	20·56	4·96	3·52	44·26	1·50		6·64
September	10·79	22¼	75·3	91·9	17·62	19·6	6·69	20·19	5·20	3·98	45·38	1·37		6·78
December	9·13	15¼	68·3	78·0	16·64	16·0	6·10	16·06	4·68	3·71	39·79	1·32		5·65
1930														
March	8·67	14	69·2	74·5	14·74	14·2	5·56	15·25	4·68	3·43	36·81	1·15	98	4·94
June	8·31	13⅜	50·0	79·0	13·21	15·2	5·31	12·38	3·56	3·28	30·30	1·05	92	4·45
September	6·26	12	46·3	91·7	10·15	14·6	5·35	8·19	2·93	3·14	29·64	·87	91	4·27
December	6·16	10½	46·8	64·9	9·16	10·7	4·95	8·94	2·69	3·29	25·27	·77	86	4·09

SOURCE: *Commodity Yearbook, 1939,* New York, 1939, for all but copper. For copper, see *Yearbook of the American Bureau of Metal Statistics.*

143

Indies, Argentina and Australia. While declines in copper and silk were not as dramatic, their impact on Chile and Japan was severe. Fleisig notes that where foreign investors contribute heavily to export production, as in Chilean copper, the local economy has the protection of the impact of the fall in price on foreign profits.[36] On this showing, the price declines in cocoa, coffee and silk were harder on peasant producers than those in copper, rubber and tin where much of the decline was deflected back to Europe and the United States through lower returns on investments. In Chile, this was small comfort as the country was simultaneously affected by a 70 per cent decline in exports of nitrate of soda, which made up 45 per cent of her exports in 1928–9, as a consequence of the depression and the development of synthetic nitrates in Germany.[37] The fall in raw silk was particularly painful for Japan, which had just returned the yen to parity in January 1930. Silk made up 36 per cent of exports in value in 1929 and contributed 19 per cent by value of total farm production. Two out of five families depended on it for cash income. The fall in value of silk exports from 781 million yen in 1929 to 417 million in 1930 led to gold losses of $135 million by November 1930.

The question remains why prices kept declining. Interest rates fell in the first half of 1930, but not fast enough to stimulate sufficient investment to enable primary producers to hold goods off the market. The weight of old inventories was heavy, and made the position altogether different from that of 1920–21, in which prices had been bid way up, and allowed to fall as expectations were belied, but without the burden of stocks accumulated over several years. Exchange depreciation in the first half of 1930 exerted deflationary pressure on world prices in coffee, hides, wheat and wool, and tariff increases and quota restrictions in copper, form, cotton, hides, lead, wheat and zinc forced an unchanged export supply on to a restricted world market.

New lending stopped because of falling prices, and prices kept falling because of no new lending. As the less-developed countries

36. Fleisig, doctoral dissertation, p. 42.

37. Stephen Triantis, *Cyclical Changes in Trade Balances of Countries Exporting Primary Products, 1927–33*, University of Toronto Press, Toronto, 1967, p. 32.

lost access to loans and spent their gold and foreign-exchange reserves, they were forced to sell old quantities of primary products for what the market would bring. Deflation spiralled.

But the process remains puzzling. Did the decline in lending emanate from the demand or the supply side? The rapid reduction in interest rates suggests the former, but the New York capital market may well have been rationed, as London was unwilling to lend at lower rates because of the dubious prospects for debt service in a world of falling prices. Would a more experienced capital market have carried through a sustained revival of lending in recession, whereas New York, having overdone it in one direction, overdid it in the other? The decline in prices and the halt of the precarious revival of long-term lending in the spring of 1930 are critical to the length and depth of the depression, as they led to the financial crisis of 1931. Their explication is still unclear, although they had nothing to do with the money supply.

7. 1931

Price declines continued into 1931 from the end of 1930. Some contribution to the trend came from the continued depreciation of the Argentine peso and the new break in the Australian and the New Zealand pounds. A determined optimist could find some hope for an upturn in prices. Norddeutsche Wollkämmerei, a German wool-combing undertaking known as Nordwolle, bought a year's supply of wool on funds borrowed from the Darmstädter und Nationalbank (the Danatbank) in early 1931, anticipating higher prices.[1] But deflation was widespread and spreading wider. As commodity prices fell, business profits declined, and with them security prices. As security and commodity prices fell, many bank loans became uncollectable. Pressure mounted against all banking systems, but in the beginning especially against those systems and banks which had overborrowed, overlent or lent to dubious risks. In Europe the number was legion.

The Banque Adam closed its doors in Paris in November 1930, and the Banque Oustric failed, unleashing a scandal which implicated three government officials and led to a new cabinet.[2] This had a brief life, but was followed in January 1931 by the Laval government, which was committed to deflation. The weight of foreign short-term indebtedness was heavy throughout Europe. In November, at the time of the first Paris bank troubles, market tightness drew French funds from London in such volume that gold could not be shipped fast enough to keep the exchange within

1. Karl Erich Born, *Die deutsche Bankenkrise, 1931, Finanzen und Politik*, R. Piper, Munich, 1967, p. 75.
2. Alfred Sauvy, *Histoire économique de la France entre les deux guerres, 1918–1931*, Fayard, Paris, 1965, pp. 413 ff.

the gold points.[3] The Bank of France came to the market's assistance, but Quesnay, now of the Bank for International Settlements, suggested that the British should float a loan in France to fund a portion of the French sterling holdings. Norman explored the matter with Moret in December 1930, but without success.[4] A month later, the President of the Reichsbank, Luther, wrote to the United States ambassador in Berlin to suggest the funding of perhaps $350 million to $475 million of American short-term claims on Germany. This proposal evoked no response in Washington.[5] Still another suggestion was the so-called Norman Plan, originated by Sir Robert Kindersley, that the Bank for International Settlements should create a subsidiary to raise money in Paris and New York, to be used to assist 'those borrowers whose relief and rehabilitation are an agreed object of policy'. It was envisaged that the body might have some £25 million to £50 million of capital, and perhaps £100 million of debt, which would be used, according to Skidelsky, to assist Germany and Eastern Europe, Australia and South America – Britain's traditional markets.[6] It aroused enthusiasm in neither France nor the United States. The French were willing to contemplate a long-term loan to Britain in French francs, though not an indirect one. If French funds were going to be lent, it would be the French who did it. The British were unwilling to borrow francs rather than sterling, although it is not entirely clear why the creditor should take any exchange risk. In New York, Jay Crane, in charge of foreign operations for the Federal Reserve Bank, wrote that international

3. The exact position of the gold points in 1930 was subject to change as the Bank of France refused to accept standard gold instead of fine gold. The gold points then depended upon the costs of refining and delays in getting standard gold refined when refinery capacity was fully utilized, or the possibility of exchanging standard gold for fine in a third country such as Germany, with its extra costs of transport. See Paul Einzig, *International Gold Movements*, 2nd edition, Macmillan, London, 1932, Chapter 12, and esp. pp. 101 ff. This point, among many others, has been brought to my attention by D. E. Moggridge.

4. Stephen V. O. Clarke, *Central Bank Co-operation, 1924–31*, Federal Reserve Bank of New York, New York, 1967, p. 178.

5. ibid., p. 177.

6. Robert Skidelsky, *Politicians and the Slump, The Labour Government of 1929–31*, Macmillan, London, 1967, pp. 285–6.

control raised serious difficulties and would not overcome the reluctance of New York to purchase foreign securities. J. P. Morgan & Co. cabled the Bank for International Settlements that, like the French, it was unwilling to surrender its judgement to an institution open to political influence.[7]

The Credit-Anstalt [7a]

Just as in July 1914, with the tension growing among Germany, France and Britain, the crack, when it came, appeared in Austria; in the early spring of 1931, a Dutch bank wrote a polite letter to the Credit-Anstalt in Vienna saying that it was obliged to raise the charge on its acceptance credits from $\frac{1}{4}$ per cent a month to $\frac{3}{8}$ per cent. It was a timorous letter, says Beyen, not a prescient one, and the bank was somewhat surprised when the Credit-Anstalt chose to pay off the loan rather than renew at the higher rate.[8] Three months later the Credit-Anstalt could have used the money.

The Austrian economy had been in disarray since the Treaty of St Germain of 1920. Its finances had required help from League of Nations loans, which entailed international supervision between 1922 and 1926. Austrian tradition involved close ties of industry with banks, which provided fixed as well as circulating capital, but the Austrian banks had lost their most profitable areas of operations in the Sudetenland and Trieste. Industrial capital was consumed in the postwar inflation, and numbers of industrial firms went into bankruptcy in the depression of 1924. In other instances, the banks had acquired industrial shares. There was no real recovery after 1924. Unemployment remained high in 1925 and 1926, decreased slightly in 1927 and 1928, only to rise again in 1929. For the period as a whole it averaged 10 to 15 per cent. The Austrian government had no economic policy.[9] Wages rose 24

7. Clarke, *Central Bank Co-operation, 1924–31*, p. 180.

7a. I have been unable to consult F. G. Pressburger's 'Die Krise der Österreichischer Creditanstalt' in *Revue Internationale d'Histoire de la Banque*, II (1969), which came late to my attention.

8. J. W. Beyen, *Money in a Maelstrom*, Macmillan Co., New York, 1949; Macmillan, London, 1951, p. 52.

9. K. W. Rothschild, *Austria's Economic Development between the Two Wars*, Muller, London, 1947, p. 47.

per cent from 1925 to 1929, contributing to the unemployment. The cost of social benefits rose from 258 million schillings annually to 383 million. This in turn led to high taxes.[10] The banking system, hurt by both the break-up of the Austro-Hungarian Empire and inflation, had adjusted haphazardly, placing heavy reliance on short-term credits from abroad. The Credit-Anstalt in particular was said to have been demoralized by the easy availability of credit from British and American lenders to its customers.[11]

Banking weakness showed up well before the fall of world prices. After 1924, one by one, small weak banks were taken over by larger, sometimes stronger banks. At the beginning of 1927, the Bodenkreditanstalt took over the Unionbank and the Verkehrbank. In 1929, the Bodenkreditanstalt was itself fused overnight with the Credit-Anstalt. The Bodenkreditanstalt brought to the Credit-Anstalt large loans to industrial concerns which could be maintained only by the device of ignoring market values. Like the German banks, the Bodenkreditanstalt had bought in its own shares to maintain their price and depositors' confidence. When the Credit-Anstalt took over the Bodenkreditanstalt, it acquired 80 million schillings of capital but 140 million of accumulated losses, as it learned later when a British chartered accountant revealed the truth. The government, the National Bank and the House of Rothschild, the last with help of the Amsterdam branch, furnished 100 million, 30 million and 22·5 million schillings, respectively. But the announcement of the support operation on 11 May 1931 started a run, partly foreign, partly Austrian.[12]

It is widely maintained that the Austrian Credit-Anstalt closed its doors as a consequence of French withdrawals of credits provoked by the proposed Austrian-German customs union. This proposal went back to a German working paper for the World Economic Conference of 1927. It had been discussed between

10. Vera Micheles Dean, 'Austria: The Paralysis of a Nation', *Foreign Policy Reports*, vol. VIII, No. 22 (4 January 1933), p. 259.

11. ibid., p. 259.

12. Walter Federn, 'Der Zusammenbruch der Österreichischen Kreditanstalt', *Archiv für Sozialwissenschaft und Sozialpolitik*, 67 Band, 4 Heft (June 1932), pp. 403–35.

Curtius, the German Foreign Minister, and Chancellor Schober of Austria at the first Hague conference on the Young Plan in August 1929, and again on the occasion of Schober's visit to Berlin in the following month.[13] Initially seen as a device to improve German-Austrian relations, it was taken up by Brüning as an item of positive foreign policy to divert the electorate from National Socialist gains in September 1930. Official German circles appeared to be painfully surprised that France objected to a customs union as being contrary to the Treaty of Versailles, which forbade only the much more far-reaching step of *Anschluss*. There is some doubt whether this surprise was genuine.[14] Whether Germany was naïve or disingenuous, however, the French foreign office objected, but French banks did not on instructions pull out French credits.[15] There were probably few such credits to begin with, and total foreign deposits declined only from 466 million schillings ($67 million) at the end of 1930 to 442 million ($63 million) at the end of April 1931.[16]

The run started as the news of the Credit-Anstalt's difficulties became known. The country needed foreign exchange to help with the run, and sought a loan of 150 million schillings ($21 million). It went to the League of Nations Financial Committee, which in turn referred it to the Bank for International Settlements (B.I.S.). Under the leadership of its president, Gates W. McGarrah, the B.I.S. arranged a loan of 100 million schillings ($14 million) from eleven countries. The process took from about 14 to 31 May. On 14 May, when McGarrah approached the Federal Reserve Bank of New York, he had already lined up the Reichsbank, the Bank of England and the National Bank of Belgium. Whether the further delay was the result of a French request for the renunciation of the Customs Union, as most

13. Julius Curtius, *Sechs Jahre Minister der Deutschen Republik*, Carl Winter Universitätsverlag, Heidelberg, 1948, pp. 118–19.

14. See Ambassador Sackett's dispatch to the Secretary of State of 24 March 1931: 'A portion of the German press evidently considers the agreement as a first step toward evading treaty rights' – Department of State, *Foreign Relations of the United States, 1931*, vol. I, U.S. Government Printing Office, Washington, D.C., 1946, p. 570.

15. Born, *Die deutsche Bankenkrise, 1931*, p. 56.

16. Federn, in *Archiv für Sozialwissenschaft und Sozialpolitik*, p. 421.

observers think, or merely the time required to arrange for a standstill among the Credit-Anstalt's creditors and to obtain the Austrian government's guarantee of Credit-Anstalt's borrowing, as Clarke asserts,[17] is not self-evident. The niggardliness of the sum and the delay together proved disastrous.

By 5 June, the credit was exhausted and the Austrian National Bank requested another. This was also arranged by the B.I.S., by 14 June this time, but subject to the condition that the Austrian government should obtain a two- to three-year loan abroad for 150 million schillings. At this point the French interposed the condition that the Austrian government should abandon the Zollunion with Germany. The Austrian government refused, and it fell. A new government took office. But meanwhile, on 16 June, Governor Norman of the Bank of England took on unilaterally a 50 million schilling ($7 million) credit to the Austrian National Bank for one week.[18] The gesture was a rebuke to the French for mixing politics and finance. It is widely thought to have deepened the Bank of France's antagonism towards Norman, and to have inspired the conversion of its sterling into gold. Regardless of the consequences in this direction, the vital point is that it marks the end of Britain as a lender of last resort: $7 million for one week! Shades of the advice of Walter Bagehot: 'In a crisis, discount and discount freely.' The loan was renewed each week through June and July until in August, the pound coming under pressure and the League of Nations arranging a 250 million schilling loan from seven governments, the Bank of England requested repayment.

The Hoover moratorium

During the course of his speaking tour of the United States denouncing reparations in October 1930, Schacht paid a visit to Mellon, the Secretary of the Treasury, who asked whether Germany could pay reparations better after a two- or three-year moratorium. The idea of a temporary postponement was widely

17. Clarke, *Central Bank Co-operation, 1924–31*, p. 189.
18. Born, *Die deutsche Bankenkrise, 1931*, p. 66, wrongly believes that Norman lent the whole 150 million schillings.

discussed at the time.[19] Hoover's proposal nine months later was not original.

At the end of May 1931, Austrian financial difficulties ramified widely and led to runs on the banks of Hungary, Czechoslovakia, Romania, Poland and Germany. Some wondered whether American creditors knew the difference between Austria and Germany.[20] But President Hoover was aware, and if his account is to be believed, prescient. Ambassador Sackett arrived from Berlin on 7 May with news from Brüning of a disastrously developing financial situation, with credits drying up, currency difficulties, pressures for repayment of debts, refusal to renew accounts. This was before the Credit-Anstalt. On 11 May, still before he had heard of the Credit-Anstalt difficulties, Hoover asked Stimson and Mellon for suggestions. They had none to offer. He called in the Federal Reserve Board. They thought he was seeing ghosts. On 5 June he suggested a moratorium to Mellon. The secretary objected that it was Europe's mess. The European press kept insisting that United States policies sucked up gold and undermined European financial systems. Hoover 'knew this to be untrue, and another example of Europe blaming the United States for its own failures'.[21] But he was prepared to concede, in a phrase he used twice in his *Memoirs*, that gold and short-term credit behaved like 'a loose cannon on the deck of the world in a tempest-tossed era'.[22]

The pressure on Germany began in May. Deposits at the banks fell in that month from 15,448 million RM to 15,070 million. The Reichsbank lost no gold, partly because of the placement of 120 million marks of the newly founded Berlin Power and Light Company with a foreign syndicate, the last commercial loan. The major difficulties were at the larger banks, with withdrawals in May of 97 million RM at the Danatbank, 70 million RM at the Dresdner, 59 million RM at the Deutsche. At the time of the Credit-Anstalt,

19. Edward W. Bennett, *Germany and the Diplomacy of the Financial Crisis*, Harvard University Press, Cambridge, Mass., 1962, p. 23.

20. ibid., p. 117, quoting the *Deutsche Allgemeine Zeitung* of 27 May and 10 June 1931.

21. *The Memoirs of Herbert Hoover*, vol. III: *The Great Depression, 1929–1941*, Macmillan Co., New York: Hollis & Carter, London, 1952, pp. 64–7.

22. ibid., p. 67; see also p. 189.

a commercial concern, the Karstadt company in warehousing, was reported to be in difficulty; at the end of May the Nordstern insurance company.

June was the difficult month. In the first six days, the Reichsbank lost 164 million RM in gold, and then matters worsened. The trouble was partly self-induced. The Brüning government on 5 June published a decree lowering the salaries of civil servants, decreasing unemployment assistance and levying a new crisis tax. To sugar the pill it remarked that Germany had reached the limit of its capacity to deal with reparations – a statement intended for internal consumption. Visiting London with Luther, the Governor of the Reichsbank, and Curtius, the Foreign Minister, in search of help, Brüning said that the German government had no intention of taking any steps on reparations before November 1931 at the earliest, provided foreign credits were not withdrawn. He spoke of the German need for new foreign loans. Norman stated that the real problem was presented by Austria and that Germany would get by.

Norman had not, however, taken into account the internal political position in Germany. On 10/11 June, the Socialist, Communist and Centre parties asked for a convening of the Reichstag to lift Brüning's power to govern by decree. This *Aufruf*, or summons, produced a heavy drain of funds. Within four days the Reichsbank had lost 400 million RM in gold. On 13 June it raised its discount rate from 5 to 7 per cent; this slowed down the movement. On 17 June, the withdrawal died away, having cost Germany 1,400 million RM in gold losses – more than half of its total at the end of May – and reduced its reserve ratio from 60 to 48 per cent. Then came the announcement of the failure of Nordwolle, the wool concern that had earlier in the year gambled on a rise in the price of wool. The company had borrowed heavily from the Danatbank, and sought to hide its losses by transferring its inventories, at cost, to its Dutch subsidiary, Ultramarine. The extent of the eventual losses was not known on 17 June when the company announced merely that it had a loss of 24 million RM covered by a reserve of 22·5 million.[23] The withdrawals picked up again, and the Reichsbank lost 90 million RM on 19 June.

23. Born, *Die deutsche Bankenkrise, 1931*, p. 75.

On 20 June, the picture was again reversed, but briefly. As early as 5 June President Hoover laid before Mellon, Mills and Stimson a 'bold, emphatic proposal' to assume leadership himself and to place a moratorium on all intergovernmental debts. The Treasury was apathetic. Mills said he needed the debt payment to balance the budget. Hoover went ahead. Adding Governor Eugene Meyer, Chairman of the Board of Governors of the Federal Reserve System, President Harrison of the New York Federal Reserve Bank and Dwight Morrow, the former Morgan partner and Ambassador to Mexico to his group, he got advice from 6 to 16 June. The group wanted a two-year moratorium, but chose one of one year in deference to the anticipated attitude of Senator Borah. Stimson states that Hoover was beset by fears and very difficult to work with. One of his fears was that the moratorium might connect war debts and reparations. Dwight Morrow strongly urged that France should be consulted beforehand, but the decision not to do so was taken so as to evoke the maximum shock effect. It was arranged that President Hindenburg would write to Hoover to ask for the moratorium. Ambassador Claudel was informed on 19 June. The moratorium was announced on the 20th.[24]

The Hoover moratorium was received in France as a bombshell. The response would have been even more bitter, Stimson believed, had it not been for the skill and force with which Laval managed the extremists. But the French refused a direct acceptance. They insisted on different treatment for the conditional and unconditional payments in the reparation schedules under the Young Plan, asking for discussions which would take 'a day or two'. Secretary Mellon was in Europe and visited Paris to negotiate the details. The talks stretched out and the favourable response in international financial markets flagged. On 25 June a credit of $100 million was arranged, with $25 million each from the Bank for International Settlements, the Bank of England, the Bank of France and the Federal Reserve Bank of New York until 16 July. It was not in time to help the Reichsbank statement of 23

24. See Elting E. Morison, *Turmoil and Tradition, a Study of the Life and Times of Henry L. Stimson*, Houghton Mifflin, Boston, 1960, pp. 347–50; and Henry L. Stimson and MacGeorge Bundy, *On Active Service in Peace and War*, Harper & Bros., New York, 1947, pp. 202–6.

June, which would have shown a reserve ratio below 40 per cent had it not been for an overnight deposit of $5 million from the Bank of England.[25] By 30 June, $70 million of the loan had been used up. By 5 July, it was gone. Hoover threatened to isolate France by dealing separately with each country over the moratorium. On 6 July the French agreed and the moratorium took effect.

The French had a real point. In urging the French to cooperate, the U.S. government had stated that the French stood to lose only $100 million in reparations from the moratorium, while the United States lost $250 million.[26] In reply, the French noted that one principle of reparations was that the unconditional annuities should be on a par with commercial obligations, whereas the moratorium made them inferior. The French had 52 per cent of reparation payments, which were lost, but only a miniscule proportion of the commercial debts, which were preserved.[27]

The run on Germany

Neither the credit nor French agreement to the moratorium was able to stop the run on Germany. The 30 June statements revealed how heavily foreigners had drawn down their claims on German banks. On 1 July, the extent of Nordwolle's losses were made known. On 5 July, a newspaper in Basle, the home of the Bank for International Settlements, reported that a German bank was in trouble. A few days later the Danatbank was named. The German banking crisis exploded. On 9 July, Luther left for a flying trip to London, Paris and Basle. The Bank of England was unable to

25. Clarke, *Central Bank Co-operation, 1924–31*, p. 193. Clarke notes that the Federal Reserve Bank of New York had been authorized by the board to lend $50 million to the Reichsbank. Luther had asked for much more, and when only $100 million was provided, asked for the announcement of the amount to be withheld so as not to reveal its inadequacy. Through inadvertence, however, the amount was made known. Foreign credit calls were resumed on 27 June. See Born, *Die deutsche Bankenkrise, 1931*, pp. 82–3.

26. Department of State, *Foreign Relations of the United States, 1931*, p. 46.

27. For a contemporary account, highly sympathetic to the French viewpoint but ignoring the wider impact, see H. F. Armstrong, 'France and the Hoover Plan', *Foreign Affairs,* vol. x, No. 1 (October 1931), pp. 23–33.

help; the French were prepared to do so, provided they received some indications of German intentions which inspired trust – specifically, the abandonment of the Austro-German customs union, cancellation of the Panzer cruiser under construction and the forbidding of military demonstrations, including those of the National Socialists. Brüning returned to Berlin for two days. On 13 July the banks closed briefly. When they reopened on 16 July, foreign credits were blocked and the discount rate was raised from 7 to 10 per cent. On 18 July all banks except the Danatbank joined in a *Haftungsgemeinschaft* ('Community of Liabilities') under the leadership of the Golddiskontobank, and a new acceptance and guaranty bank was started to provide a third name on paper so as to make it eligible to discount at the Reichsbank. This opened for business on 1 August with a discount rate of 15 per cent.

French and German opinion each agreed that the German banking crisis should be resolved by a fresh loan. On the terms of the loan, however, there was a wide difference. The French clung to the idea of a private loan, guaranteed by the governments of France, Britain and the United States, with political guarantees being given by Germany. The Germans were persuaded of the necessity for a guaranteed extension of the stabilization of existing short-term credits to the German economy, and in addition for a new loan, but one free of political conditions. The French had in mind $500 million; the Germans preferred to think in terms of $1,000 million.[28]

The Secretary of State, Henry L. Stimson, left Washington for a vacation in Europe on 27 June, and was visiting European capitals when he encountered the issue. He favoured the idea of

28. For an account of one rescue loan from the Warburg bank in New York to the Warburg bank in Hamburg, which cost Paul M. Warburg half his fortune, see James P. Warburg, *The Long Road Home*, *the Autobiography of a Maverick*, Doubleday, Garden City, New York, 1964, pp. 92 and 98. Warburg states that the New York banks accumulated a fund of 50 million RM to be used to shore up the weakest German bank, which proved to be the Danatbank, but that Brüning turned down the offer of this rescue loan, with tears in his eyes but without explanation. This was later revealed to have been because the Danatbank had a mysterious 10 million RM bad loan to President Hindenburg's son, Oskar, which the government did not want to come to light.

a new loan to Germany, and opposed political conditions. But he was unable to win Hoover's support. Hoover noted the U.S. prospective budget deficit of $1,600 million, and thought it preposterous to expect Congress to lend more money to Germany in such circumstances. Moreover, he thought a private loan was impossible. He recommended instead the stabilization of existing credits. In Britain, Arthur Henderson, the Foreign Minister in the Labour government, was attracted to the idea of a loan, but Governor Norman maintained that the Bank of England had 'already lent quite as much as is entirely convenient in Austria, Hungary and Germany to avoid financial collapse'.[29] He was also fearful that if Germany obtained a government guaranteed loan, these would be sought by Australia, India and many other countries.[30] A meeting of ministers was called on 20 July in London. During the course of it, the idea of a loan of new money gradually died as neither the British nor the Americans were willing to agree. The meeting produced an extension for three months of the $100 million central banks' loan of 25 June, and a standstill agreement on withdrawals of foreign credits. To ascertain what these amounted to, a special committee was appointed under Albert Wiggins to work with the Bank for International Settlements.

Stimson liked the 'excitement of the moratorium'[31] and thought the standstill agreement' the neatest and most successful [negotiation] of his career'.[32] In his view, the moratorium was 'one of the best things Mr Hoover ever did'.[33] It is difficult to approve the superlatives, unless Stimson is trying to say something about other negotiations and other things.

The attack shifts to sterling

In mid July sterling weakened. The usual explanation is that the publication of the Macmillan Report on 13 July worried sterling holders as it revealed to the world the extent of foreign sterling

29. Federal Reserve Bank of New York files, cable Norman to Harrison, 3 July 1931.
30. Clarke, *Central Bank Co-operation, 1924–31*, p. 199.
31. Morison, *Turmoil and Tradition*, p. 353.
32. Stimson and Bundy, *On Active Service in Peace and War*, p. 209.
33. ibid., p. 208.

balances. This interpretation suffers from the fact that the press failed to note the figures.[34] Several sources suggest that the French were taking revenge on the British for failing to support French views over exacting political conditions from Austria and Germany.[35] This is probably incorrect. The pressure seems to have come from the commercial banks in the smaller countries of Europe – Belgium, the Netherlands, Sweden and Switzerland – which had lost liquidity through the blocking of German credits, and sold sterling to increase their gold reserves.[36] The Macmillan Report tended, if anything, to underestimate Britain's sterling liabilities;[37] its contribution to policy was confused. Keynes and McKenna came out for expansionist policies, with existing exchange rates but import controls. The majority supported the maintenance of the exchange rate, but Ernest Bevin advocated devaluation. The central recommendation was that all three countries – Britain, France and the United States – should expand spending simultaneously, but the emphasis on tariffs and/or devaluation of the minority conveyed a more nationalistic flavour.

A more profoundly discouraging impact on the foreign-exchange market for sterling was conveyed by the May Report, the work of a committee set up in March 1931 under the chairmanship of Sir George May to make recommendations on the Labour government's budget proposals. The draft was communicated to Snowden on 24 July and published a week later. Both majority and minority on the committee agreed that there would be a budget deficit of £120 million, though neither took account of the fact that this included provision for sinking funds. The majority blamed it on government extravagance and proposed cutting unemployment insurance (to the extent of two thirds of the total saving of £100 million), while the Labour minority blamed it on deflation and suggested taxing the rich. The report called for

34. Skidelsky, *Politicians and the Slump*, p. 340.

35. Born, *Die deutsche Bankenkrise, 1931*, p. 66; see also Bennett, *Germany and the Diplomacy of the Financial Crisis*, p. 152.

36. Willard Hurst, 'Holland, Switzerland and Belgium and the English Gold Crisis of 1931', *Journal of Political Economy*, vol. XL, No. 5 (October 1932), pp. 638–60.

37. David Williams, 'London and the 1931 Financial Crisis', *Economic History Review*, second series, vol. XV, No. 3 (April 1963), pp. 527 ff.

foreign loans. Efforts in this direction had begun earlier with a loan of £50 million arranged with the Federal Reserve System as early as 24 July, Sir Robert Kindersley going to Paris for a loan of similar amount from the Bank of France on the 26th. These two loans were announced on 1 August. The Bank of England raised its discount rate from $2\frac{1}{2}$ to $3\frac{1}{2}$ per cent on 23 July, and to $4\frac{1}{2}$ per cent on the 30th. In all, it lost $200 million in reserves during the second half of July. David Williams comments that the Bank ceased to use discount policy as a means to combat the crisis because of large-scale unemployment.[38] With liquidity tight abroad, and confidence in sterling shaky, it is doubtful whether the crisis could have been corrected by a 10 per cent bank rate, which, according to tradition, would draw gold from the moon.

The crisis proceeded to its climax without Governor Norman, who became ill on 29 July, and was sent away to convalesce after he had recovered. The last entry in his diary on 27 July was, 'Danger of suspension of gold payments'.[39]

The £100 million were not used when the foreign-exchange market reopened on 4 August after the bank holiday. The French share had been divided between the Bank of France and the commercial banks, and the French wanted the two to be drawn simultaneously in equal amounts. This would have informed the French money market of the state of British exchange support, so the Bank postponed using the credit until the matter could be straightened out. The process took several days. The Bank was also slow to support sterling as a means of putting pressure on the government, with which it strongly disagreed. During the resulting interval, the psychological benefit of the credit was lost and pressure on sterling was maintained.[40]

The May Report provided encouragement to deflationists in Britain and abroad, and set the stage for a classic political struggle. MacDonald and Snowden became convinced that Britain could not maintain the gold standard without further loans. The Bank of England and private bankers in New York and Paris were persuaded that, to be creditworthy, Britain had to correct its

38. ibid., p. 524.
39. Andrew Boyle, *Montagu Norman*, Cassell, London, 1967, p. 266.
40. Clarke, *Central Bank Co-operation, 1924–31*, pp. 207–9.

deficit by the methods outlined by the majority in the May Report, i.e. by a cut in the dole. Henderson strongly opposed this policy and proposed instead a 10 per cent tariff for revenue. The Bank of England reported that a serious cut in the dole was necessary before foreign loans could be obtained. The trade unions, led by Ernest Bevin, who favoured devaluation and a turning inward from the world economy to the Empire, withdrew their support from the Labour government, which fell on 24 August. The loans, amounting to $200 million each from Paris and New York, were provided on 28 August, after the formation of the National government with MacDonald still Prime Minister and Snowden still Chancellor.[41] The division within the Labour party was deep, as the left wing accused the right of submitting to 'a bankers' ramp'. The bankers replied that they had merely found out from abroad whether certain actions would be sufficient to restore confidence in the currency.[42]

On 10 September the National government introduced a new budget designed to levy new taxation of £80 million a year and to provide economies of £70 million. Within a few days, however, there were new bankruptcies in Germany, which communicated tension to Amsterdam, which in turn drew funds from London. On 16 September, there was unrest among naval personnel at Invergorden over the prospect of pay reductions. This was exaggerated by the press into a mutiny in the Royal Navy.[43] If the Royal Navy were to go, how long would that other mainstay of nineteenth-century liberalism last – the gold standard run by the City of London? The pace of withdrawals accelerated. On 21 September, Great Britain left the gold standard. The initial intention was that this would be for a matter of six months.

41. For a detailed account of the formation of the National government, see R. Bassett, *Nineteen Thirty-One: Political Crisis*, Macmillan, London, 1958.

42. P. J. Grigg, *Prejudice and Judgement*, Jonathan Cape, London, 1948, p. 257.

43. According to David Divine, *Indictment of Incompetence*, *Mutiny at Invergorden*, Macdonald, London, 1970, it was more a strike than a mutiny. Vansittart called it a 'demonstration' in *The Mist Procession, the Autobiography of Lord Vansittart*, Hutchinson, London, 1958, but notes that 'Europe thought that revolution had started, that troops were unpaid, and mobs starving' (p. 425).

The Bank of France was in no way implicated in the September withdrawals as it probably was not in July. Leith-Ross states how cooperative the Bank of France was in the provision of the 28 August loan. The Bank of France was left with £65 million on 21 September when sterling went off gold, and Clément Moret, the Governor of the Bank of France, was decorated by Britain with a K.B.E. in October.[44]

The role of the small central banks has been criticized by Born, Bennett, Hurst, Einzig and others. Einzig tells the story of Vissering of the Netherlands Bank, who asked the Bank of England for a gold guarantee, was scornfully invited to take his total balance of £11 million in gold, and decided against it. Later the Netherlands Bank briefly contemplated a suit against the Bank of England for the implicit guarantee contained in a telegram from Sir Ernest Harvey to Vissering:

> Confidential – With reference to our conversation on Wednesday last [26 August] you will no doubt have seen the official announcement today of the conclusion by our government of large credits in New York and Paris. I trust this announcement will serve to abolish all doubts as to the safety of foreign funds in London.[45]

The Swiss National Bank sold all but £300,000 by 20 September.[46] A folk-tale has it that the National Bank of Belgium, asking a week ahead of the event whether sterling would be devalued, was told 'no'. Complaining later, it was informed that if it asked illegitimate questions it would get illegitimate answers. While this

44. Sir Frederick Leith-Ross, *Money Talks, Fifty Years of International Finance*, Hutchinson, London, 1968, p. 139n. The author adds that central-bank cooperation was much more close than with some of his predecessors. This dictum stands in some contradiction to the thesis of Clarke (*Central Bank Co-operation, 1924–31, passim* and esp. p. 220) that central-bank cooperation was effective up to mid 1928 and a failure thereafter.

45. Public Record Office, Treasury File T 160/439/F12712 Dutch Sterling Balances at Bank of England, Aide Memoire left by M. R. Van Swinderen at Foreign Office, 21 January 1932. Paul Einzig, *The Comedy of the Pound*, Kegan Paul, London, 1933, p. 44, has an almost literal rendering of this telegram. The exact reference has been furnished by D. E. Moggridge.

46. See Clarke, *Central Bank Co-operation, 1924–31*, p. 214 n. 104; and the Annual Report of the Swiss National Bank, *Federal Reserve Bulletin*, April 1932, p. 252.

story is doubtless apocryphal, the record does contain revealing comment. Baudhuin notes that Belgium had had £25 million on deposit some time prior to devaluation, but 'had always applied itself to reduce this figure to the point where the Bank of England would have been willing to complain'. This appears to have been £12,643,000, the balance at 21 September 1931. At a meeting that morning, while the London market was closed for two days, it was decided that Belgium was not able to liquidate its remaining sterling since this would have been unfriendly to the Bank of England. 'They thus held back before this act which would have appeared remiss in the light of the duties imposed by international solidarity.'[47] As will shortly appear, however, this solidarity, attuned to what would lead to complaint, did not prevent the large-scale conversion of dollars into gold.

The problem goes to the roots of international relations. When the large countries provide no leadership, is it the duty of the small to supply it through self-denial, or to protect themselves?

The depreciation of sterling

The pound fell from $4·86 with remarkable speed. Within a few days it was off 25 per cent, to $3·75, before recovering slightly to $3·90. The authorities made no attempt to intervene in the market, or even to maintain orderly conditions. Many people anticipated a decline comparable to the postwar falls of the French franc or the Italian lira, and were anxious to liquidate their holdings. The Bank of France participated in this liquidation. According to Einzig, it offered to forbear from selling sterling against an exchange guarantee, but the British government was not prepared to take on commitments in foreign exchange.[48] By December, the rate had reached a low of $3·25, 30 per cent below par, averaging $3·47 for the month. This involved a 40 per cent appreciation in those currencies which had not immediately followed sterling off gold. Grigg later commented: '. . . Britain had gone off gold, not

47. Fernand Baudhuin, *Histoire économique de la Belgique, 1914–1938*, vol. I, Établissements Émile Bruyles, Brussels, 1946, pp. 249–50.

48. Einzig, *The Comedy of the Pound*, pp. 32–3 and 43–4. Treasury records on French balances do not confirm this plausible account.

in a genteel way, but with a catastrophic fall of 30 per cent or more, which destroyed whatever basis of coherence and stability the world had at that time.'[49]

By December 1931, the Chancellor of the Exchequer adopted a policy with respect to sterling, proposed by Governor Norman of the Bank of England, which provided for the authorities to refrain from dealing unnecessarily; to ignore the question of profit and loss; to avoid deliberate depreciation – even at the risk of allowing reserves to fall dangerously low; to allow sterling to find its own long-run level; and to avoid an attempt to fix the rate prematurely.[50] Omitted from the list, which Clay states was maintained up till the outbreak of war in 1939, is a consideration of the impact of depreciation on other countries.

Twenty-five countries in all followed Britain off gold, largely in the Empire, Scandinavia, Eastern Europe and such trading partners as Argentina, Egypt and Portugal. Canada split the difference between the U.S. dollar and sterling, experiencing some depreciation against the U.S. dollar, but appreciation against sterling, and, especially painful, against the Swedish krone (newsprint) and the Argentine and Australian currencies (wheat). The Union of South Africa resisted depreciation, together with the U.S. dollar, the gold bloc and the German mark.

Dark hints have been given as to why Germany did not devalue to alleviate the deflationary pressure from appreciation. Schumpeter has been told by a 'man who ought to know' that Britain would not consent, but himself asked how that was relevant since what could she do?[51] Born asserts that Germany was bound by the Young Plan to maintain its exchange fixed in terms of gold, and that when Ernst Wagemann proposed devaluation in 1931 (before Standstill?), the French government and the directors of the Bank of France threatened to call German credits.[52] Hodson

49. Grigg, *Prejudice and Judgement*, p. 184.
50. Sir Henry Clay, *Lord Norman*, Macmillan, London, 1957, p. 405.
51. Joseph A. Schumpeter, *Business Cycles, A Theoretical, Historical and Statistical Analysis of the Capitalistic Process*, McGraw-Hill, New York and London, 1939, p. 943.
52. Born, *Die deutsche Bankenkrise, 1931*, p. 45. The French are cited in this connection also by Dietmar Keese, 'Die volkswirtschaftlichten Gesamt-grössen für das Deutsche Reich in den Jahren 1925–36', in *Die Staats- und*

gives as the reason the desire to hold down the local-currency cost of foreign debts.[53] The truth appears to be more simple. The British devaluation was regarded by Brüning and Luther as inflationary and dangerous.[54] A number of economic heretics recommended devaluation, notably Rudolf Dahlberg, Albert Hahn, Wilhelm Grotkopp, et al.[55] But anyone who recommended devaluation 'was almost in danger of his life'. The slogan generally was 'Hands off the exchange rate'.[56] Luther returned from a holiday on 21 September to find that the cabinet had already agreed not to attach the mark to the pound on the grounds that, eight years after the inflation, the public would have reacted strongly against devaluation. He expressed his complete agreement with the decision.[57] In a speech in November, Brüning admitted that many people 'have the opinion that now that the pound has fallen we ought to make a dash for it and devalue. I shall defend to the end against taking any inflationary measure of any kind.'[58] The leading Marxist theorist and former Social Demo-

---

Wirtschaftskrise des Deutschen Reiches, 1929/1933, Ernst Klett, Stuttgart, 1967, p. 41.

53. H. V. Hodson, *Slump and Recovery, 1929–37*, Oxford University Press, London, 1938, p. 90.

54. Hans Luther, *Vor dem Abgrund, 1930–1933: Reichsbankpräsident in Krisenzeiten*, Propyläen, Berlin, n.d. (1964?), p. 154; Heinrich Brüning, *Memoiren, 1918–1934*, Deutsche Verlags-Anstalt, Stuttgart, 1970, p. 395, states that Schacht came to him on 23 September with the suggestion that he should link the mark to the pound, but that he rejected the idea categorically. His memoirs do not explain why.

55. Wilhelm Grotkopp, *Die Grosse Krise*, Econ-Verlag, Düsseldorf, 1954, Chapter 5, esp. pp. 198 ff., and Anlage IV, an article recommending devaluation (by Dahlberg and Grävell, reprinted from the *Deutsche Ökonomist* of 11 December 1931).

56. L. Albert Hahn, *Fünfzig Jahre zwischen Inflation und Deflation*, J. C. B. Mohr (Paul Siebeck), Tübingen, 1963, pp. 103 and 106–7.

57. Hans Luther, *Vor dem Abgrund, 1930–1933*, pp. 153–5.

58. Heinrich Brüning, 'Keine Reparationen mehr', a speech before the Reichsparteiausschuss of the German Centre party on 5 November 1933, in Wilhelm Vernehohl (ed.), *Reden und Aufsätze eines deutschen Staatsman*, Verlag Regensburg, Münster, 1968, p. 75. Note Brüning's view (*Memoiren, 1918–1934*, p. 431) that the October conversions of gold were a device by which the Quai d'Orsay put pressure on the United States to support the French view on German reparations.

crat Minister of Finance, Rudolf Hilferding, asserted in a debate with Woytinsky that it was:

... insanity that London had abdicated its role as the economic centre of the world ... Germany's main task continued to be to protect its currency. He predicted increased unemployment in England as a result of depreciation.

To Woytinsky, who counter-argued that Britain's credit would be stronger, and that others would devalue, increase their exports and reduce their unemployment, Hilferding shouted 'Nonsense'.[59] The error was expensive for Germany. Following the exchange appreciation of the Deutsche Mark in 1961, Hahn said that if a 5 per cent upward valuation aroused such opposition in industry, what must the deflationary pressure of a 40 per cent revaluation have felt like.[60]

The German government pursued a policy of deflation, and so did the British. The gold bloc and the United States had serious balance-of-payments problems; in neither the British nor the German case was this true, thanks respectively to depreciation and the Standstill Agreement. Both fought an inflation which did not exist. The necessary wedge between British and world prices created by depreciation developed through the reduction of world or gold prices, not the rise of those denominated in sterling or the countries which devalued with sterling.

The contrast is with Japan: after the fall of the pound, the market sold yen. Within three months the Bank of Japan had lost

59. W. S. Woytinsky, *Stormy Passage, a Personal History through Two Russian Revolutions to Democracy and Freedom, 1905–1960*, Vanguard Press, New York, 1961, p. 467. For an account of the conservative character of Marxist ideas on depression remedies, see Adolf Sturmthal, *The Tragedy of European Labor, 1918–1939*, Columbia University Press, New York, 1943: Gollancz, London, 1944, Part III, 'Labor in the Great Depression', and Chapter 7. Sturmthal quotes Fritz Naphtali, a leading Socialist expert, who had written a book on *Wirtschaftskrise und Arbeitslosungkeit*, Berlin, 1930, to the effect that it was necessary for the crisis to run its course (pp. 86–7). 'No tampering with the currency' was the almost unanimous slogan of the left, partly because of *laissez faire* principles, and partly because of the memory of the 1923 inflation when wages failed to keep up with prices and when trade-union funds lost all value overnight (pp. 87–8).

60. Hahn, *Fünfzig Jahre zwischen Inflation und Deflation*, p. 80.

675 million yen in gold, prohibiting the export of gold on 14 December, and suspending the gold standard on 17 December 1931. What followed, Patrick says, could not have been anticipated from the record of Japanese behaviour or economic analysis, one of the most brilliant and highly successful combinations of fiscal, monetary and foreign-exchange rate policies the world has ever seen.[61]

During the 1920s, a small minority opposition had campaigned against the restoration of the yen to par, holding out for a lower rate. Led by Tanzan Ishibashi and Kemekicki Takahashi, a distinguished journalist, it had fed on the views of Gustav Cassel, and later of Keynes, whose *Tract on Monetary Reform* was translated into Japanese in 1924, and *Treatise on Money* in 1932. These works did not anticipate the theory of public spending, but impressed Ishibashi and Takahashi with their advocacy of a managed currency.

With the failure of the return of the yen to par, the view of the heretics came to the fore. The journalist Takahashi was initially critical of the theories of Korekiyo Takahashi, the former Prime Minister (1921–2) and Minister of Finance (1918–22) and Minister of Finance in the new cabinet which took power after the depreciation of the yen. But the politician Takahashi intuitively understood the potentiality of deficit financing with a flexible exchange rate, and his writing of the period showed that he already understood the mechanism of the Keynesian multiplier, without any indication of contact with the R. F. Kahn 1931 *Economic Journal* article. The balance of payments was protected not only by the flexible exchange rate, but also by the foreign exchange control laws of July 1932 and March 1933. The Bank of Japan lowered discount rates from 6·57 per cent in March 1932 to 2·29 per cent in April 1936. The fiduciary issue of the Bank of Japan was raised from 120 million yen to 1,000 million.[62] But the primary refla-

61. Hugh T. Patrick, 'Some Aspects of the Interwar Economy', prepared for VIth Seminar of the Conference on Modern Japan: 'Dilemmas of Growth in Prewar Japan', a conference held in Puerto Rico, 2–7 January 1968, p. 42.

62. Eigo Fukai, 'The Recent Monetary Policy of Japan', in A. D. Gayer (ed.), *The Lessons of Monetary Experience, Essays in Honour of Irving Fisher*, Farrar & Rinehart, New York: Allen & Unwin, London, 1937, p. 391.

tionary mechanism was government spending. Under Takahashi's finance ministry, central-government expenditures rose 20 per cent in each year of 1932, 1933 and 1934, and, in all, from 31 to 38 per cent of net domestic product. Sufficient to produce recovery, this expansion failed to satisfy the militarists, who wanted unlimited military expenditures. In consequence, they assassinated Takahashi the politician, aged eighty-two, in 1936.[63] The Japanese share in imports of such an area as the Netherlands East Indies, as a consequence of exchange depreciation, rose from 12 per cent in 1930 to 31 per cent in 1933 when the Indies government took protective measures.[64]

Liquidation of dollars

On 21 September 1931, the day sterling was devalued, Governor Moret of the Bank of France asked the Federal Reserve Bank of New York whether it minded the conversion of dollars into gold. Harrison assured him it did not. On 22 September, the Bank of France converted $50 million to gold, and the National Bank of Belgium $106·6 million. The Bank of France explained to Crane, in charge of foreign operations, that it had sold forward a certain amount of gold to Belgium and Switzerland and wanted to replace

63. The gist of the foregoing paragraphs was communicated to me by Ryutaro Komiya, who observed that there is no standard historical work on the reflationary policies of the Takahashi finance ministry. *Who's Who in Japan, 1930–1931* notes that Takahashi was born in July 1854, studied English at Yokohama, was 'sent to America to study, in 1867, and was for several months treated as a slave through the treachery American [*sic*] of his knavish guardian; returned home the following year. Principal of Osaka English School, 1875. President of the Patent Bureau which he resigned in 1890; went to Peru to exploit the silver mine being defrauded by a German swindler.' His banking career in Japan started in 1891, and his public career in 1904 when he was 'Financial Agent for raising loans in England and America, and dispatched there twice on that Important Mission [*sic*]'.

64. A. Neytzell de Wilde and J. Th. Moll, assisted by A. J. Gooszen, *The Netherlands Indies during the Depression, a Brief Economic Survey*, J. M. Meulenhoff, Amsterdam, 1936, pp. 57 and 58. The expansion had started before depreciation, but after the loss of half the outlet for its silk in the United States. In cotton textiles, Japan had 30 per cent of the Netherlands East Indies market in 1928, 48 per cent in 1931 and 76 per cent in 1933 (ibid., p. 54).

it before delivery so as not to show a loss in its statement.[65] Gold losses in the statement of the Federal Reserve System were unavoidable, and when they were reported they disturbed the foreign-exchange market. On 1 October, the Bank of France earmarked another $25 million, on 8 October another, and on 13 October $20 million. Moret explained to Harrison on 7 October that the 'considerable losses sustained by the Bank of France on balances it maintained in London by solidarity and politeness induce me to consider *a priori* the matter [of converting dollar balances] in a special light'.[66] A memorandum from Governor Hamlin to Eugene Meyer at the Board of Governors of the Federal Reserve System quotes reports from Paris, based on discussions with the Bank of France and newspaper articles, to the effect that the Bank of France will maintain its holdings of dollars 'provided that the [Federal Reserve] follow a conservative policy likely to uphold and maintain the dollar at its present value, and not resort to inflation'.[67] This produced a reaction by letter from Harrison to Meyer on 18 December to the effect that the New York bank would make no commitments. The Bank of France was free to take gold and the Federal Reserve Bank was free to adopt any credit policy it chose. Bank of France acceptances and deposits held with the bank, which had been $190 million, were down to $86 million. Harrison had been told that the French had decided not to take any more gold now, as the directors were worried about the loss of earnings.[68] The loss of gold from the Federal Reserve System from mid September to the end of October amounted to $755 million. A memorandum of 17 December 1931 from W. R. Gardner of the board staff to Governor Meyer noted that the National Bank of Belgium had acquired $131 million in gold, the Netherlands Bank $77 million and the Swiss National Bank $188 million, and referred to panic among the central banks.[69] The bulk of the rest went to France. It is hard to see what was meant by the statement in the Annual Report of the Bank of

65. Correspondence, Federal Reserve Bank of New York.
66. ibid.
67. ibid., memorandum of 24 November 1931.
68. ibid., letter of 18 December 1931.
69. ibid.

France for 1932: 'The Bank abstained from disposing of its dollar assets in the autumn of 1931 when the United States was faced with important withdrawals.'

The monetary authorities in the United States responded to the gold loss in the classic way by raising the discount rate. A rise of a full percentage point on 9 October, followed by another a week later, brought the New York bank rate only to $3\frac{1}{2}$ per cent. Even this bothered Harrison, who pressed to have the effects offset by open-market operations. But the system was hesitant about disturbing European confidence, which might lead to more gold withdrawals and more currency hoarding.[70] The end of November meeting of the Open-Market Committee authorized purchases of $200 million but only $75 million were bought in December. Banks outside the main financial centres rediscounted heavily. Bank failures spread.

Friedman and Schwartz maintain that the pressure on the United States gold supply following British suspension of the gold standard was not critical in United States economic life, which continued to decline consistently from March 1931 to mid 1932.[71] It is difficult to accept this verdict. Not only the money supply, but commodity prices, security prices, imports and, to a lesser extent, industrial production declined faster after devaluation than before.[72] European and especially French pressure on the United

70. Elmus R. Wicker, *Federal Reserve Monetary Policy, 1917–33*, Random House, New York, 1966, p. 169.

71. Milton Friedman and Anna Jacobson Schwartz, *A Monetary History of the United States, 1867–1960*, Princeton University Press, Princeton, 1963, p. 322.

72. See the following:

U.S. Economic Indicators, March 1931 to June 1933
(seasonally adjusted, 1923–5 = 100)

	Industrial production	Construction contracts	Factory employment	Factory payrolls	Freight car loadings	Prices
March 1931	87	77	78	75	80	76
August 1931	78	59	74	64	72	72
September 1931	76	59	73	62	69	71
June 1932	59	27	60	43	52	64

States gold stock was to be resumed in the early months of 1932, although it would then be offset. The double-barrelled impact of the appreciation of the dollar and capital outflow maintained and accelerated the deflationary pressure.

	Currency in circulation and demand deposits adjusted (in 1,000 millions of dollars)	Imports (unadjusted) (in millions of dollars)
March 1931	24·8	205·7
August 1931	23·4	168·7
September 1931	23·4	174·7
June 1932	20·4	112·5

SOURCE: *Federal Reserve Bulletin*, various issues.

8. More Deflation

The depreciation of sterling, and the responses of the gold bloc to the depreciation and to German restrictions, applied powerful deflationary pressure to Germany from abroad. World trade declined sharply, as Figure 8 shows, but German exports fell even more sharply. Britain not only depreciated sterling in September, as Bevin recommended; in November and December 1931 she also raised tariff rates, as Keynes had advised, to provide another example of the tendency, when alternative courses have long been debated, to do both.[1] Denmark also raised tariffs in October, together with depreciation, and Sweden in February 1932. In the months from October 1931 to March 1932, the Netherlands, France, Belgium/Luxemburg and Switzerland applied across-the-board tariffs, imposed quotas, and in the Swiss case denounced an outstanding German-Swiss trade agreement. The German export surplus, which had reached almost 400 million RM a month in September and October, fell sharply to 100 million in January and to 97 million in February to remove an expansionary source of spending.

Deflation came not only from abroad, but was applied at home. The Acceptance Bank and the Reichsbank provided funds for banks in trouble, the latter furnishing 1,600 million RM on the third signature of the former, and brought the rate down from the 10 to 15 per cent level of July and August 1931. Not, however, a great deal: to 8 per cent in October, 7 per cent in December. Deflation was still the order of the day.

---

1. Keynes himself, however, felt that with sterling off gold, the tariff was unnecessary. See his letter to *The Times* of 28 September 1931, reprinted in J. M. Keynes, *Essays in Persuasion*, Macmillan, London, 1931; Harcourt Brace, New York, 1932, pp. 286–7.

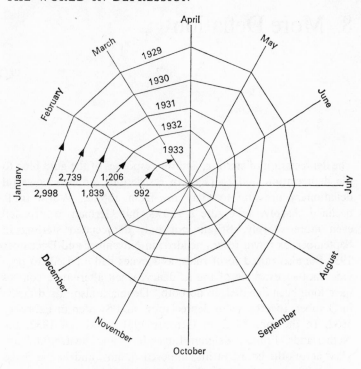

(in millions of dollars)

Figure 8. The contracting spiral of world trade, January 1929 to March 1933: total imports of seventy-five countries (monthly values in terms of old U.S. gold dollars (millions)).

	1929	1930	1931	1932	1933
I	2,997·7	2,738·9	1,838·9	1,206·0	992·4
II	2,630·3	2,454·6	1,700·5	1,186·7	944·0
III	2,814·8	2,563·9	1,889·1	1,230·4	1,056·9
IV	3,039·1	2,449·9	1,796·4	1,212·8	
V	2,967·6	2,447·0	1,764·3	1,150·5	
VI	2,791·0	2,325·7	1,732·3	1,144·7	
VII	2,813·9	2,189·5	1,679·6	993·7	
VIII	2,818·5	2,137·7	1,585·9	1,004·6	
IX	2,773·9	2,164·8	1,572·1	1,029·6	
X	2,966·8	2,300·8	1,556·3	1,090·4	
XI	2,888·8	2,051·3	1,470·0	1,093·3	
XII	2,793·9	2,095·9	1,426·9	1,121·2	
Average:	2,858·0	2,326·7	1,667·7	1,122·0	

Source: League of Nations, *Monthly Bulletin of Statistics,* February 1934, p. 51.

Luther was a straightforward deflationist. Chapter 7 of his autobiography is entitled 'Brüning's Policy: There was no Alternative',[2] an expression which Treviranus, who was in the Brüning cabinet, mocks by quoting the Cockney expression, 'Blimey, there's nothing else to do.'[3]

But there were alternatives. Wilhelm Lautenbach, an official in the Economics Ministry, had a plan for expanding bank credit for public works by several thousands of millions Reichmarks.[4] These proposals for credit creation were later taken up by Wagemann.[5] Woytinsky for the trade unions, at first alone and later with Baade and Tarnow, became obsessed, as he says, with programmes

2. Hans Luther, *Vor dem Abgrund, 1930–1933: Reichsbankpräsident in Krisenzeite,* Propyläen, Berlin, n.d. (1964?), pp. 131 ff.

3. Gottfried Reinhold Treviranus, *Das Ende von Weimar, Heinrich Brüning und seine Zeit,* Econ-Verlag, Düsseldorf, 1968, p. 173.

4. The nearest thing to a text of the Lautenbach plan is his memorandum 'Defizitpolitik? Reichsbankzusage als Katalysator der Verzweiflungsweg – ohne Auslandskapital!' [Deficit policy? Reichsbank endorsements as Catalyst of the Way out of Despair – without Foreign Capital!], in Wilhelm Lautenbach, *Zins, Kredit und Produktion,* J. C. B. Mohr (Paul Siebeck), Tübingen, 1952, pp. 137–56. This memorandum is printed in the original version of 9 August 1931 and the revised 9 September version in parallel columns where they differ and follows an earlier undated essay for the Brauns Commission on Unemployment (on which Röpke also sat) on 'Auslandskapital als Katalysator' ('Foreign Capital as Catalyst'), which dealt with recovery through public works financed from abroad.

Zins, Kredit und Produktion was edited by Wolfgang Stützel after Lautenbach's death, and contains a foreword by Röpke with an appreciation of Lautenbach's contribution to economic thought from the Economics Ministry. A full account of Lautenbach's ideas is also found in Wilhelm Grotkopp, *Die grosse Krise, Lehren aus der Überwindung der Wirtschaftskrise, 1929–32,* Econ-Verlag, Düsseldorf, 1954, which contains thirty-three index citations to the name and a short biography on p. 38 n. 4.

The Lautenbach plan was actively discussed in the Reichsbank in a meeting on 15 September 1931, and opposed by, among others, Salin, Hilferding and Röpke. After the departure of sterling from gold, however, Salin came to Berlin from Basle on 3 October to argue with Luther for the Lautenbach plan, which he said was supported by some officials at the Bank for International Settlements. See his preface to Luther, *Vor dem Abgrund, 1930–1933,* p. 23.

5. Grotkopp, *Die grosse Krise,* pp. 179 ff. Wagemann's plan was the basis for the German banking reform of 1934.

for public works, international, and if not that way, on a national basis.[6] Luther argued them all down. In this he had plenty of orthodox economic assistance.[7] But the major point was that Brüning adopted deflation as a means of getting rid of reparations. His detractors suggested that he was a tool of the Reichswehr, having been put in office by Kurt von Schleicher two weeks after the ratification of the Young Plan in March 1930, and removed

6. See ibid., *passim*; W. S. Woytinsky, *Stormy Passage, A Personal History through Two Russian Revolutions to Democracy and Freedom, 1905–1960*, Vanguard Press, New York, 1961, pp. 466 ff. Baade states that Woytinsky made the most important contribution to the Woytinsky-Tarnow-Baade plan for domestic public works which was drafted in December 1931, although not published by the German Federation of Trade Unions (A.D.B.G.) until 13 April 1932. See his essay 'Fighting Depression in Germany' in Emma S. Woytinsky (ed.) *So Much Alive, the Life and Work of W. S. Woytinsky*, Vanguard Press, New York, 1962, pp. 64–5. Woytinsky had written *Internationale Hebung der Preise als Ausweg der Krise* (Leipzig, 1931) early in 1931, and an article in the *International Labor Review*, 'International Measures to Create Employment: A Remedy for the Depression', vol. xxv, No. 1 (January 1932), pp. 1–22, at the end of the year. Among his various colleagues was Gerhard Colm. In *Stormy Passage* (p. 471) Woytinsky quotes Hilferding, whom the trade unions were accustomed to think of as the greatest authority on economic theory since Karl Marx (p. 465), as saying, 'If Colm and Woytinsky think they can mitigate a depression by public works, they are merely showing they are not Marxists.'

Grotkopp insists that Woytinsky, among others, had a well-worked-out version of the Keynes-Kahn multiplier, and claims originality for them in pushing for public works. But Keynes and Henderson had a version of public spending to counteract depression in a pamphlet *Can Lloyd George Do It?* in 1929, though without the multiplier, and the multiplier was published by Kahn in June 1931 (R. F. Kahn, 'The Relation of Home Investment to Unemployment', *Economic Journal*, vol. xli, No. 2 (June 1931), pp. 193–8). Keynes himself, of course, was familiar with this idea as early as 1930, and discussed it publicly in the Norman Wait Harris Foundation lecture in June–July 1931. See his 'An Economic Analysis of Unemployment', in Q. Wright (ed.), *Unemployment as a World Problem*, University of Chicago Press, Chicago, 1931, pp. 3–42.

7. Heinrich Dräger, an expansionist and a merchant, wrote bitterly of the solidarity of almost all professors of economics who regarded the expansion of employment through credit creation as useless, impractical, inappropriate and at a minimum inexpedient ('*unbrauchbar, undurchfuhrbahr, ungeeignet und zum mindestens als unzweckmässig*'), quoted by Grotkopp, *Die grosse Krise*, p. 38 n. 3.

by von Schleicher on a thin pretext of agricultural policy in May 1932, six weeks before the Lausanne Conference which ended reparations: 100 metres from the goal, as Brüning claimed.[8]

Whether or not it was part of a conspiracy against the Weimar Republic, as the Communists claimed, Brüning's policy from the elections of September 1930 was first and foremost to concentrate on removing reparations, and to use deflation as a means to that end.[9] Luther puts it that a foreign-policy success was needed to take the wind out of the sails of the radicals. The Brüning government had three objectives in order of priority: (a) foreign policy, to end reparations; (b) economic policy, to eliminate unemployment; and (c) internal policy, to strengthen the centre against the extremes. It seemed to Brüning vital to settle reparations before moving on to the next two priority objectives.[10] A default on the Young Plan would lead to new negotiations, which would result in unthinkable internal conditions. It was necessary for Germany to demonstrate to her creditors that it was impossible to pay. Treviranus claims that the plans for government employment lay on Brüning's table and would be used after Germany was free of reparations.[11] Woytinsky thinks Brüning less Machiavellian: 'His suicidal policy stemmed from his general philosophy. He feared the phantom of a runaway inflation; he did not like the idea of pampering the unemployed by creating jobs; and he thought that a public works programme was a luxury Germany could not afford.'[12]

8. See Bernhard Menne, *The Case of Dr Brüning*, Hutchinson (pamphlet), London, 1943, who regards Brüning as a member of a conspiracy against the German republic. That Brüning had army support and was later destroyed by the army is also stated by Vansittart in *The Mist Procession, The Autobiography of Lord Vansittart*, Hutchinson, London, 1958, pp. 418 and 446. Menne quotes Thyssen as having said at a meeting at Haus Hügel of Krupp in the spring of 1929, 'I need that crisis now. It offers the only chance of settling wages and reparations questions at one and the same time' (pp. 47–8).

9. Luther, *Vor dem Abgrund, 1930–1933*, pp. 137–8. Heinrich Brüning, *Memoiren, 1918–1934*, Deutsche Verlags-Anstalt, Stuttgart, p. 221, speaks of a 'seemingly flawless deflationary policy to be followed in order to induce the world at its own initiative to cancel reparations'.

10. Luther, *Vor dem Abgrund, 1930–1933*, p. 141.

11. Treviranus, *Das Ende von Weimar*, p. 175.

12. Woytinsky, *Stormy Passage*, p. 466.

Brüning communicated to Sackett his scenario by which deflation would lead to the cancellation of reparations. Hoover was to call a five-power conference in Washington to address the question of the world economy, and in the course of the conference it would become clear that it was necessary to cancel reparations. According to Brüning's memoirs, Hoover thought enough of the suggestion to send Joseph Cotton, the Undersecretary of State, on an exploratory trip to Europe. Cotton's death on 27 January 1931 brought the effort to a conclusion.[13] But the exact mechanism which would lead from deflation to cancellation is never made clear. Menne is persuaded that bankruptcy was the aim of Brüning's extraordinary campaign of retrenchment, which earned for him the derisive name of 'Hunger Chancellor'.[14] In his speech on the end of reparations, Brüning is less precise:

The balance of German finance and the German economy stand clear in the world for everyone to see. That is the strongest weapon that the administration can have.[15]

Suggestions for devaluation, credit expansion or public works were rejected out of hand on the grounds that 'only through the subsequent carrying out of the deflationary policy could he hope to maintain the goodwill of the Allies, and this conviction seemed to him a necessary condition of the final ending of reparations'.[16] There is frequent mention of possible Allied objection to the Lautenbach and Wagemann plans, including a protest by Benjamin Anderson, the conservative economist of the Chase Bank in New York,[17] but little explicit conception how deflation would end reparations by demonstrating the impossibility of payment.

Whatever Brüning's thought, he proceeded on 8 December 1931, by a fourth emergency decree, to reduce wages, interest rates, and the prices of cartellized industry. Wages were required to be lowered across the board to the level prevailing on 10

13. Brüning, *Memoiren, 1918–1934*, pp. 222–3.
14. Menne, *The Case of Dr Brüning*, p. 60.
15. Heinrich Brüning, *Reden und Aufsätze eines deutschen Staatsmanes*, edited by Wilhelm Vernehohl, Regensburg, Münster, 1968, p. 76.
16. Salin in Preface to Luther, *Vor dem Abgrund, 1930–1933*, p. 23.
17. Treviranus, *Das Ende von Weimar*, p. 177.

January 1927. It failed to help with unemployment. The year-to-year figures, which had shown an increase in unemployment of 1·3 million in August 1931 over 1930 and 1·4 million in September, showed a small decline to 1·1 million over the previous year in January and February 1932 before rising to 1·5 million increases in May and June. The social cement in the country crumbled. The Nazi party continued to gain.

Whether one blames the rise to power of the Nazis on reparations, the occupation of the Ruhr, the 1922–3 inflation, the failure to devalue in 1931 or the Brüning deflation, the verdict is unanimous that Brüning failed. Reparations were cancelled *de facto* at the Lausanne Conference of June and July 1932, but Brüning had been dismissed as Chancellor by von Hindenburg in May, falling '100 metres from the tape'. His successor, von Papen, adopted the credit creation and spending policies of the reformers, including a device of Lautenbach's to pay for public works with certificates which could be used by business to pay taxes to the Reich in the years 1934–8, when they would presumably be paid off out of budget surpluses. The certificates were negotiable and eligible for discount at the Reichsbank. In addition to the tax certificates, issued to the amount of 1,500 million RM, von Papen, and after him Gereke, the Reichs Commissioner for Employment, and still later Reinhard, undertook public works on the basis of bills issued to governmental organizations (which were also eligible for discount at the Reichsbank): 300 million under Papen, 600 million under Gereke, and 1,000 million under Reinhard, prior to Hitler, who took office on 30 January 1933, the numbers reaching 5,500 million by the end of 1933 and 40,000 million by the end of 1939.[18] The reformers were politically opposed to Hitler, and sceptical of his programme, which concentrated initially on autobahns (as well as assistance to farmers under Gregor Strasser, who was killed in 1934), and later on rearmament. They furnished him with the ideas which Brüning had refused to use.

18. C. R. S. Harris, *Germany's Foreign Indebtedness*, Oxford University Press, London, 1935, p. 44.

The end of reparations

In October 1931, Laval paid a visit to Washington to discuss war debts and reparations after the elapse of the year's moratorium. Hoover suggested that European countries might confer to re-examine German capacity to pay reparations, and that after a display of Continental initiative it might be possible to re-examine the question of all international debts on the basis of capacity to pay during the depression.[19]

In so far as inter-governmental obligations are concerned, we recognize that prior to the expiration of the Hoover year of postponement some agreement regarding them may be necessary covering the period of business depression, as to the terms and conditions of which the two governments make all reservations.

This sentence gave rise to the view a year later that if reparations were further postponed or cancelled, similar treatment should be accorded to war debts.

Europe did take the initiative and called a Special Advisory Committee on the Young Plan to meet in December 1931 under the auspices of the Bank for International Settlements. The committee concluded that the depression had altered the conditions under which the Young Plan had been agreed, and recommended a conference of governments. In an *aide-mémoire* at the conclusion of the meeting, and periodically throughout the following months, the United States insisted that war debts had no connection with reparations. The conference to settle the question was postponed for the French elections of April 1932, and again for the Prussian elections of May, and was finally held in June and July at Lausanne. The meeting was a difficult one, but resulted in an agreement which all but wiped out reparations. Three thousand million marks of German debt were issued to the Bank for International Settlements, which was to sell them commercially on the open market after three years, but not below 90. Any bonds left unsold after fifteen years would be cancelled. Ratification of the agreement

19. Elting E. Morison, *Turmoil and Tradition: A Study of the Life and Times of Henry L. Stimson*, Houghton Mifflin, Boston, 1960, p. 425.

was delayed to give a chance to settle war debts, mainly those with the United States, but Italian-British and French-British as well. The question of war debts arose in November 1932 when the French and British ambassadors in Washington asked the United States for a review of war debts and postponement of the 15 December payment. This is characterized by Stimson as a bombshell. It helped to complicate still further the transfer of power from Hoover, who had been defeated in his attempt at re-election to the presidency, to Roosevelt, who had won – a transfer which proved to be difficult enough.

Britain emerges from the depression

The upturn of the pound began in the first months of 1932. In part it had been oversold as importers had rushed to buy before the prospective import duties were levied. A more significant factor was the recovery of confidence in January 1932 engendered by the knowledge that French holdings of sterling were no longer overhanging the market, and that the Bank of England would meet the payments due on the 1931 summer credits without dipping into its gold stock. Another factor may have been the early voluntary payment of income tax due at the end of March shortly after the issuance of first notices on 1 January.[20] The dollar was under evident pressure. In early March, the market started to bid the pound up from below $3·50. At the end of the month it reached $3·80.

Einzig regarded the turn in sentiment in favour of the pound as a lost opportunity to stabilize the pound in terms of gold, at such a rate as $3·50 to the dollar, and to re-establish London as a world financial centre.[21] This time the rate was important. When

20. Paul Einzig, *The Comedy of the Pound*, Kegan Paul, London, 1933, p. 56.

21. ibid. This view was not held long. In 1935 Einzig wrote: 'The author views with growing suspicion the conversion of some radical economists, such as Sir Arthur Salter, Mr J. M. Keynes, and Mr Hubert Henderson, in favour of some form of immediate stabilization . . . this step should not be taken prematurely . . . ingenious traps laid by orthodox adherents of stabilization, who . . . would like to lure Great Britain and other countries into stabilization' – see Paul Einzig, *Bankers, Statesmen, Economists*, Macmillan, London, 1935, p. vii.

it rose from \$3·50 to \$3·80 there was a cry of protest from industrial and exporting circles. But after the difficulties of 1931, Britain was far from ready to reassert a world position. Leadership in free trade was jettisoned in favour of the Import Duties Act of February 1932, levying a 10 per cent tariff on most imports, but excepting the Empire. An Imports Advisory Committee was established to recommend additional duties, and in April this advised doubling the initial level. An Exchange Equalization Account (E.E.A.) was established with £150 million in rights to issue Treasury bills, with the task of holding the pound stable – a euphemism for preventing the rise. It proved to be a highly useful device for insulating the exchange rate and the London money market from hot-money movements, issuing pounds in exchange for gold to those who wanted pounds, and holding gold in readiness to exchange for pounds when the foreign holder reversed the initial process. Equipped with the E.E.A., the monetary authorities felt no need to stabilize for reasons of national policy. They had given up responsibility for the international economic system more generally.

In February 1932, Britain also reversed its deflationary policy applied with such determination since the abandonment of gold. In six steps, from 18 February to the end of June, the Bank of England discount rate was reduced from 6 per cent, fixed on 21 September, to 2 per cent on 30 June. The main effort, however, was to convert the 5 per cent War Loan of 1929–47, which held the short-term rate structure up, into a $3\frac{1}{2}$ per cent War Loan repayable at the government's option after 1952. It was a major operation, since the issue amounted to £2,085 million, or 27 per cent of the national debt and 38 per cent of quoted British securities on the London Stock Exchange.[22] The conversion was a success; 92 per cent of the loan was exchanged. Treasury bill rate dropped from 4·94 per cent in January to 0·55 per cent in September, and the bankers' allowance on deposits from 4 per cent in January to $\frac{1}{2}$ per cent in June. In the light of modern monetary theory, it is useful to note that the emphasis was on cheap money, not money

22. Edward Nevin, *The Mechanism of Cheap Money: A Study in British Monetary Policy, 1931–1939,* University of Wales Press, Cardiff, 1955, p. 92.

supply. The latter, as measured by the deposits of the ten London clearing banks, had declined from £1,900 million in May 1931 to £1,700 million in September and £1,650 million in February 1932. It rose sensibly thereafter to £1,750 million in June, and £2,000 million in December 1932. But the conscious focus of policy was on cheapening money.

Cheap money made a substantial contribution to British prosperity during the 1930s through its effect on housing. It did not operate in a vacuum. There was a backlog of unsatisfied demand accumulated during the 1920s when building had been held back by high interest rates. A 1930 Housing Act gave financial assistance to slum clearance. Improvement in the terms of trade of Britain from cheaper imports of necessities gave consumers a surplus to spend. Cheap money assisted. Building plans picked up in the autumn of 1932 after the conversion of War Loan. The increase in private building between 1931 and 1933 amounted to 70 per cent.

The improvement in the terms of trade runs contrary to the classical expectation that currency depreciation worsens them. In the classical model, exports are specialized, and more can be sold only at lower prices, whereas the depreciating country has to pay the same price in foreign exchange for its imports. British experience was otherwise. Its import market was so important to so many foreign exporters that it had a monopsony advantage. Attempting to buy less obtained Britain its imports cheaper. Exports fell in price in foreign exchange but imports fell as much, after having fallen much more from 1928 to 1931. Depreciation of sterling put strong downward pressure on world prices expressed in gold, dollars or other undepreciated currencies, on import prices as much as on export. A direct impact was felt on building costs, which were reduced. In addition, British wage and salary earners had £250 million more in 1932, after buying their food, drink and tobacco and clothes, than they had in 1924–7, and much of it was spent on housing.[23]

23. See Harold Bellman, 'The Building Trades', in *Britain in Recovery*, Pitman, London, 1938, p. 432. For a different view which emphasizes changes in policy between the 1920s and 1930s, see H. W. Richardson and D. Aldcroft, *Building in the British Economy between the Wars*, Allen & Unwin, London,

Swedish anti-depression policy

Swedish depression and recovery have given rise to widespread debate. It is generally conceded that the depression came from abroad, although the suicide of Ivar Kreuger in March 1932 proved sufficiently upsetting to world markets to constitute a small Swedish contribution to contraction.[24] The more significant issue is the extent to which Sweden recovered through its own efforts, and especially through developing a public works policy to accompany cheap money, and to what extent the recovery represented simple exchange depreciation in excess of that of the pound, plus spillover from the British building and later armament boom.

Sweden early adopted unorthodox budgetary policies. The 1 January 1933 budget of the Minister of Finance, Ernst Wigfors, based on ideas of Gunnar Myrdal, and adopting the Danish device of dividing the governmental budget between current and capital expenditures, called for public works of 160 million kroner to be paid off in four years out of an increase in death duties.[25] The amount of deficit financing in the period to rearmament, however, was small. The public debt rose in five years from the end of 1932 only from 2,202 million kroner to 2,342 million. Swedish economists regarded the favourable 'international margin' from an improvement in the terms of trade and the British boom as making recovery through public works possible. A Danish economist insists that it was the international margin which produced the recovery.[26] At the time of the Kreuger suicide, the

1969, and H. W. Richardson, *Economic Recovery in Britain, 1932–9*, Weidenfeld & Nicolson, London, 1967, Chapter 7, 'The Housing Boom'.

24. Kreuger organized Kreuger & Toll, a match conglomerate, which lent money to governments on favourable terms in exchange for the grant of match monopolies. When tight credit made it difficult for Kreuger & Toll to borrow the money to relend, Kreuger forged collateral. For a detailed account of his operations and the events leading to his suicide, see Robert Shaplen, *Kreuger, Genius and Swindler*, Alfred A. Knopf, New York, 1960; André Deutsch, London, 1961.

25. Brinley Thomas, *Monetary Policy and Crisis: A Study of Swedish Experience*, Routledge, London, 1936, p. 208.

26. C. Iversen, 'The Importance of the International Margin', in *Explora-*

182

Riksbank with limited reserves, allowed the rate to decline from 18 kroner to the pound to 19·50. Thomas notes explicitly that the advantage of a small country is that it can undertake beggar-thy-neighbour policies of currency depreciation and (moderate) tariffs without eliciting retaliation.[27] Danish exports were restricted in recovery, despite depreciation competitive to that of New Zealand, by British quotas on bacon, ham and butter, and increased only from a monthly average of 91 million kroner in 1932 to 107 million in 1935. Besides Japan, Sweden was the only country in the world with a greater increase in exports than in industrial production.[28] The monthly average value of exports rose from 70 million kroner in 1932 to 108 million in 1935, or 54 per cent compared with 17 per cent for Denmark. Finland, without the well-worked-out theory of public spending, recovered as much as Sweden did with it.[29]

French pressure on United States gold

In December 1931, a Reconstruction Finance Corporation was initiated in the United States to provide finance for banks and firms in need of liquidity. The rapid decline in governmental revenue led to a substantial deficit. These factors struck H. Parker Willis, Professor of Banking at Columbia University, as highly

tions in International Economics: Notes and Essays in Honor of F. W. Taussig, McGraw-Hill, New York, 1936, pp. 68–93.

27. Thomas, Monetary Policy and Crisis, p. 154. Marcus claims that the greater depreciation of the krone, while the Canadian dollar appreciated against the pound, enabled Scandinavian countries to offer newsprint, and presumably pulp and paper, in Europe at prices $10 to $12 below Canadian mills – see Edward Marcus, Canada and the International Business Cycle, 1927–39, Bookman Associates, New York, 1954, p. 105. The price of Canadian newsprint had fallen from $65 a ton in the spring of 1928 to $32 under N.R.A. in June 1933.

28. H. W. Arndt, The Economic Lessons of the 1930s, Oxford University Press, London, 1944, p. 215.

29. Arthur Montgomery, How Sweden Overcame the Depression, 1930–1933 (1938), cited in Per Jacobsson, 'A Comparison of the Business Developments in Great Britain, the United States and Sweden, 1932–1934', in Some Monetary Problems, International and National, Oxford University Press, London, 1958, pp. 115–16 and 124.

inflationary, and he said so in a famous dispatch to Agence Économique in Paris. It disturbed French official and private opinion. Governor Moret of the Bank of France cited it in asking the Federal Reserve Bank of New York to resume earmarking gold and the shipping of it. Operations were to be carried out in an orderly way, without undue haste, and without adverse publicity, but there were to be two shipments a week.

Harrison was unwilling to ask Moret to stop taking gold. On the contrary, at every stage he offered to assist the Bank of France in converting all or any part of its dollars, which amounted to some $600 million in mid January. But the Willis view that the United States ran grave risks of inflation produced a reaction. On 15 January Harrison explained that the country had experienced the most drastic deflation of bank credit in history, and that the policy of the Federal Reserve System was not to stimulate inflation, but to halt deflation. The next day he added that Kemmerer, Hollander, Taussig, Carver, Seligman, Durand and Wilcox, economists of reputations as conservative and prestigious as Willis, believed that the general contraction of credit and prices had gone far enough, and that what was needed was a liberal policy to encourage the expansion of credit. Moret replied that French opinion still felt some hesitation in forming a judgement about the decisions taken in the United States, but that recent dollar sales had originated in London.[30]

After the gold withdrawals of the autumn of 1931, member-bank discounting left indebtedness to the system at $836 million on the average in February, the highest level since November 1929. Free gold of the Federal Reserve System was down to $400 million. While, with close to $4,000 million, the system had more than enough gold to meet the 35 per cent gold cover for its liabilities, it lacked the eligible paper needed to make up the difference between 35 and 100 per cent, and could count only gold in its place. As early as July 1931, the Federal Reserve Bank of St Louis had stood aside from participation in the system loan to the Bank of England because of a shortage of free gold. By

30. Federal Reserve Bank of New York correspondence, January 1932.

184

December 1931, free gold was beginning to be a problem.[31] In his presidential campaign in October, Hoover claimed that the United States had come within two weeks of going off the gold standard. This referred to the fact that, before the Glass-Steagall Act of 27 February, free gold had fallen to $350 million, with gold losses at a rate of $150 million a week. The Glass-Steagall Act, however, enabled the Federal Reserve System to count government securities together with eligible paper as reserves against the system's liabilities. Its passage was the signal both for a substantial campaign of open-market operations, converting net borrowings (gross borrowings minus excess reserves) of $792 million in February to net excess reserves of almost $100 million in July, and for a renewed outflow of French funds. The open-market campaign was inspired by congressional pressure, and was voted in the Open-Market Committee by three to two against strenuous opposition.

On 1 March, three days after passage of the Glass-Steagall Act, the U.S. Ambassador to France referred to the withdrawals by the Bank of France as politically inspired by the demands of parliamentary deputies, nervous over the large loss in sterling, which was then being transferred from the Bank of France to the French Treasury. A week later Moret wrote to Harrison, explaining French devotion to the gold standard; the monetary law of June 1928, which allegedly required the Bank of France to liquidate foreign assets, a task which presented a problem when the French balance of payments was in surplus; and the necessity for the Bank of France to set an example in demonstrating the operation of the true gold standard, as opposed to the makeshift arrangements which the 1931 crisis had demonstrated as unsatisfactory. This required liquidation of French holdings of foreign exchange.

31. Elmus R. Wicker, *Federal Reserve Monetary Policy, 1917–1933*, Random House, New York, 1966, p. 169. Friedman and Schwartz hold that the shortage of free gold did not seriously limit the alternatives open to the system – see Milton Friedman and Anna Jacobson Schwartz, *A Monetary History of the United States, 1867–1960*, Princeton University Press, Princeton, 1963, p. 406 – but Wicker (p. 172) notes that the references to the free gold issue are too frequent in January and February 1932 to permit this conclusion.

By April, French conversions of dollars into gold were proceeding at $12,500,000 a week. Following the French example, the Netherlands Bank converted $40 million. At the end of May, Moret hinted strongly that he would like to increase the rate. Harrison first suggested that he should do what he liked, and then, when Moret went to $25 million a week, recommended him to convert the entire $93 million left. This was done, except for $10 million which were left as an exchange reserve. The gold-exchange standard was wound up in mid June 1932 at the bottom of the depression.

It made no difference. Open-market operations under the Glass-Steagall Act had belatedly relieved the pressure on the banks. But not equally throughout the system.

The country banks

Simple monetary theory suggesting that business conditions ought to follow the money supply fails to take adequate account of the country banks. Table 10 shows the breakdown of net excess reserves, or, with a minus sign, net borrowings from the Federal Reserve System, divided among central-reserve city, reserve city and country banks. The figures are monthly averages for the last month in the quarter from 1929 to 1933 (except for March 1933, when it is necessary because of the bank holiday to use February). In 1929, New York, Chicago, reserve cities and country banks were all net borrowers from the system to supply the call-loan market. With the open-market operations following the crash, central-reserve cities virtually got out of debt, and by September 1930 reserve cities cut their indebtedness to a low figure. Country banks remained substantially in debt to the system, largely, it is hypothesized, because of the need to carry loans of farmers and small business, and the lack of government bonds which could be sold off. The increase in borrowings after the pound left gold took place in reserve cities and country banks. Withdrawals of foreign funds occurred largely from New York, but tighter money in that centre drew funds from smaller communities. Moreover, open-market operations after March 1932 quickly produced excess reserves in central-reserve cities, and sharply reduced the net

Table 10.   Federal Reserve member bank net excess reserves or net borrowing (−), by class of bank: monthly averages, end of quarter, 1929–33 (in millions of dollars).

		TOTAL	New York	Chicago	Reserve cities	Country banks
1929	March	−915	−147	−118	−414	−236
	June	−932	−167	−62	−397	−305
	September	−927	−159	−20	−486	−260
	December	−753	−90	−33	−339	−293
1930	March	−216	−7	1	−60	−150
	June	−196	−20	2	−26	−153
	September	−129	1	1	−12	−119
	December	−264	−15	3	−88	−165
1931	March	−110	6	2	−10	−108
	June	−58	67	1	−18	−105
	September	−160	41	16	−90	−137
	December	−703	−27	−3	−344	−323
1932	March	−647	11	3	−312	−357
	June	−260	89	57	−110	−292
	September	−41	192	82	−74	−242
	December	245	283	163	−19	−182
1933	February*	111	65	169	25	−174
	June	.179	69	78	62	−30
	September	572	152	197	160	63
	December	671	95	211	246	118

*March figures incomplete owing to bank holiday.

SOURCE: Federal Reserve System, *Banking and Monetary Statistics*, Washington, D.C., 1943, pp. 396–9.

indebtedness of reserve cities. It was much slower to assist country banks, which remained substantially indebted until after the 1933 bank holiday. The figures for December 1932, following the open-market programme of $1,000 million, are of particular interest: high net excess reserves in New York and Chicago, small net borrowing in reserve cities, but close on $200 million of net borrowed reserves of country banks.

These figures cast doubt on the efficacy of open-market operations in relieving the squeeze on the economy outside financial

Table 11. Prices of specified commodities, selected months, 1931–3.

	cocoa ¢ per lb	coffee ¢ per lb	copper ¢ per lb	corn ¢ per bu.	cotton ¢ per lb	hides ¢ per lb	lead ¢ per lb	rubber ¢ per lb	silk $ per lb	sugar ¢ per lb	tin ¢ per lb	wheat ¢ per bu.	wool ¢ per lb	zinc ¢ per lb
1931														
March	5·41	8½	9·9	57·5	10·15	9·0	4·28	7·13	2·77	3·28	27·07	76	80	4·01
June	5·17	9½	8·0	53·8	8·42	10·0	3·76	6·38	2·40	3·32	23·41	76	75	3·40
September	4·47	8	7·0	43·2	5·83	9·0	4·22	5·00	2·57	3·41	24·68	71	77	3·74
December	3·97	8⅜	6·6	34·5	5·78	7·8	3·59	4·63	2·18	3·14	21·35	74	72	3·15
1932														
March	4·44	9	5·8	32·2	6·44	6·4	2·99	3·31	1·71	2·76	21·84	72	69	2·79
June	3·99	10⅛	5·1	29·4	4·99	4·3	2·89	2·69	1·27	2·72	19·24	64	54	2·79
September	4·63	15	6·0	28·0	7·40	8·1	3·32	3·88	1·89	3·16	24·76	59	63	3·30
December	3·71	10½	4·8	18·8	5·72	5·5	2·88	3·25	1·60	2·83	22·69	49	55	3·12
1933														
March	3·40	9¼	5·0	20·6	6·19	5·2	3·03	3·03	1·25	2·96	24·34	54	55	3·00
June	4·60	9	7·8	40·2	9·28	12·2	4·02	6·09	2·17	3·44	44·21	81	90	4·35

SOURCE: *Commodity Yearbook, 1939*, New York, 1939, *passim.*

188

markets. Commodity prices continued to decline, as Table 11 shows. Certain commodities, like sugar and coffee, were unaffected by appreciation of the dollar (depreciation of sterling), but the decline in most was accentuated after September 1931, especially in the last quarter of 1931, when the pound went to $3·30, and again in the last half of 1932, when it dropped from $3·64 in June to $3·27 in December. Wheat and corn were particularly badly hit in the last quarter of 1932.

The price collapse initiated by appreciation was sufficiently fast in both the United States and Germany for export surpluses to be maintained in every quarter but one, as Table 12 shows. The composition of foreign trade helped in both cases, as did the fact that import prices fell sharply while exports of manufactures held up better in price. German foreign-exchange control played a role. It remains true that imports fell almost as fast as exports, so that while export surpluses were reduced in 1932 as compared with 1931, they were not eliminated.

Table 12.   German and United States average monthly export surplus (import surplus –), quarterly, 1931 and 1932.

		Germany (in millions of RM)	United States (in millions of dollars)
1931	I	167	68·5
	II	154	5·0
	III	334	68·3
	IV	302	78·4
1932	I	121	43·7
	II	80	16·1
	III	81	−0·7
	IV	75	32·4

SOURCE: *Federal Reserve Bulletin.*

The German export surplus hardly entered into the discussion as to whether or not the currency should be devalued, since devaluation was thought of, on the external front, as a substitute for foreign-exchange controls. In the United States, however, the export surplus was used as an argument that foreign trade was a force for expansion, and that it was beggar-thy-neighbour policy

189

to seek more by depreciation. The error, a normal one in economics, was to confuse partial with general equilibrium. In partial
equilibrium, an export surplus is inflationary compared to balance
or net imports, other things equal. In general equilibrium, the
appreciation of the exchange rate can be so deflationary that the
fall in income spread through bank failure can wipe out the
expected import surplus. In such a case the surplus cannot be
regarded as expansive.

The export economies

After the initial squeeze from the halt in lending, business decline
in industrial countries spread to the less developed countries of
the world, primarily by means of reduced exports. In these economies, the level of exports is generally a critical autonomous
variable in the determination of national income – more important
than investment, which is often dependent on export sales, and
surely more so than government expenditure, which cannot be
independent because of the lack of a domestic money market at
home. As noted earlier (see page 149), a country's local population
may find a partial cushion in the decline of foreign profits after
a fall in exports. In Java, foreign planters suffered more serious
losses in income than the native population, which obtained much
of its income in kind; and natives associated with foreign-owned
plantations had more serious income losses than those only
loosely tied to the export sector. But the losses of exports and
income were highly impressive in percentage terms. Triantis
prepared a table to show the decline in exports value by various
periods. From 1928–9 to 1932–3, Chile led the list, as shown in
Table 13. Where each country fared depended to a great extent on
the character of the products it sold. Triantis divided primary
products into four classes: (a) staple foodstuffs, which face low
elasticity of demand; (b) semi-luxury foodstuffs, such as dairy
products, meat and fruit, which declined less than goods in (a) because of higher price elasticity; (c) raw materials, except fuel,
including especially metallic minerals, timber and hides, which have
very high income elasticity; and (d) materials with low income
elasticity, notably oil and paper. In general, the countries special-

izing in (c) goods, like Chile, Bolivia, Malaya and Peru, did worst, while oil exporters, like Venezuela, were protected by income inelasticity of demand. Exporters of wheat and coffee did less well than those selling butter and meat abroad. Exceptions occurred everywhere. Denmark and New Zealand hurt each other and themselves by engaging in competitive exchange depreciation in 1932 and 1933 in a fight for the British butter market. Britain obtained its butter cheaper from both.[32]

Table 13. Forty-nine primary-exporting countries classified by percentage of decline in exports, 1928/9 to 1932/3.

Percentage decline in exports	Country
Over 80	Chile
75–80	China
70–75	Bolivia, Cuba, Malaya, Peru, Salvador
65–70	Argentina, Canada, Ceylon, Netherlands Indies, Estonia, Guatemala, India, Irish Free State, Latvia, Mexico, Siam, Spain
60–65	Brazil, Dominican Republic, Egypt, Greece, Haiti, Hungary, Netherlands, Nicaragua, Nigeria, Poland, Yugoslavia
55–60	Denmark, Ecuador, Honduras, New Zealand
50–55	Australia, Bulgaria, Colombia, Costa Rica, Finland, Panama, Paraguay
45–50	Norway, Persia, Portugal, Romania
30–45	Lithuania, Philippines, Turkey, Venezuela

SOURCE: S. G. Triantis, *Cyclical Changes in Trade Balances of Countries Exporting Primary Products, 1927–1933*, University of Toronto Press, Toronto, 1967, p. 19.

In such a country as Canada, depression and subsequent recovery were governed almost entirely by exports. With a branch banking system, Canada suffered no bank failures. Between 1929 and 1933, the supply of money fell only 13 per cent, as compared with 33 per cent in the United States. But monetary velocity, which

32. C. P. Kindleberger, 'Competitive Currency Depreciation between Denmark and New Zealand', *Harvard Business Review*, vol. XII, No. 4 (July 1934), pp. 416–27.

fell 29 per cent in the United States, declined 41 per cent over the same period in Canada, so that the declines in net national product at 53 and 49 per cent respectively were of the same order of magnitude.[33] Canada gained only limited outlets in Britain from preferences prior to the Ottawa Agreement. The appreciation of the Canadian dollar against sterling, and especially against the Scandinavian currencies, which were competitors in newsprint, hurt more than Empire preference helped. Despite the depreciation against the United States, exports and industrial production plunged downward after September 1931 – exports with a lag – and recovered after April 1932, only to suffer a relapse in the second half of the year and the first months of 1933.[34]

The decline of investment

The emphasis given to stock-market speculation, the halt of international lending, the scramble for liquidity, exchange depreciation and bank failures suggest a theory of business cycles which is financial to the exclusion of real factors. Some over-expansion was allowed for in a few commodities: sugar, wheat, coffee and rubber. The decline in housing from 1925 to 1929 has been mentioned. But little notice was taken of the view, which flourished in the later 1930s and for some time after the Second World War, that depression results from an exhaustion of investment opportunities. In one version, this was caused by overshooting normal demand growth, as in commercial building, durable consumer goods such as motor-cars, radios, etc., and such materials as newsprint and copper. The overshooting results from the acceleration principle, which relates investment to increases in consumption, so that when consumption levels off, investment must decline and bring income and demand down with it. On this showing, speculative excesses, unwise bank lending and international complications may account for the depth of the depression, and help its spread to the rest of the world; the origin of the cycle, however, lies in an

33. Friedman and Schwartz, *A Monetary History of the United States, 1867–1960*, p. 352.

34. Marcus, *Canada and the International Business Cycle, 1927–39*, p. 71.

over-expansion of investment in the United States.[35] A further view goes beyond the mechanical connections between multiplier and accelerator into deep-seated factors responsible for the decline in investment: changes in population growth, waves of innovation and exhaustion of the frontier. These autonomous influences produce now a bunching of investment leading to secular exhilaration, and at other times, as in the late 1920s and early 1930s if they work in concert, a dearth of investment outlets and secular stagnation.[36]

Experience since the 1930s has suggested that investment can be stimulated by fiscal policy – and, in the views of some, by maintaining the money supply stable – and that it is not as intractable as is implied by the stagnation theories. Whether the 1929 depression owes its depth to special circumstances of particularly excessive over-expansion of investment in the 1920s may also be doubted, in as much as the boom was not as far-reaching as this would imply. Over-expansion in wheat, copper, rubber and sugar were a factor in the depression in some countries, but the over-expansion of investment in general hardly was.

If it is difficult to explain the decline in investment, except on the accelerator principle combined with financial factors, the fact that gross investment has a limit of zero is useful in explaining that the depression must end. Gross domestic investment in the United States amounted to $16,000 million in 1929. It fell to $1,000 million in 1932 and net investment to −$6,600 million. Inventories declined, durable goods wore out, depreciation reduced fixed capital. At some point, gross investment turns up again and the acceleration principle comes back into its own.[37] With purely

35. Robert A. Gordon, *Business Fluctuations*, 2nd edition, Harper & Row, New York, 1952, pp. 410 ff.

36. A. H. Hansen, *Full Recovery or Stagnation*, W. W. Norton, New York: A. & C. Black, London, 1938.

37. W. W. Rostow ascribes the length of the depression in the United States to the importance of automobiles and other durable goods in total spending, and the consequent need to wait for an autonomous rise in consumers' durable-goods spending to set leading sectors in motion again. In his view, this altered the business cycle from the nineteenth-century model, in which a fall in interest rates, raw material prices and money wages could lead to resumed investment; or where population expansion and urbaniza-

financial theories of the business cycle, there is no need for the up-turn. Liquidity squeezes, bank failures, price declines have no nat-ural limits until the monetary system has been entirely wiped out and the system converted to barter. With gross investment close to zero in 1932, the system was ready for the upturn. It was first ne-cessary, however, to have an apocalyptic climax in bank failures.

The 1932 election and interregnum

The depression appeared to be bottoming out in the spring of 1932 after the recovery of sterling from its December 1931 low. Whole-sale prices in the United States stopped falling. In July, industrial production turned up. Whether one ascribes this to the $1,000 million of open-market operations, to the end of appreciation, or to the multiplier-accelerator turning point which comes when gross investment hits the bottom, the arrival of the upturn was unmistakable. The suggestion of a world economic conference to plan cooperative recovery, mentioned by Hoover to Laval in October 1931, was revived in May, and further discussed at the Lausanne Conference in July. But there was still an election to come in the United States.

In the electoral campaign, Roosevelt charged Hoover with total responsibility for the depression. Its origin, he said, was entirely within the United States. As Secretary of Commerce and President, Hoover had been responsible for the orgy of speculation in the stock market, the overbuilding of industry and the flood of loans abroad which caused depression through default. The Smoot-Hawley Tariff Act made it impossible for other countries to pay their debts and gave rise to trade reprisals all over the world. A wildly extravagant government budget produced a huge Federal deficit which strangled the country.

Hoover, in reply, insisted that the depression had originated

---

tion at steady rates could make profitable the opening up of new agricultural territories in response to increased demand for grain. See his 'The Strategic Role of Theory: A Comment', *Journal of Economic History*, vol. xxxi, No. 1 (March 1971), p. 84. Of course, the larger the proportion of investment plus postponable consumption, the deeper the depression may go, but it is not self-evident that durable goods behave differently from investment in plant, equipment or inventories in producing the upturn.

abroad, starting well before the crash of October 1929, that the heritage of war had led to a financial collapse in Europe, which made it impossible for the United States to collect its debts, and had come within two weeks of forcing the United States off the gold standard. Tariffs were necessary to protect American farmers. Agriculture was recovering, employment gaining. The American dollar rang honestly on the counter. Since July 1932, gold had been gained from abroad, and currency and gold were returning from hoarding.

Roosevelt attacked on no other aspect of foreign economic policy than the tariff, nor did he fault Hoover's handling of the banks. On his side, Hoover kept war debts out of the campaign. They were united in opposition to deficits and support of balanced budgets in principle, though Roosevelt characterized Hoover's efforts as inadequate in practice. In a speech at Des Moines on 4 October, Hoover described how close the country had come to going off the gold standard. This elicited speculation against the dollar and a reply by Senator Carter Glass that there had never been the slightest danger. There was no hint in the campaign oratory of new experimental policies in either domestic or foreign economic fields, nor of a shift of focus in policy from international to national concerns. Both candidates represented the domestic and Middle Western wings of their parties; though Roosevelt from New York had connections with internationalists, his foremost advisers, Moley and Tugwell, represented a Middle Western point of view.[38]

With Roosevelt's sweeping victory in November, two issues requiring urgent attention became caught in the interregnum: one was foreign – war debts; the other domestic – the banks. Neither had played a role in the campaign, but Hoover, the lame duck, wanted to engage Roosevelt's cooperation in their handling for the sake of continuity; Roosevelt was wary of accepting responsibility until he assumed authority.

British and French notes asking for deferment of the payment of 15 December and a review of the war-debt issue were presented

38. Herbert Feis stated that the knowledge of foreign affairs possessed by Roosevelt's assistants seemed to be slighter than their intellectual assurance – see *1933: Characters in Crisis*, Little Brown, Boston, 1966, p. 13.

on 10 November, two days after the election. Hoover asked Roosevelt to assist in framing the United States reply. Conferences on 17 and 22 November, and 20 January, produced agreement on broad principles of American policy: the debts were a business matter with no connection with reparations or the prospective world economic conference, and each debtor should be treated separately, taking into account ability to pay; the Allies should pay first and talk later. But this was all. Roosevelt was not as upset as Hoover by the suggestion in the British note that the United States was committed to revision by the terms of the Hoover-Laval communiqué; he would not endorse Hoover's proposal for a review commission made up of Executive and Congressional representatives; he was not prepared to follow up Hoover's suggestion of exchanging war debts for some specific benefit, such as enlarged markets for United States agricultural exports. He issued separate statements, and left the task of replying to the British and French to Hoover.[39]

Hoover had strong views on war debts; Roosevelt did not. Tugwell notes that Roosevelt viewed them as a bargaining problem on the one hand, and a political complication on the other. On the latter score, public opinion, both at home and abroad, was singularly determined: on the one side, not to cancel; on the other, not to pay. This made temporizing necessary. The realities would have their way in the long run, but political considerations had to be taken into account.[40] After 28 January 1933, when Sir Ronald Lindsay, the British Ambassador, saw the President-elect in Warm Springs, the British apparently stopped pushing the question. But the Herriot government had fallen over the issue of whether to pay on 15 December; the British offered to pay with U.S. agreement that it did not imply resumption of regular payments. The Department of State replied that if payment was made, the debts would undoubtedly be reviewed, but that if

39. For a full account of the meetings, which he attended, and the text of Roosevelt's briefing instructions, see Raymond Moley, with the assistance of Elliott Rosen, *The First New Deal*, Harcourt Brace & World, New York, 1966, pp. 27 ff. and 555–6. There are numerous other accounts.

40. Rexford G. Tugwell, *Notes on a New Deal Diary*, pp. 71–3, quoted in ibid., p. 55.

agreement to a review was a condition of payment, the United States would have to reject it. The payment was finally made without qualification. There was no agreement, no indication by the United States of what would constitute a solution.

The banking collapse of early 1933 had complex political roots. One strand was the attempt of the vice-presidential candidate, and Speaker of the House, John N. Garner, to insist on Reconstruction Finance Corporation (R.F.C.) loans to banks being publicized. In July 1932, it had become known that the Central Republic National Bank and Trust Company of Chicago had received a $90 million loan from the R.F.C. Since this was a Dawes-controlled bank, there was political advantage in charging that the second 'Dawes loan' represented political favouritism; but publicity for banks receiving R.F.C. loans would tend to speed up bank runs. Accordingly, when the requirement was enacted in January 1933, banks in trouble stopped seeking R.F.C. aid. On 17 January, Hoover asked Roosevelt, among other things, to advise congressional leaders to stop publication of the names of R.F.C. borrowers. Roosevelt refused.

The 17 January letter contained other requests from Hoover to Roosevelt: that there could be no tampering with the currency, no inflation, that the budget could be balanced even if it meant more taxation, and that government credit would be maintained through limiting government debt. Earlier, in December, the President had called in congressional leaders proposing increased taxes and a cut in expenditure, to carry out Roosevelt's campaign promises. In a Lincoln Day address, he asked the President-elect to commit himself to stabilizing currencies and forswearing funny money. These actions were partly a response to the rising tide of demand for inflationary measures by South-western and Western Senators, notably Connally of Texas, Thomas of Oklahoma and Wheeler of Montana, and to the formation of a Committee for the Nation committed to raising prices by monetary means. On 31 January, the designated Secretary of Agriculture in the new cabinet, Henry Wallace, had said, 'The smart thing would be to go off the gold standard a little further than England has.' Whether markets reacted to the inflationary suggestions or to Hoover's calling them to national attention is not self-evident, but bank failures spread

197

in the Middle West in December, and more widely in January. There was widespread hoarding of currency, and in February 1933, loss of gold. Hoover wrote to Senator Reed on 10 February, stating that the panic and gold outflow were the result of a loss of confidence in the new administration.

Gradually the Federal Reserve System became demoralized. It undertook contraction in January by selling off government bonds. During the troubles of February, the Open-Market Committee did not meet. In response to an express invitation of President Hoover to make suggestions, the Board of Governors on 25 February had none to offer. On 2 March it was not prepared to recommend a Federal guarantee for bank deposits, nor were there any additional measures which it felt it would be justified in recommending.[41]

Bank holidays started in Nevada in October 1932 when the state's banks were shut for twelve days. In mid February, a feud between Henry Ford and Senator James Couzens over two rival groups of Detroit banks required the Governor of Michigan to close the banks to prevent Ford from withdrawing a large deposit from the rival system. This was 14 February. A week later, the banks were closed in New Jersey. On the eve of Roosevelt's inauguration, Governor Lehman closed the banks of New York. On 4 March, as President, Roosevelt invoked the Trading with the Enemy Act of 1917 to close all banks in the country.

Hoover blames the panic of February–March 1933 squarely on Roosevelt – 'the most senseless and easily prevented panic in all history'.[42] In his view, Roosevelt wanted to close the banks and blame the débâcle on Hoover. Roosevelt, on the other hand, had his hands full in organizing to take power as well as resting after his campaign, and was unwilling to commit himself to any of Hoover's explicit proposals.

The current administration was exhausted by the depression. Everywhere there was strain and confusion. Antipathy existed between Hoover and Roosevelt, the former regarding the latter as shallow and dangerous, the latter the former as doctrinaire. There was no standard to follow.

41. *The Memoirs of Herbert Hoover*, vol. III: *The Great Depression, 1929–1941*, Macmillan Co., New York: Hollis & Carter, London, 1952, pp. 211–12.
42. ibid., p. 215.

9. The World Economic Conference

The inaugural speech

During the campaign and after the election up to the eve of the inauguration, there was considerable question over Roosevelt's attitude towards foreign economic questions. Roosevelt came from an internationalist tradition. As a candidate for vice-president in 1920, he had strongly backed the League of Nations. He was, however, responsive to pressure. When the Hearst press violently attacked the League during 1932, he backed away from it, saying that the League had changed, but went on to hedge by saying that this did not preclude future international cooperation. Tugwell, who with Moley belonged to the national school in Roosevelt's staff, noted that the internationalists in the Democratic party – Baker, Daniels, House and Hull – were dismayed by his equivocation.[1]

The internationalist leader in the Roosevelt inner group was Norman Davis, a banker, who had had wide experience in Europe. Moley was worried that Davis, and Henry Stimson, Hoover's Secretary of State who negotiated with Roosevelt during the transition on foreign economic matters, might swing Roosevelt into the internationalist camp. The draft agenda for the World Economic Conference, calling for restoration of the gold standard, tariff reduction and other measures of international cooperation, in his view threatened to inhibit the programme for domestic recovery.[2]

1. Rexford G. Tugwell, *The Brains Trust*, Viking Press, New York, 1968, p. 76.
2. Raymond Moley, with the assistance of Elliott Rosen, *The First New Deal*, Harcourt Brace & World, New York, 1966, p. 39.

Tugwell and Moley won. The inaugural speech on 4 March 1933 enunciated the commitment of priority to domestic recovery that Moley had sought, and which he took to be 'final and irrevocable'.[3]

> Our international relations, though vastly important, are in point of time and necessity secondary to the establishment of a sound national economy. I favour as a practical policy the putting of first things first.

While he insisted that his programme was not narrowly nationalistic, Roosevelt's attention was inward. The day following the inauguration, Adolf Hitler was given full powers to govern by decree in Germany.

There were campaign promises, but no programme. Counsels on the domestic front were divided among at least five groups: (a) the orthodox, who favoured putting the economy through the wringer, including Bernard Baruch, an adviser, Lewis Douglas, Director of the Bureau of the Budget, Jesse Jones of the Reconstruction Finance Corporation (R.F.C.), and William Woodin, the new Secretary of the Treasury; (b) monetary manipulators, including Senators Key Pittman, Elmer Thomas and Burton Wheeler, and Professor James Harvey Rogers of Yale; (c) trustbusters, including Justice Louis Brandeis and Professor Felix Frankfurter of the Harvard Law School; (d) those who believed in government ownership, notably Senator George Norris and Harold Ickes, Secretary of the Interior designate; and (e) the planners, including the advisers Adolph A. Berle, Hugh Johnson, Raymond Moley and Rexford Tugwell, and the new Secretary of Agriculture, Henry Wallace.[4] Moley was made an assistant secretary of state in charge of economic questions, notably foreign debts, the World Economic Conference, 'and such additional duties as the President may direct in the field of foreign and domestic government'. He worked from the White House, rather than the Department of State, and regarded his task in part as preventing foreign considerations from interfering with the domestic programme. His nominal superior, Cordell Hull, the Secretary of State, had only one formula: stop raising tariffs and

3. See page 26, n. 14, above.
4. Moley, *The First New Deal*, p. 228.

start lowering them. It was hard to see the mechanism by which this could lead to recovery.

First, it was necessary to open the banks. This was done within eight days. The next ninety-two of the 'Hundred Days' of Roosevelt's first administration were devoted to developing programmes on a variety of domestic fronts. In agriculture, major emphasis was given to production control as a means of raising prices. The Agricultural Adjustment Act (A.A.A.) was passed in May 1933, restricting output and removing surpluses from the market, making direct payments to farmers for reducing production; levying excise taxes on food processors to raise funds for paying benefits; and establishing marketing agreements under government supervision. In June 1933, the National Recovery Act (N.R.A.) provided for industrial agreements or codes on production and prices, but including protection for labour through the specification of maximum hours and minimum wages and a guarantee of the right to join a union. A Tennessee Valley Authority (T.V.A.) was created in May 1933 to establish government authority over the operation of the hydroelectric dam and nitrate plants built at Muscle Shoals on the Tennessee River during the First World War, as well as to coordinate power production, flood control and river transport. Relief was provided through the Emergency Relief Act of 1933, following similar legislation in 1932 under Hoover, but creating a new agency. Later the Civil Works Agency was established for work relief (in November 1933); this ultimately developed into the Works Progress Administration (W.P.A.) for public works and work relief for the unemployed. Among the more far-reaching items of legislation was bank deposit insurance, resisted by both Hoover and Roosevelt for fear that the weak banks would pull down the strong, and initiated by the Congress rather than the Democratic administration.

The two major parts of the programme of the Hundred Days, the N.R.A. and the A.A.A., were both later declared unconstitutional (in 1935 and 1936, respectively). The A.A.A. was replaced by other legislation, to accomplish the same purpose of holding production down and prices up; N.R.A., which had been progressively undermined by industrial competition, was quietly forgotten. Neither earned the approval of economists or of ordinary folk; A.A.A. because of the ploughing under of cotton when people were badly clothed, and of the killing off of pigs when people were hungry; and N.R.A. because it emerged as industrial cartels policed by government sanction. During the 'Hundred Days', however, the measures were looked on by farmers and industry as the way to salvation.

For the orthodox school, Roosevelt cut $400 million in veterans' payments and $100 million in federal employees' salaries to redeem his campaign promise of balancing the budget.

Going off gold

While planners and government-owners were occupied with restricting output and the slower process of governmental public works, the monetary manipulators in the Congress were at work. Silver interests attached an amendment to the farm Bill, requiring the President to coin silver at a ratio of 16 to 1 with gold. The President threatened to veto this Wheeler amendment; the farmer-monetary bloc substituted the Thomas amendment, which allowed the President (a) to issue greenback currency (currency outside the Federal Reserve System, not backed by metal) up to a limit of $3,000 million; (b) to fix the value of silver in terms of gold; and (c) to fix the weight of gold by proclamation. On the evening of 18 April, President Roosevelt announced his decision to accept the Thomas amendment. Lewis Douglas commented later that evening, 'This is the end of Western civilization.'

In the bank-holiday legislation, gold exports had been prohibited except under licence. Until the Thomas amendment, licences had been issued. Increasingly, as April wore on and the inflationary bloc in Congress grew in strength, the question was raised as to whether this was a good idea.[5] With the acceptance of the Thomas amendment, the decision was taken to stop issuing licences. The outflow of capital picked up. By 24 April, the pound had risen from $3·24 in the first half of April to $3·86.

5. See the excerpt from James Warburg's oral history statement in Jordan Schwartz, *1933: Roosevelt's Decision: The United States Leaves the Gold Standard*, Chelsea House, New York, 1969, p. 141; and Herbert Feis, *1933: Characters in Crisis*, Little Brown, Boston, 1966, p. 121.

In January, twenty economists had recommended that the United States should settle war debts, reduce tariffs and cling unflinchingly to the gold standard.[6] At the time of the bank holiday, Paris saw it as utter madness for the United States to attempt to go off gold. It would solve nothing, and only bring United States internal problems to a world level.[7] On 7 March, *The Times* in London declared the abandonment of the gold standard by the United States so unlikely as almost to be left out of account. None of the causes which drove the United Kingdom off gold were to be found in the United States. There was no run on United States funds or securities by foreign creditors. There was no remedy for any problem in devaluation.[8] At the same time, a cynical Frenchman, Édouard Daladier, who replaced Paul-Boncour as Prime Minister of France at the end of January, thought that going off gold was the inevitable answer of the dollar to the fluctuating pound.[9]

The pound was comfortable. In his annual speech as chairman of the Midland Bank, Reginald McKenna opposed Britain returning to gold, claiming that it had been off the gold standard for sixteen months and that nothing catastrophic had happened.[10] The Chancellor of the Exchequer, Neville Chamberlain, said on 28 January that the United Kingdom would return to gold only when it felt assured that the system would work well.[11] The action by the United States in halting gold exports took place while Ramsay MacDonald was *en route* to Washington to discuss

6. *New York Times*, 3 January 1933, p. 1.

7. *New York Times*, 3 March 1933, p. 21. This conclusion was insufficient to free French officials of thought of what would be required in the event of devaluation of the dollar. At French-British discussions, headed by Neville Chamberlain, Chancellor of the Exchequer, and Georges Bonnet, French Minister of Finance, in London on 17 March to discuss the World Economic Conference, it was agreed that further discussions would be useful if the dollar were to be devalued – see *Documents diplomatiques français, 1932–1939*, 1er série (1932–5), III (Imprimerie Nationale, Paris, 1966), # 1, p. 12.

8. *New York Times*, 7 March 1933, p. 6.

9. Department of State, *Foreign Relations of the United States, 1933*, vol. I, U.S. Government Printing Office, Washington, D.C., 1948, p. 576.

10. *New York Times*, 28 January 1933.

11. *New York Times*, 30 January 1933.

preparations for the World Economic Conference with Roosevelt. It changed the bargaining position.

Preparing for the World Economic Conference

The idea of a world economic conference to formulate recovery plans perhaps goes back to a discussion of December 1930 between the U.S. Ambassador, Sackett, and Chancellor Brüning in Germany, in which the latter suggested the possibility of a conference in which the great related questions of disarmament, reparations, debt retirement and international loan requirements could be dealt with as one package, and settled on a political basis rather than treating each question separately by economic experts.[12]

The more proximate origin of the conference, as noted earlier, was the Laval-Hoover discussions of October 1931 and the Hoover-MacDonald exchange of May 1932. On the latter occasion, the British government had expressed some concern that gold prices had suffered a further fall. Stimson's reply to MacDonald on behalf of President Hoover had indicated that the conference should have two purposes: (a) to raise commodity prices by easier credit, and possibly by some programme of synchronized public expenditure; and (b) to encourage private business groups throughout the world.[13]

The conference was formally called by the Lausanne Conference resolution of 9 July 1932, following up an International Labour Office (I.L.O.) proposal adopted by the League of Nations on 21 May. Its official title was 'International Conference on Mone-

12. Edward W. Bennett, *Germany and the Diplomacy of the Financial Crisis, 1931*, Harvard University Press, Cambridge, Mass., 1962, p. 32. James M. Cox, the former governor of Ohio and presidential candidate on the Democratic ticket in 1920, traces the origin to a resolution of the Democratic Congress elected in 1930, calling for international action to reduce excessive duties and eliminate destructive and unfair trade practices by means of an international economic conference on the one hand, and reciprocal trade agreements negotiated by the President on the other. The resolution was, of course, directed against the President's signature of the Smoot-Hawley Tariff Act. President Hoover vetoed it. See James M. Cox, *Journey through My Years*, Simon & Schuster, New York, 1946, p. 353.

13. Feis, *1933: Characters in Crisis*, pp. 21 and 23.

tary and Economic Questions', after the United States had objected to calling the questions 'Financial and Economic', on the
grounds that 'Financial' would allow the discussion of war debts,
which it sought to keep off the agenda. The Lausanne resolution
provided for an organizing committee and a preparatory commission of experts to draw up an agenda. The topics to be covered
were designated (a) under monetary (and financial) questions:
monetary and credit policy, exchange stabilization and the level of
prices and the movement of capital; and (b) under economic
questions: improved conditions of production and trade, with
particular attention to tariff policy, quantitative restrictions and
agreements among producers.

The organizing committee stayed away from substance, and the
preparatory commission of experts did not do much better.
Professor John H. Williams, who with E. E. Day served as one of
the United States experts, reported to W. Randolph Burgess of
the Federal Reserve Bank of New York after the first meeting of
the experts in Geneva in November that the discussion started with
the British asking: 'How can prices be raised?' and the others
replying, 'When will sterling be stabilized?' The British were
reluctant to discuss the second question at any length, but indicated that there would be no stabilization until prices were higher,
or at least until war debts were settled.[14]

Roosevelt's primary response was to delay the conference; first,
until he took over, and secondly until his domestic programmes
had had an opportunity to take hold. Like Hoover, he was against
allowing war debts into the discussion.

The second meeting of the preparatory commission took place
in January and February, before the bank holiday and before the
dollar went off gold. Leith-Ross stated for the British that the
world economy had deteriorated since the previous meeting, that
a premature restoration of the gold standard would be extremely
dangerous, and that there was need to close the gap between costs
and prices before restoring gold, plus clearing up war debts and
reparations, undertaking monetary reform to economize gold,
providing for financial reconstruction and lowering tariffs and

14. Federal Reserve Bank of New York files, memorandum from Burgess
to Harrison, 23 November 1932.

quotas.[15] Émile Francqui of the National Bank of Belgium proposed a plan for an international credit institute which would make short-term funds available to countries running temporary balance-of-payments deficits in the course of stabilizing their currencies and undertaking domestic recovery measures. An I.L.O. plan for international public works financed by a common credit pool followed the lines of Woytinsky's proposal noted in the previous chapter. Echoes of the 1930 Kindersley or Norman plan were heard at the conference. But the experts ultimately put aside these ideas in favour of first raising prices directly in so far as it could be done with balanced budgets and sound monetary measures; and secondly, of dismantling the system of national defensive measures based on concerted action over a broad front: the United Kingdom would stabilize the pound, although it was agreed that the timing and the rate posed tricky questions; Germany would relax foreign-exchange control; France would reduce its quota restrictions; and the United States would settle war debts and lower the tariff.[16] Herbert Feis, in a memorandum of 29 January, stated that this programme was impracticable because workers and politicians in the United States wanted bolder monetary and banking measures and that stabilization at present rates of the franc and pound would be premature. This statement led to an angry intellectual brawl.[17]

It was agreed that the meeting would be held in London. Ramsay MacDonald hoped to go out in a blaze of glory at the conference.[18] In his memoirs, Warburg says this was a mistake and that the conference should have been held in Washington.[19]

15. Federal Reserve Bank of New York files, memorandum of 7 January 1933. An account of the opening session is also contained in *Documents diplomatiques français*, II #180, Geneva to Paris, p. 386, and notes that Professor J. H. Williams, the United States expert, called Great Britain and Germany 'key countries', anticipating his 'key-currency' view of ten years later.

16. Department of State, *Foreign Relations of the United States*, I, p. 462.

17. Feis, *1933: Characters in Crisis*, p. 116.

18. Department of State, *Foreign Relations of the United States*, I, 1933, p. 477.

19. James P. Warburg, *The Long Road Home, the Autobiography of a Maverick*, Doubleday, Garden City, New York, 1964, p. 122. A desire to hold the conference in Washington was expressed by Roosevelt to the French

As a preliminary, the heads of various delegations came to Washington to confer with President Roosevelt. 'For a time it seemed that America was assuming the leadership in an enterprise that held out every hope of success.'[20]

Roosevelt, Hull and Moley took only a minor part in the consultations, however. Warburg handled financial questions, Feis tariff and trade; Bullitt handled politics.

The departure of the dollar from gold while MacDonald and Herriot were at sea shifted the focus from war debts to stabilization. Warburg seized the initiative, and with agreement from President Roosevelt, proposed a stabilization plan in which the United States would depreciate the dollar by 15 to 25 per cent, and thereafter the three currencies would be stabilized and managed by a three-country stabilization fund. Leith-Ross for the British was shocked by a depreciation of the dollar as high as 15 per cent. He felt the United States could easily maintain its old gold parity and stated as a final position that, if the stabilization of the dollar took place at a lower rate, the pound would be lowered to a parallel extent.[21] Charles Rist for the French thought it would be impossible to get the Chamber of Deputies to agree, since francs might be used to buy dollars, and these might subsequently depreciate to saddle the French treasury with a loss. These discussions took place over the period 26–30 April with the dollar

---

Ambassador, Claudel, on 21 February, and the possibility was again taken up by Ramsay MacDonald and the French Premier, Édouard Daladier, in Paris on 10 March. It was stated that President Roosevelt was willing to send a delegation to London, but preferred Washington as a site. The French had no preference, and MacDonald asserted that he would go to Washington, if it would help, but the Prime Minister of Britain could hardly spend several months across the ocean. Sir John Simon, the Foreign Minister, added that Washington was hot in summer. At the 17 March meeting between Chamberlain and Bonnet, it was noted that London was a preferable location for the time of year, but that Washington would have helped to educate United States public opinion. See *Documents diplomatiques français*, ii, #s 318 and 392, 21 February and 10 March on pp. 671 and 778, respectively, and iii, #1, 17 March, p. 3.

20. Cox, *Journey through My Years*, p. 355.

21. This was *à propos* a suggestion that the U.S. dollar might be depreciated by 15 per cent in respect of gold, and the pound held at $3·75. See *Documents diplomatiques français*, iii, #190, Washington to Paris, p. 328.

steady – the pound moving down from $3·85 on 25 April to $3·73 on the 27th and back again to $3·85 on the 29th. President Roosevelt expressed relief when the stabilization proposal fell through.[22] The communiqué issued by the President and Guido Jung of the Bank of Italy, however, came out in favour of currency stabilization.

As the dollar fell on international exchanges in May – going from $3·85 to the pound on 29 April to $4·00 on 31 May – Roosevelt became less and less interested in stabilization. Moley records that he experienced a 'dangerous euphoria'. He was prepared to agree on the date of the conference – in mid June. Nothing else was decided.

Hull and Feis worked on the tariff truce. It was difficult to the point of impossibility to give it content. Every country wanted exceptions. The United States wanted to put up tariffs on agricultural commodities subject to a processing tax under the A.A.A.; Britain had some unfinished tariff increases on eggs and bacon under the Ottawa Conference of 1932. France reserved its position until it saw whether prices in the United States rose the full amount of the depreciation of the dollar; otherwise they would be obliged

22. Feis, *1933: Characters in Crisis*, pp. 144–7. Jeannette P. Nichols claims that Bonnet as Minister of Finance in Paris rejected the agreement as likely to be interpreted as inflationary – see 'Roosevelt's Monetary Diplomacy, 1933', *American Historical Review*, LVI, No. 2 (January 1951), p. 302. This seems less compelling than the fear of loss which was cited by Governor Moret of the Bank of France in 1932. See *supra*, p. 169. No explicit message on Paris's reasoning is contained in *Documents diplomatiques français*, in which a statement of a position against the common stabilization fund is given in III, #258, note of the Section on Commercial Policy (Paris), p. 457. Bullitt later expressed the discouragement of the United States government over the restrained attitude of the British government and the lack of response of the French to the common stabilization fund (ibid., #262 of 10 May, p. 465). In reply, the French Foreign Office expressed the willingness of its government and the Bank of France to enter into immediate conversations on tripartite monetary cooperation as soon as they were approached (ibid., #274 of 14 May, p. 482). The French ambassador in London asked for immediate stabilization discussions on 17 May (ibid., #288, p. 500). He was told that the British thought that too little time had elapsed since the dollar had gone off gold. It took six months for sterling to find a certain equilibrium. As much would be required of the dollar, especially in the light of the conflicts between Wall Street and Washington, and the President and the Congress.

to apply import surtaxes. But when Brazil demurred to the tariff truce, stating that it had some increases in process, Feis told them sharply that all countries had to make sacrifices in the general interest.[23]

The Washington consultations brought up a number of points of national economic interest. Schacht asked for access to colonies, and hinted that Germany might cut off external debt service unilaterally. On 20 May, service in fact was suspended on debts amounting to perhaps $5,000 million.[24] An Australian submission pointed out that gold prices for the country's exports had fallen to 30 per cent of the 1928 level, and sterling prices to 42 per cent, imposing a heavy burden of debt service in sterling and gold currencies. Interest alone absorbed one third of a greatly increased volume of exports.[25] T. V. Soong, the Chinese Minister of Finance, was disturbed at the rising price of silver, since China (as well as Mexico) were stabilized on a silver standard and found its rising price draining their countries of money.[26] The Japanese representative made it clear that under no circumstances in a world stabilization agreement would his country allow the yen to go back to 49 cents. Twenty cents would be all right, and it might compromise at 25 cents if it could not go lower.[27]

The Swedish minister could not understand how the dollar

23. Department of State, *Foreign Relations of the United States*, I, pp. 515, 587 and 608. The text of the truce, with some of the reservations verbal, was announced in London by the Organizing Committee of the Conference, but was good only for the duration of the conference.

24. ibid., pp. 532 and 534.

25. ibid., p. 511.

26. ibid., pp. 532 and 763 ff.

27. ibid., pp. 536 and 538. *Documents diplomatiques français*, III, #242, Tokyo to Paris, 4 May 1933, p. 423, sets out the Japanese attitude before the arrival of Viscount Iichi in Washington: without rejecting a return to the gold standard, Japan considers this measure should be subordinated to a redistribution of world gold and increases in reserves in all countries. It should also be connected with free circulation of capital . . . 'In other words, Japan is not proceeding otherwise than other governments, and under its adherence to principles, it is easy to discern the concern to safeguard above all its national economic interests. It refuses to lower its tariffs significantly, objecting that it has not, unlike other countries, significantly raised them since the war. At the same time, and in apparent contradiction, it refuses to revalue its exchange rate for fear of upsetting the conditions of exporting.'

needed to be protected by a gold embargo, when the balance of payments was in surplus. Ambassador Lawrence Steinhardt, working with Warburg, explained that the United States had been experiencing a capital flight based on the possibility that the dollar might be devalued, and on that account had to devalue.[28]

Of more far-reaching importance were the answers given to the Japanese and the Poles on international public works. Mr Tusushima of the Japanese delegation stated that he understood that the International Labour Office at Geneva was going to propose some international programme of international public works. Mr Warburg said that the United States felt that each nation must raise its own funds. 'We would oppose without any ambiguity a proposal that we finance someone else's programme.'[29] The Polish ambassador found the proposals of the American government too indefinite to provide any basis for understanding between the two governments. Dr Feis replied that the United States did not want to enter the conference with a programme

28. Department of State, *Foreign Relations of the United States*, I, 1933, p. 566.

29. ibid., p. 538. In this the United States was following the French, who, as reported by Cochran (Department of State, *Foreign Relations of the United States*, vol. I, 1932, p. 831), with regard to the work of the Preparatory Commission had stated their objection to the Francqui and Kindersley plans: 'If she is called upon to make a big investment, she desires to be free to make her own terms as she has done before. She looks on loans as political as well as trade means and desires her independence of action. She is not willing to help the British or Americans retrieve bad loans unless her funds are involved.'

The Francqui plan was referred to earlier. The Kindersley plan is probably the same as the Norman plan, noted in the previous chapter.

In addition to the International Credit Institute proposed by Francqui, the Preparatory Commission also discussed, and was cool towards, a Monetary Normalization Fund, first brought forward at the Stresa Conference for the Economic Restoration of Central and Eastern Europe, held from 5–20 September 1932, and an I.L.O. proposal for financing international public works, probably along the lines of Woytinsky's article in the *International Labour Review* discussed above. See James W. Angell, *The Program for the World Economic Conference: The Experts' Agenda and the Document*, World Peace Foundation, Boston, 1933, p. 52, and Department of State, *Foreign Relations of the United States*, I, 1933, p. 457.

For a reference to a Turkish proposal for an International Credit Bank, see ibid., p. 570.

binding itself to a series of propositions. It was not an American conference, and the United States had less to gain and less to lose than other countries. The ambassador referred to the question of the synchronization of public works undertaken for the purpose of increasing employment and trade and asked how funds would be provided.

He was informed that proposals had been made for the creation of an international fund ... The United States could not participate in such a fund. In the first place it would be impossible to come to any international agreement ... An international fund of the nature proposed would only cause greater dissension among the countries. In the second place, the United States could not possibly participate in such a fund since the Congress would not provide money for that purpose. American experience with respect to international loans has not been sufficiently happy to encourage it to enter into additional ventures.[30]

In talking to the Polish ambassador, Feis mentioned a proposal put forward by the Special British Mission. This is referred to in a brief memorandum of conversation by Feis. The British financial attaché in Washington, Kenneth S. Bewley, waited on Feis with a memorandum on 15 April, but did not leave it with him. The British government proposed the creation of an international fund of between $1,500 to $2,000 million by the contribution of various governments for the purpose of making loans to central banks, which in turn would end exchange controls, and reduce trade barriers. Bewley and Feis agreed that there were three questions which would have to be answered with respect to the suggestion: (a) Was it practical? (b) Would it achieve the desired end of reducing trade barriers and raising prices? And (c) would it be politically possible to win support for it in the United States? Feis suggested that there was doubt on all three issues, and especially the third in the light of the opposition in the United States to proposals under which the government would obligate itself to furnish any more money to foreign governments – particularly in the light of threatened default on all past loans. Bewley was so impressed that he left, taking with him the copy of the British government's memorandum.[31]

30. ibid., pp. 560–61.
31. ibid., pp. 574–5.

The Bewley proposal represents a watered-down Treasury version of a memorandum by Hubert Henderson which was adopted by the Economic Advisory Council in its Fourth Report and revived when the prime minister asked an E.A.C. Committee on International Economic Policy, consisting of Sir Charles Addis, Lord Astor, Sir Basil Blackett, Lord Essendon, Keynes, Layton, Salter, Stamp and Henderson, for advice on the World Economic Conference. It strongly resembles the Henderson 'Monetary Proposal for Lausanne', dated 12 May 1932, which called for special currency International Certificates to be issued by the Bank for International Settlements, to the value of 50 per cent of a country's gold value exports in 1928 (as an illustration);[32] and the Keynes proposal published in letters to *The Times* in March and April 1933, and reproduced as Chapter 5 of *The Means to Prosperity*.[33] The Keynes proposal provided for $5,000 million in paper gold to be issued to countries of the world based on their gold holdings at the end of 1928, but with an upper limit of $450 million which would be granted to Great Britain, the United States, France, Germany, Spain, Argentina and Japan.

The Henderson memorandum for the E.A.C. is dated 1 July 1932 and calls for the issue by the Bank for International Settlements of new notes, equivalent to gold, in the amount of £1,000 million.[34] The basis for distribution is not stated. Of particular interest, however, is the analysis leading up to the proposal. Henderson recalled the central theme of Bagehot's *Lombard Street* of the danger of a run on London and the necessity to curb it by suspending the Bank Act of 1844 (which limited the note issue). He stated that Britain used to assist in maintaining solvency everywhere in difficult times, by shipping gold to centres of financial crisis and by drawing gold from centres which were not affected:

32. See Hubert Henderson, *The Inter-War Years and Other Papers*, Clarendon Press, Oxford, 1955, pp. 103–106.

33. Macmillan, London: Harcourt Brace, New York, 1933. My personal copy has the date of 1 May 1933 written in it.

34. D. E. Moggridge has kindly traced the history of the Bewley memorandum for me in the Public Record Office, and sent me a copy of the Henderson memorandum.

It is of the essence of the present world difficulties that London has failed in the discharge of that vital function, and that no other centre has been willing and able to discharge it.[35]

Henderson suggested that the departure of Great Britain from gold had had national advantages, but from the general world standpoint had seriously intensified the instability of international financial relations.

... general lack of confidence serves to render precarious even currencies like the dollar which are impregnable against a purely external drain. This makes it impossible for the United States and perhaps for any country to step into the breach and discharge the functions of a world banker by advancing money to embarrassed countries.[36]

Henderson recognized that to issue new money on a uniform basis to all governments, debtor and creditor alike, would be a departure from Bagehot's principle of making notes available in internal panics to applicants, but thought it would be effective. The resemblance to the Special Drawing Rights of the International Monetary Fund, agreed upon in 1968, is striking. But whether or not the United States could participate in such a scheme, it would not. Bewley's conversation with Feis, based on the cut-down version of the Henderson report, was enough to kill the idea.

Earlier Chamberlain had sounded out Bonnet on the Keynes version of the plan, including the provision for public works, in a London meeting of the two financial heads on 17 March. He introduced the subject by stating that Keynes was not infallible, briefly described the Keynes proposal for public works by the United States, France and Great Britain, together with the creation of purchasing power, noted that since the war Great Britain had undertaken public works without the results forecast by Keynes, and asked for Bonnet's views. Bonnet replied that there had been little British help for Daladier when he had supported a programme of international public works at Geneva in October 1932, worried about the financing, but was not reassured by the discussion of new credits put at the disposition of central banks. He asserted that France had practised public

35. Henderson memorandum, p. 4.
36. ibid., p. 5.

works programmes for several years without any noticeable increase of prices. The budgetary deficits disquieted the Minister of Finance. The real need was to restore confidence.[37] There was no support for the feeble British initiative from this quarter.

Apart from Hull, who was to head the delegation, and who thought exclusively about tariff truce and long-run tariff reduction, there was little enthusiasm for the conference as the date grew near. Norman Davis kept cabling from London that while MacDonald was away in Washington, there were grave doubts at home whether Britain might not do better to move to an Empire rather than a world solution. The country wanted to cooperate, but its only interest was war debts, now widened by the unhinging of the dollar.[38] In a speech made over the radio on 20 May and approved by Roosevelt, Moley suggested that not much would result from the World Economic Conference apart from comparing domestic experience:

> Too many people are likely to think that because the depression is world-wide, its causes rest solely on international conditions or that the solution for this world-wide depression is solely through international remedies . . . The fact is that a good many of the economic ills of each country are domestic . . . They are predominantly internal, not external. Much of the remedy, then, must be what the nations do themselves.[39]

37. *Documents diplomatiques français*, iii, #1, London to Paris, 17 March 1933, p. 607.

38. ibid., pp. 586 and 598–9.

39. Moley, *The First New Deal*, pp. 404–5. The sardonic Lord Vansittart, who accompanied MacDonald to Washington, put it thus: '. . . we find that discussion of war-debts, reparations and tariffs might be difficult at the World Conference. We could present *Hamlet* without the Prince of Denmark, Ophelia and Polonius; it would be shortened. So would the Conference. Failure was assured' – *The Mist Procession, the Autobiography of Lord Vansittart*, Hutchinson, London, 1958, p. 465.

At the time he sought Washington conversations, Roosevelt indicated to Claudel, the French ambassador, his concern that the programme was insufficiently prepared, the assemblage too large, exposed to publicity and divided by irreconcilable views – *Documents diplomatiques français*, iii, #54, Washington to Paris, 27 March 1933, p. 94. The Washington talks helped to remedy these defects but little. See also *The Economist*, 10 June 1933, p. 1229: 'France is sceptical; the American delegation, perplexed by an extremely complex situation at home, is new to the international game; while Germany

War debts were separated from the agenda of the conference, and so was currency stabilization, although Governor Harrison of the Federal Reserve Bank of New York, O. M. W. Sprague, a former adviser to the Bank of England, and Warburg were to negotiate an agreement on stabilization among the central banks parallel to the general conference. United States instructions to the delegation called for action along six (overlapping) fronts, and furnished draft resolutions:

(1) A tariff truce.

(2) Coordinated monetary and fiscal policy, with the monetary policy consisting of open-market operations (to which the French objected) and no content given to coordinated fiscal policy, which was to be the object of study.

(3) The removal of foreign exchange restrictions.

(4) Laying the groundwork for an adequate and enduring monetary standard.

(5) Basic agreement on the gradual abolition of barriers to trade.

(6) Basic agreement on the control of production and distribution of world commodities.[40]

As the Polish ambassador commented, the degree of specificity was low.

---

is deeply absorbed in her ideas of national revival at home. England, in her turn, shows signs of a dangerous complacency, due perhaps, to the happy chance that she has escaped the worst crises of the past year' – quoted by Abdul Hasib, *Monetary Negotiations in the World Economic Conference*, Publications of the Faculty of Arts, Muslim University, Alijar, 1958, p. 82.

40. *Foreign Relations of the United States*, I, 1933, p. 623. At an earlier stage, when the United States was still committed to the gold standard, proposals for monetary reform – put forward by the United States as a basis of discussion – included a reduction of gold reserve requirements to a uniform 30 or 25 per cent, the abandonment of internal convertibility of currencies into gold, and the adoption of fixed gold points, perhaps 5 per cent apart, rather than gold points which altered with such circumstances as geographical distance. See *Documents diplomatiques français*, III, #106, Washington to Paris, 8 April 1933. With the abandonment of the gold standard, this proposal dropped by the wayside.

The suggestion regarding open-market operations goes back to the second Preparatory Commission, but it was difficult to have much faith in open-market operations in the United States with excess reserves of over $1,000 million.

215

The World Economic Conference

Meeting in London on 12 June, the conference was thronged with prime ministers – Daladier of France, Beneš of Czechoslovakia, Bennett of Canada, Dollfuss of Austria, Smuts of the Union of South Africa, Bruce of Australia; foreign ministers, such as Hull of the United States, Colijn of the Netherlands, Litvinov of the Soviet Union; ministers of finance, including Neville Chamberlain, the British Chancellor of the Exchequer, Bonnet of France, T. V. Soong of China; presidents of central banks, among them Hjalmar Schacht of Germany, Trip of the Netherlands, Kienbock of Austria, Jung of Italy. The United States delegation, headed by Hull, included an odd assortment of personalities and experts, among them three isolationists who were ultimately pleased with the conference failure – Key Pittman and James Couzens, Senators respectively of Nevada and Michigan, and an industrialist named Morrison. There was a round of opening speeches. That of Hull had to be delayed while it was rewritten in Washington to play down international solutions to the depression, provided in the Hull draft, and to emphasize domestic ones. MacDonald scandalized the American delegation by mentioning war debts.

In the course of organization, a contest emerged between James Cox of the United States and Georges Bonnet of France for the post of presiding officer of the financial committee. The French suggested that it was inappropriate to have the representative of a country which had left the gold standard presiding; in reply, it was pointed out that it was unsuitable to elect the representative of a country which had repudiated its debts. The British had paid the 15 June instalment on war debts by transferring silver which they were able to buy in the market at half the price for which they were credited. The French defaulted. Feis notes that Roosevelt showed no animus against the French on this score, and shelved the issue for the duration of the conference. He added, 'It is probable that the default washed away the remnants of Roosevelt's tolerance for the French effort to cause us to return to the international gold standard . . .'[41]

41. Feis, *1933: Characters in Crisis*, p. 182. Roosevelt had been urging the French to make a gesture of a token payment in arrears for the 15 December

216

The first business was to take place outside the conference: the conclusion of an agreement to stabilize the pound and the dollar in terms of gold for the duration of the conference. This had been agreed on 31 May, when the pound was $4·00. On 12 June, as the conference opened, the rate was $4·15. More important, while the dollar was falling from $3·42 to the pound to $4·00, Moody's index of staple commodity prices had risen from 86 to 120, and the Dow-Jones industrial stock index from 56 to 90. By 12 June the two indexes were 124 and 97 respectively.

The deal worked out among the financial representatives called for the dollar to be stabilized at $4·00 to the pound and ·04662 to the franc, with a 3 per cent spread on either side, from $3·88 to $4·12 for the pound (and ·04893 to ·047331 for the franc). Each of the three central banks would support its currency up by selling gold, to a limit of four or five million ounces, equivalent to $80–$100 million. When this was used up, the agreement would be re-examined.

The news of stabilization leaked to the press, and the exchange market firmed from $4·12 to $4·02; the commodity and stock markets declined. The Committee for the Nation sent President Roosevelt a telegram calling for the dollar to be cut 43 per cent, based on calculations for restoring United States prices, which implied a pound rate of $5·70. Roosevelt sent the delegation telegrams on 17 June from Washington (and on the 19th and 20th from the destroyer U.S.S. *Ellis*, accompanying him sailing), saying that $4·00 was unacceptable. While stabilization was an ultimate objective, one needed worldwide action to achieve it, not just action taken by three or four countries. It was as well to avoid even a tentative commitment to a definite programme to control fluctuations in the dollar. When the pound reached $4·25, the United States would contemplate unilateral action to hold the level. As an afterthought, he added that he would consider a median rate of $4·15. Too much importance was attached to

---

1932 instalment, but without promising them anything concrete in exchange. See *Documents diplomatiques français*, III, #86, Washington to Paris, 5 April, pp. 148–9, *à propos* of Herriot's visit: 'For the due date of 15 June, I hope in one way or another to have the necessary powers, but France must understand that it is impossible for me to undertake any explicit engagements now.'

stabilization by banker-influenced cabinets. In the case of the United States, 'it means only a very small (perhaps 3) per cent of our total trade'.[42] He then took off for a sailing vacation which made communication difficult with both Washington and London.

The rejection of the stabilization agreement on 17 June restored the downward progress of the dollar, and the upward march of commodity and stock prices. Harrison returned from London. In London Warburg began to draft a new stabilization agreement. Moley flew from Washington to Martha's Vineyard to confer with Roosevelt aboard his boat, and then returned to New York to sail for London on 21 June. In the Federal Reserve Bank of New York, J. H. Williams suggested that if the French, and to some extent the British, insisted on stabilization, and the United States that currency stabilization must not be allowed to interfere with the domestic programme of raising prices, 'we say to the British what they said to us at Geneva last fall: we cannot undertake currency stabilization except as part of a general program, to be entered into by at least three leading countries, to raise prices by means of credit expansion, public works and other suitable measures, and that any stabilization agreement must be flexible and subject to change in accordance with domestic and international forces, especially relative changes in price levels.'[43] The gold bloc told the British that unless something were done to stabilize the dollar, it would have to go off gold.

Moley arrived in London on 28 June and went to work with Warburg to effect a compromise. He refers to a declaration drawn up by Cox, Warburg and Sprague and agreed by the French, Dutch and Italians – largely a paraphrase of Warburg's instructions from Washington with no mention of rates, and stabilization mentioned only as an ultimate objective – and calls it unconditional surrender on the part of the gold-bloc countries.[44] Bonnet's report to his government suggests that he drew up the statement in response to a request of MacDonald, and transmitted a copy before

42. Department of State, *Foreign Relations of the United States*, I, 1933, pp. 646, 649 and 650.

43. Federal Reserve Bank of New York files, J. H. Williams memorandum to Secretary of the Treasury Woodin, 19 June 1933.

44. Moley, *The First New Deal*, p. 435.

the British and American delegations signed it, which they ultimately did on 30 June.[45] The agreement provided for appropriate measures to limit speculation and for central-bank cooperation in stabilization on an interim basis. It is hard to understand Moley's characterization of the agreement as unconditional surrender.

The draft was cabled to Washington and to Roosevelt in his Campobello summer home in New Brunswick, Canada, across the border from easternmost Maine. Baruch, Woodin and Acheson supported the plan from Washington. Roosevelt, who had no advisers with him, and only Henry Morgenthau of the Farm Credit Board as a friend and Louis Howe, his secretary, rejected the compromise, twice. By this time the dollar had reached $4·33 against the pound, commodity prices had risen to 130 and the Dow-Jones industrial average reached 100. On 1 July Roosevelt stated that stabilization was a matter for private (i.e. central) banks, not governments, that it would permit unbalanced budgets and that he could not obligate the United States now or later to approve the export of gold. A second message on 3 July was worded more pungently for public release.

I would regard it as a catastrophe, amounting to a world tragedy, if the great Conference of Nations . . . should . . . allow itself to be diverted by the proposal of a purely artificial and temporary experiment affecting the monetary exchange of a few nations only . . . I do not relish the thought that insistence on such action should be an excuse for the continuance of basic economic errors that underly so much of the present worldwide depression.

The world will not long be lulled by the specious fallacy of achieving a temporary and probably an artificial stability in foreign exchange on the part of a few large countries only.

The sound internal economic situation of a nation is a greater factor in its well-being than the price of its currency . . .

The old fetishes of so-called international bankers are being replaced by efforts to plan national currencies with the objective of giving those currencies a continuing purchasing power . . . the U.S. seeks the kind of dollar which a generation hence will have the same purchasing power and debt-paying power as the dollar value we hope to attain in the near future . . .

45. *Documents diplomatiques français*, III, #s 426, 436 and 438, Bonnet to Paris, pp. 776, 795 and 799, respectively.

Our broad purpose is the permanent stabilization of every nation's currency . . . When the world works out concerted policies in the majority of nations to produce balanced budgets and living within their means, then we can properly discuss a better distribution of the world's gold and silver . . .[46]

The message was a bombshell. Criticized for its rhetoric, which Roosevelt later admitted was excessive, its substance has been debated to this day. It broke up the World Economic Conference, which limped along at United States insistence for a week or two before closing up shop with one agreement on silver, pushed through by Senator Pittman. British Empire countries met in a formal conference and formed the sterling area. The gold bloc organized itself defensively more fully. A number of economists – notably Harrod, Meade and Keynes, who called Roosevelt 'magnificently right' – approved. They could hardly have approved the analysis, which contained some unusual economic ideas and even *non sequiturs*: fear of gold losses, when the United States had one third of the world stock; concern that two or three currencies only would stabilize, when the rest of the world could stabilize only in terms of key currencies; distinctions between governments and central banks, which make it appropriate for the latter to undertake agreements the former should avoid; the unimportance of trade to the United States but the crucial importance of a declining dollar; and the suggestion that stabilization leads to unbalanced budgets, which are in themselves abhorrent. Nor could they have endorsed reasoning which spoke of stabilizing currencies in terms of purchasing power from generation to generation when it was evident that Roosevelt's agreement to stabilize gave way under the impact of a decline in the stock market from 96·8 to 89·2 in four days in mid June. Moley talked to Lippmann and Keynes in London about a proposal for a new international currency unit – the *dinard* – the value of which would be stabilized in terms of many commodities and not merely gold. 'None of them knew how this could be done.'[47]

Presumably Roosevelt was saying that the United States was not

46. Department of State, *Foreign Relations of the United States*, I, 1933, pp. 673–4.
47. Feis, *1933: Characters in Crisis*, p. 211.

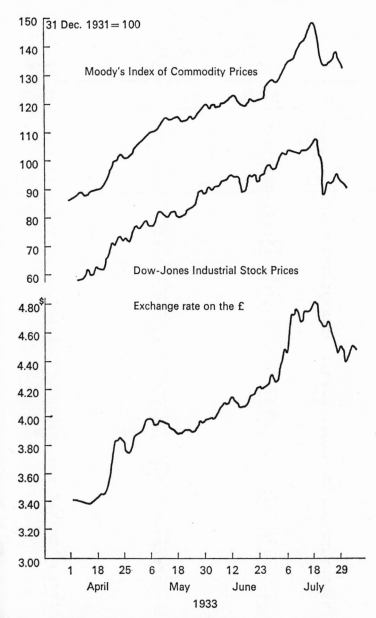

Figure 9. Daily exchange rates, commodity prices and stock prices, New York, April–July 1933.

221

		Moody's Daily Index of Staple Commodity Prices	Exchange rate on the £	Dow-Jones Industrial Average closing
		(Base: 100 = 31 Dec. 1931		
1933:				
April	1	86·4	3·42	55·7
Sun.	2	X	X	X
	3	86·7	3·42	55·7
	4	86·8	3·42	56·1
	5	87·5	3·42	57·5
	6	88·8	3·42	58·8
	7	88·5	3·42	58·8
	8	87·9	3·42	59·3
	9	X	X	X
	10	88·6	3·41	62·1
	11	90·2	3·41	61·2
	12	89·7	3·41	60·3
	13	90·9	3·41	62·7
	14	Holiday	3·44	X
	15	Holiday	3·45	62·9
	16	X	X	X
	17	91·3	3·49	61·6
	18	92·5	3·45	62·7
	19	95·1	3·49	68·3
	20	99·9	3·61	72·3
	21	99·7	3·84	69·8
	22	100·5	3·81	72·2
	23	X	X	X
	24	102·9	3·86	73·7
	25	102·2	3·85	72·4
	26	102·4	3·79	72·6
	27	102·4	3·73	71·7
	28	101·5	3·77	73·1
	29	103·8	3·85	77·7
	30	X	X	X
May	1	105·9	3·88	77·8
	2	106·6	3·88	77·3
	3	108·1	3·91	77·4
	4	109·0	3·91	79·2
	5	110·0	3·98	79·8
	6	109·8	3·99	77·6
	7	X	X	X
	8	111·0	3·97	76·6
	9	110·9	3·94	77·2
	10	111·6	3·93	80·8
	11	114·1	3·96	82·5
	12	115·6	3·98	82·1
	13	115·8	3·97	80·9
	14	X	X	X
	15	115·0	3·96	79·7
	16	115·3	3·94	81·3
	17	116·4	3·91	82·6
	18	116·0	3·90	82·6
	19	114·9	3·88	81·8
	20	113·7	3·87	80·2
	21	X	X	X
	22	113·6	3·89	79·9
	23	114·7	3·91	83·1
	24	115·7	3·92	84·3
	25	115·4	3·92	83·7
	26	116·9	3·91	86·6
	27	118·5	3·97	89·6
	28	X	X	X

		Moody's Daily Index of Staple Commodity Prices	Exchange rate on the £	Dow-Jones Industrial Average closing
		(Base: 100 = 31 Dec. 1931		
	29	119·5	3·97	90·0
	30	Holiday	X	X
	31	120·7	4·00	88·1
June	1	120·3	4·00	89·1
	2	120·9	3·99	92·2
	3	120·5	4·01	90·0
	4	X	X	X
	5	120·2	4·01	91·9
	6	120·9	4·02	91·9
	7	121·4	4·06	93·0
	8	120·6	4·12	93·5
	9	121·6	4·10	94·3
	10	122·7	4·14	94·4
	11	X	X	X
	12	123·7	4·15	96·8
	13	123·8	4·14	94·8
	14	121·8	4·09	94·1
	15	120·1	4·06	88·9
	16	120·1	4·07	89·2
	17	119·5	4·07	90·2
	18	X	X	X
	19	121·7	4·14	96·0
	20	121·7	4·18	95·2
	21	121·9	4·16	95·9
	22	122·4	4·23	92·9
	23	122·7	4·22	95·5
	24	123·4	4·22	95·7
	25	X	X	X
	26	127·4	4·21	98·5
	27	130·3	4·24	98·7
	28	128·9	4·34	97·7
	29	128·8	4·30	97·0
	30	128·6	4·26	98·1
July	1	129·9	4·33	100·9
	2	X	X	X
	3	132·4	4·41	103·8
	4	Holiday	X	X
	5	132·9	4·52	102·7
	6	134·6	4·47	105·0
	7	135·4	4·73	105·4
	8	135·5	4·70	105·2
	9	X	X	X
	10	136·9	4·80	104·1
	11	139·0	4·74	103·1
	12	142·6	4·68	104·6
	13	143·0	4·77	105·5
	14	143·7	4·78	105·0
	15	145·3	4·78	106·1
	16	X	X	X
	17	148·5	4·78	108·3
	18	148·9	4·84	108·7
	19	145·2	4·83	103·6
	20	137·8	4·75	96·3
	21	134·1	4·65	88·7
	22	133·5	4·64	88·4
	23	X	X	X
	24	135·4	4·64	94·3
	25	135·2	4·68	92·8
	26	137·4	4·61	95·1

	Moody's Daily Index of Staple Commodity Prices	Exchange rate on the £	Dow-Jones Industrial Average closing
	(Base: 100 = 12/31/31)		
27	140·0	4·56	96·0
28	137·4	4·48	94·5
29	·135·3	4·53	X
30	X	X	X
31	132·1	4·53	90·8
August 1		4·41	
2		4·45	
3		4·53	
4		4·50	

Source: Commercial and Financial Chronicle, 1933.

ready to enter into international agreement until it had pushed further with attempting to raise prices by exchange depreciation. The experiment did not last long. On 17 July the pound approached $4·86 and Roosevelt ordered the Federal Reserve Bank of New York to support the dollar, up to perhaps $30 million, in an effort to fend off possible retaliation.[48] The bank bought only $1·3 million when the exchange, commodity and stock markets all turned around. There was a substantial rise in the dollar, and falls in the commodity and stock markets. As Figure 9 shows, however, the rise in the stock market did not keep up with the depreciation of the dollar, and the decline went further than the depreciation. The dollar went to $5·15 in the autumn; the stock market did not reach its July 1933 peak again until well into 1934.

The official reaction was well expressed by MacDonald, who cabled Roosevelt that Europe had no desire to interfere with domestic American policies, but had counted on the United States finding an arrangement which would not bring chaos to Europe as the price of American success; Jung of Italy added that Europe could not throw overboard the accumulated experience of centuries for an untested theory and would have to leave such experimentation to those with sufficient resources to be able to afford it.[49]

48. Federal Reserve Bank of New York files, Crane memorandum, 20 July 1933.

49. *Foreign Relations of the United States*, I, 1933, pp. 682–3. Roosevelt's reply to MacDonald was unenlightening: there is no inconsistency between

Experimenting with the gold price

The collapse of the conference and the rise of the dollar set prices down again, and Roosevelt looked around for a new expedient. It was not far to seek. Henry Morgenthau, who was with him at Campobello and coming home on the *Indianapolis*, brought Roosevelt charts showing weekly prices of agricultural prices and of gold prepared by Professor George Warren, an agricultural economist of Cornell.

A week after the bombshell, Roosevelt had Warren to tea. Roosevelt was impressed. On 16 August he told Morgenthau that he would like to buy gold in the open market at more than the prevailing price in an effort to raise commodity prices. The day before he had authorized Warburg to form a monetary study group consisting of Acheson, Eugene Black, Douglas, Harrison, James Harvey Rogers, Sprague and Walter Stewart. This group urged strongly against the Warren Plan, but had no alternative to offer. Accordingly, on 8 September, Roosevelt raised the domestic price of gold from $20·67 an ounce, where it had been for more than a century, with the exception of twenty years during and after the Civil War, to $29·82.

The initial results were satisfactory. Sterling rose above $5·00 and, with the depreciation of the dollar, stocks and commodities went up. Warburg's diary for 21 September records a conversation with the President in which he accused the President of always wanting a lower dollar than existed. In April, when the dollar was $3·75, he wanted $3·85. In May, when it was $3·85, he said he would be satisfied with $4·00. On 17 June, when he was offered $4·00, he wanted $4·25. In August, when the pound was $4·50,

---

the U.S. programme for economic recovery and international cooperation for the purpose of restoring prices, maintaining purchasing power stable over a generation, stimulating business activity, public works, managed farm production, increased purchasing power through high wages, and balanced expenditure and government taxes. The programme might be jeopardized by exposure to concerted competition. The United States wanted to stop the drift to nationalist exclusionism. There could be no other response than the present programme until a general international programme was worked out (ibid., p. 686).

he wanted $5·00. The process could go on indefinitely. Roosevelt's reply was, 'Well what would you do?' Warburg had to confess that he and his study committee had no panacea.[50]

But prices fell again, and in October, after some weeks looking for the requisite authority, Roosevelt undertook to buy newly mined gold on the open market through a subsidiary of the R.F.C. The policy was announced in a fireside chat on 22 October. The permanent value of the dollar would not be fixed until the price level had been restored. The United States must take firmly into its own hands the control of the gold value of the dollar, too greatly influenced by the accidents of international trade. The new gold purchases were a policy and not an expedient. Morgenthau reported that the President was not surprised or upset by the scepticism of the press or the angry uproar of the gold bloc, and laughed at the news from Harrison that Governor Norman – 'old pink whiskers', as he referred to him – had complained that the whole world would be put into bankruptcy.[51]

Beginning on 25 October, Morgenthau, working with Roosevelt, set the price higher each day by amounts which varied arbitrarily and about which they joked.[52] They began by buying only newly mined domestic gold, but it proved impossible to get the London price up the full amount of the rise inside the United States. On 29 October, therefore, the R.F.C. started to buy gold abroad. Harrison and Black were worried that the move would push France off the gold standard.[53] The President, however, was insistent that the time had not come to stabilize the dollar.

50. Warburg, *The Long Road Home*, p. 147.

51. John Morton Blum, *From the Morgenthau Diaries*, vol. 1: *Years of Crisis, 1928–1938*, Houghton Mifflin, Boston, 1959, p. 73. Feis comments (*1933: Characters in Crisis*, p. 287) that Morgenthau had a juvenile sense of humour.

52. Morgenthau reported that Roosevelt once proposed raising the price 21 cents because it was three times 7 cents and seven was a lucky number. Morgenthau claims Roosevelt was making a joke to relieve a tense and gloomy moment (Blum, *From the Morgenthau Diaries*, 1, p. 70). Moley, on the other hand, comments that Roosevelt gravely marred his image as a responsible statesman by his early-morning bedside guesses as to what the price of gold would be that day (*The First New Deal*, p. 303).

53. The Board of Directors of the Federal Reserve Bank of New York

It came quickly. Farm prices sagged again in November and December, and the gap between the New York and the London gold price widened. Morgenthau, who had been appointed Acting Secretary of the Treasury in November to replace Woodin, who was gravely ill, telephoned Harrison asking him to approach Governor Norman to ask whether the British government would join the United States in *de jure* stabilization of the pound and the dollar. Two days later, Norman telephoned that he had consulted Leith-Ross and that the British government would not be willing to stabilize *de jure*, nor would it be willing to give any commitment as to a minimum rate in future. They would be glad to consider, however, *de facto* stabilization for a temporary period, through the use of an agreed amount of gold. By December, when the dollar strengthened, Harrison reported to Norman that it was impossible to press the scheme. It no longer mattered. Roosevelt and Morgenthau were bored with changing the gold price and wanted to fix it permanently. On 15 January 1934 the President sent a special monetary message to Congress. The Gold Reserve Act was passed on 30 January. On 1 February, the President fixed the price of gold at $35 an ounce.

It is not entirely clear why. Morgenthau's account has an assortment of not very compelling reasons, judged in the light of the past. Exchange fluctuations could not be permitted to disrupt trade. A fixed price for gold was necessary if the government was to realize a profit for gold and use it to create a stabilization fund. The dollar was again appreciating, and Jacob Viner reported that the American gold purchases abroad were inadequately large to hold down the value of the dollar or inflate the domestic price level.[54] Flexibility was less important than the continuous

---

contemplated refusing to assist the R.F.C. in its foreign purchases. Owen D. Young, the chairman, expressed the sense of the directors that they were determined not to cooperate in any monetary programme which threatened the government credit to such an extent as to make the issuance of fiat money inevitable. Harrison, the president, however, argued against any action to terminate the bank's participation while even a slight hope remained of a programme of dollar stability. See Federal Reserve Bank of New York files, Board Minutes, 10 November 1933.

54. Blum, *From the Morgenthau Diaries*, p. 120.

harassment by the Committee for the Nation, Father Coughlin and other inflationary groups. The policy had not worked. It was necessary to move on.

Raising prices

A long list of economists has denounced the United States for abandoning the gold standard and devaluing the dollar when it had an export surplus. To Röpke, for example:

> The abandonment of the gold dollar by the Roosevelt administration must, indeed, be viewed as one of the most disastrous acts of any government and any country in recent times, disastrous both for the country itself and the rest of the world.[55]

In the previous chapter, however, it was indicated that the appreciation of the dollar was exercising a deflationary force in the United States which was keeping ahead of any decline in exports, and leaving a small export surplus. It may be granted that Roosevelt and his closest advisers – especially Morgenthau and Howe – often had no clear idea of what they were doing. In the end, the policy may have been a good one.

Once it is agreed that it is important and necessary to raise world prices,[56] two means are available. The first is for the countries of the world to embark simultaneously on programmes of government spending, either so carefully articulated in amount and timing that each country's exports grow at the same rate as its imports; or more probably, with a fund contributed jointly to

55. Wilhelm Röpke, *Crises and Cycles*, William Hodge, London, n.d. (?1936), p. 167. See also Ragnar Nurkse, 'International Monetary Equilibrium', *Essays in International Finance*, No. 4 (Spring 1945), International Finance Section, Princeton University, reprinted in American Economic Association, *Readings in the Theory of International Trade*, Blakiston, Philadelphia, 1949: 'A country with a surplus in its balance of payments should never resort to devaluation; on the contrary, it might be asked to appreciate its currency' (p. 13).

56. Feis records a view of Keynes that the gold bloc sees no virtue in a rising price level, putting their faith in a revival of confidence which is to come somehow by itself through businessmen gradually deciding that the world is safe for them (*1933: Characters in Crisis*, p. 236).

ensure that any country whose imports got ahead of its exports – in the pursuit of the common programme, and not in an effort to acquire resources – would be financed temporarily. Such a programme was impossible in 1933, though not because it had not been thought of – the elements were all available in the Kindersley, Francqui, I.L.O. and Keynes plans. It was simply that all governments (and most politicians and economists) were opposed to government deficits, and the United States was not prepared to take the leadership in making fresh money available for a Monetary Normalization Fund or International Credit Institute, or to take the daring step of creating new international money by fiat.

The other possibility is for all countries to devalue in terms of gold simultaneously, and in the same proportion, maintaining exchange rates and creating gold profits which would be available for spending.[57] When the spending occurred, prices would rise. They might even reverse direction and start upward in expectation of increased spending. This idea had been expressed. Feis had written a memorandum to this effect on 3 March.[58] The Lippmann-

57. This is presumably what Jacobsson meant when he approved of Roosevelt's devaluation, but suggested that it would have been advantageous if it had occurred in 1931, two years earlier. (Per Jacobsson, *Some Monetary Problems, International and National*, Oxford University Press, London, 1958, pp. 117 and 124.) But the text is not altogether clear. On p. 118 he states that other means to raise prices than depreciation were not available. But Britain and the United States could not depreciate simultaneously against one another's currencies: only against gold. If all countries had depreciated against gold, with exchange rates unchanged, there would have been no lift to prices from the exchanges, and prices would have been raised, if at all, only from the spending of profits on gold reserves and enlarged gold production.

58. Feis, *1933: Characters in Crisis*, p. 119. Feis also records that he wrote a memorandum in May 1932 when the first discussions took place between Hoover and MacDonald about a world economic conference, suggesting that all the main currencies be devalued as a preliminary to stabilization (p. 113). The proposal was disliked by Ogden Mills and was on that account not put forward as a suggestion to the British. It is not clear from his account, however, whether Feis implied, in 1932 as in 1933, devaluation in gold, but no stimulus for any country from lower exchange rates. Or perhaps he wanted the pound sterling rate to be returned from $3·67½ in May 1932 back to $4·86.

Keynes discussion of a new currency encompassed the outlines of a programme for general devaluation. But there was almost no possibility of getting opinion to understand and agree on such a programme, especially since there would be much objection that it was highly inflationary.

In no event is it likely that world economic recovery could have been accomplished by truces in the fields of tariffs and exchange depreciation.

A series of national depreciations which runs through the full list of important countries is the equivalent of general devaluation. For a certain distance, the devaluations are likely to be deflationary, especially when they occur in a setting of world deflation and are not accompanied by rapid domestic expansion. Thus Argentine, Australian, sterling depreciation worsened world deflation, while depreciation of the yen, backed by rapid expansion, hurt little except perhaps in some less developed countries. The United States depreciation, however, happened to be followed by steady gold-bloc prices and rising dollar prices. It could have happened that the depreciation merely pushed gold-bloc prices lower. That it did not is probably the result of the change in expectations in the United States, plus the fact that spending had gone about as low as it could. When the gold bloc finally devalued in 1935 and 1936, general devaluation had taken place – a slow and painful process. The United States devaluation, inept and graceless as it was, can be regarded as useful, in the absence of intellectual and political readiness to move by more efficient methods to general expansion.

But this is serendipity. Surely the Roosevelt policy was clumsy in letting the World Economic Conference go forward, and then killing it in what appeared to be a vindictive way, citing the purchasing power of generations while reacting to the fall in market prices of a few days. Morgenthau's defence is puerile:

Compared to what Roosevelt might have done in setting a $40 price for gold, printing $3 billions [$3,000 million] in paperbacks, remonetizing silver, the gold-buying program was modest. European countries resented the policy, but no nation had for several years shown much regard for the economic convenience of others, and in 1933 the pressure on the President was such that he had to do something.[59]

The Democratic administration was prepared to experiment until it achieved recovery on the home front. It had little interest in or knowledge of the world economy, and lacked confidence in facing it. The memoirs are full of hesitations in dealing with the British: 'Every time we take the British into our confidence, they give us a trimming.'[60] Moley characterized the United States delegations to the World Economic Conference as, 'Untrained and unbriefed . . . pitted against foreigners who knew what they wanted.'[61] Pierrepont Moffat reported that the President wondered whether his 3 July message had been too strong; but he did not regret it. 'It counteracts an impression widespread throughout the country that at every conference we come out a loser.'[62]

It would not be for three years that the administration felt a responsibility for the operation of the international economic system.

59. Blum, *From the Morgenthau Diaries*, I, p. 75.
60. ibid., p. 71; see also p. 141: President Roosevelt said, 'The trouble is that when you sit around the table with a Britisher he usually gets 80 per cent of the deal and you get what's left.'
61. Moley, *The First New Deal*, p. 432.
62. Feis, *1933: Characters in Crisis*, pp. 246–7.

10. The Beginnings of Recovery

World economy in disarray

The upturn from the depth of the depression began in 1933, but was neither widespread nor rapid. In particular, the world economy lost its cohesion. The gold bloc sank still further into depression. Germany and Italy of the Axis pursued independent economic paths, cut off from the world economy by a system of controls. On the other side of the world, Japan was recovering on its own with speed and verve. The British Commonwealth, together with a number of other countries linked to sterling, proceeded, turning inward along its own recovery path. In the United States and Canada, recovery was under way, but unevenly and, on balance, slowly. The world capital market was moribund. Debt service for less developed countries was heavy. Default spread.

But the turn had been made. Outside the gold bloc, 1934 and 1935 saw increases in prices, exports, industrial production, national income. The largest part of this improvement came in 1934, after some recovery but much uncertainty the previous year. In 1935 the movement slowed to barely perceptible gains.

There were, of course, more exceptions than the gold bloc. The most notable was the foreign trade of the Soviet Union, which found more and more difficulty in exporting to European countries with foreign-exchange control and was obliged in consequence to squeeze down imports in 1934 and 1935 one third below the 1932 low level.

Recovery in the United States

The position of the United States was significant for the world economy and illustrated the unevenness of the pattern. The rapid rise in industrial production from 59 in March 1933 (on the basis of 1923–5 as 100) to 100 in July was not sustained. Based on inventory accumulation rather than long-term investment, with excess capacity in many lines of activity, it fell to 71 in July 1934, well below the peak of the previous year, but at the same time off the depression bottom. From this level it worked its way to 90 at July 1935 and to 100 by the end of the year. The movement in prices was broadly similar but dampened: from 63 in March 1933 (1929 = 100) to 74 in July, off again to 71, and then back to 75 in 1934 and 76·5 in 1935. Unemployment declined on one measure from more than 25 per cent of trade union membership to less than 17 per cent, but the American Federation of Labor estimate of the number of unemployed went down only from an average 13,700,000 in 1933, to 12,400,000 in 1934 and 12,000,000 in 1935. The Agricultural Adjustment Act and the National Recovery Act (N.R.A.) were declared unconstitutional by the Supreme Court, and spending for relief under the Works Progress Administration increased. Fiscal measures to expand employment were limited, however, since the Democratic administration under President Roosevelt remained committed to balanced budgets.

N.R.A. left a strong imprint on the country, however, in its effect on union membership. Since N.R.A. suspended anti-trust action against industrialists, it was felt necessary also to allow workers to combine as a means of promoting industrial peace. Union membership rose from under 3·0 million in 1933 to 3·6 million in 1934 and 3·9 million in 1935. The Committee for Industrial Organization (C.I.O.) split off from the American Federation of Labor (A.F.L.) to organize along industrial and across traditional craft lines. Among its leaders were John L. Lewis of the United Mine Workers, Walter Reuther of the United Automobile Workers and Sidney Hillman and David Dubinsky of the needle trades. Labour and anti-labour violence followed in a

233

variety of strikes in 1934 and 1935, which the National Labor Board, and a National Labor Relations Board succeeding it in 1934, sought ineffectively to contain. Sit-in strikes in automobile plants in Detroit added a new technique to the show of force in industrial and subsequently other types of disagreement. In 1935, after N.R.A. had been declared unconstitutional, the National Labor Relations Act re-enacted the labour provisions of N.R.A. to apply in interstate commerce. Parallel state laws in a number of jurisdictions extended the coverage to intra-state activity.

The National Labor Relations Act, considered by the Supreme Court to be constitutional in early 1937 following President Roosevelt's attack on the court at the end of 1936, was a signal to labour to extend its membership and its aggressive bargaining tactics. It marked the arrival of what was later called a 'labouristic' economy in the United States, and stimulated fears of inflation from higher wages, which led, in 1936 and early 1937, to industrial orders to build up inventories before prices rose too far. We return to this experience in Chapter 12.

In the relations of the United States to the world economy, the stabilization of the dollar in February 1934 has already been noted. This seems to have been less part of a positive design for foreign economic policy than an attempt to bury an experiment (judged to have failed) to raise prices by changing the price of gold. President Roosevelt seems to have been reluctant to admit the failure, although he was clearly relieved to turn from it to domestic policy concerns.[1]

The monetary experiment with silver was continued longer. Domestic purchases had begun under the Thomas amendment, and the only agreement to emerge from the World Economic Conference in December 1933 extended them to the world.

1. See John Morton Blum, *From the Morgenthau Diaries*, I: *Years of Crisis, 1928–1938*, Houghton Mifflin, Boston, 1959, p. 132. Roosevelt was not opposed to *de facto* stabilization, but neither was he excited by it. Morgenthau also records (p. 126) that Roosevelt contemplated changing the price of gold in January 1935, when the Supreme Court considered the gold clause case. Such a change would, according to Morgenthau, have been for political, not economic, reasons. The same source records that Roosevelt in August 1935 suggested changing the gold price, 'partly in fun, partly to test him [Morgenthau]'.

The price was set at 64·64 cents, or half the $1·29 price, which was one sixteenth of $20·67, the March 1933 price of gold. It was 19 cents above the market. In the eyes of the silver bloc, it was not high enough. The price of gold had been raised substantially, and in February 1934 was set at $35 an ounce. The bloc turned up the pressure. In June 1934, President Roosevelt submitted to the Congress a Bill, quickly passed, to buy silver at home and abroad until the price reached $1·29, or until silver, valued at $1·29, amounted to a quarter of the government's monetary reserve.

Silver purchases abroad provide a brilliant example of world economic irresponsibility on the part of the United States. Chapter 5 of the *Morgenthau Diaries* records how Roosevelt and Morgenthau embarked on the policy of appeasing the silver bloc at the cost of monetary disorders to Mexico and China, both countries which based their currencies on silver and found their money supply drained as the price of silver rose. Morgenthau's initial reaction was to blame the Mexicans and Chinese for creating difficulties, for failure to guard their currency system or for their standards of personal and public morality.[2] In due course, he became indignant at the action of 'speculators' who sold them silver at the high prices which the Treasury set, and set out at the end of 1935 with high moral resolve to drive the price of silver down again. 'All in all, the silver program was a fiasco.'[3] But it was more: it represented a beggar-thy-neighbour policy where the hurt to the neighbour was wanton, and provided no domestic economic and little political benefit.[4]

2. ibid., pp. 204 and 209. Morgenthau said (p. 202) that he wanted to help Mexico, but that he was concerned for his own country. At another stage he told the protesting Chinese that they should complain to the Congressmen who wrote the law (p. 207).

3. Broadus Mitchell, *Depression Decade, From New Era Through New Deal, 1929–1941*, Holt, Rinehart & Winston, New York, 1947, p. 150.

4. Some unintended benefit may have accrued to India, which, after importing silver for hoarding for almost a hundred years, turned to exporting it at the higher price. Estimated imports from 1874 to 1932 amounted to 2,900 million ounces. No estimates are available for the subsequent exports, since most of it was smuggled abroad at a rate believed to run roughly between 20 and 25 million ounces a year. See *Green's Commodity Market Comments*, 21 October 1970.

The Reciprocal Trade Agreement Act of 1934 was the very opposite: an act of piety in which the Roosevelt administration had little faith but which it undertook out of tradition and to appease the Secretary of State, Cordell Hull. During the political campaign, Roosevelt had paid little heed to the issue, though he had condemned the Smoot-Hawley Tariff. When Hoover accused him of plans to reduce tariffs on agricultural products and plunge the farmer still deeper into depression, he provided assurance that he would not. Hull, on the other hand, was 'almost fanatical' in his dedication to lower tariffs. Ernest Lindley said he had only one formula.[5] After returning from the World Economic Conference, he four times took to cabinet meetings proposals for tariff reductions. Once there he mumbled his views and did nothing more when they were ignored.[6] But in due course a proposal for reducing tariffs by executive agreement on a reciprocal basis was sent to the Congress, and was enacted into law. Hull's 'rambling, lisping speeches on the evils of protection', as Tugwell characterized them, ultimately produced the legislation which started the reversal of fifty years of rising protection, the last three of them at an unprecedented rate. It is characteristic of the chaos of Roosevelt's administration that the President decided in favour of a trade agreements programme in November 1933, but appointed George Peek, an agricultural restrictionist, to be chairman of the Executive Committee on Commercial Policy which was charged with drafting the Bill. A draft was completed under the leadership of the State Department in February 1934, and approved by the President at the end of the month. It passed the House on 20 March, and the Senate on 4 June, despite its provision for negotiation by executive agreement which did not have to be ratified by the Senate, instead of trade treaties which did. It was signed into law on 12 June.[7]

The comparison and contrast are with the Repeal of the Corn Laws in Britain in 1846. The fundamental cause for the change in

5. Raymond Moley, with the assistance of Elliott Rosen, *The First New Deal*, Harcourt Brace & World, New York, 1966, pp. 90 and 92.

6. Herbert Feis, *1933: Characters in Crisis*, Little Brown, Boston, 1966, p. 262.

7. *The Memoirs of Cordell Hull*, vol. I, Macmillan Co., New York: Hodder & Stoughton, London, 1948, pp. 353–7.

commercial policy was in each case a change in the structure of the economy, and the rise to political dominance of the group which benefited from lower tariffs: manufacturers in Britain, and mass production in the United States – that is, Manchester and Detroit respectively. In the United States, however, there was no Cobden or Bright to articulate the interest of the dominant group. On the contrary, the Republican party of the northern manufacturers went ahead with two tariff increases in 1921 and 1930, after much of its clientele had changed from import-competing to exporting in the First World War; and the spokesmen for lower tariffs were the Democrats from the agrarian South, which was on the verge of becoming industrialized and a potential beneficiary from protection. Nor was there a *causa proxima* like the potato famine of 1845. The Reciprocal Trade Agreement Act of 1934 was sold on the basis of employment, although there is a theoretical basis for believing that a balanced increase in exports and imports – the one capital-intensive, and the other labour-intensive – would increase unemployment. The action was tentative, and required execution under safeguards in separate negotiations with foreign countries. It remains a tribute to a statesman with a one-track mind with whom history has not in other respects dealt generously.

Support for the Reciprocal Trade Agreements Act came especially from United States traditional opposition to preferences, and concern that the Ottawa Agreements might isolate the country and lose British markets to Commonwealth farmers and jobs to American firms which had established plants in Canada to come within the preference system. By the end of 1937, sixteen agreements covering a third of American foreign trade had been negotiated. The Act was renewed in 1937, in 1940, and again on frequent occasions after the Second World War. The 1934 Act, at the faint beginnings of recovery, remains a remarkable and unpredictable step reversing the direction of movement in the world economy.

Much of the tariff reduction under the programme consisted in the lowering of redundant or ineffective duties. Half the early agreements under its authority were with Latin American countries, most of whose exports to the United States consisted of duty-free tropical products and raw materials. Other early

237

agreements were with countries of highly specialized manufactured exports which were not directly competitive with United States manufactures – Finland, Sweden and, to a lesser extent, Switzerland. There were, however, major accomplishments: two agreements with Canada, in 1935 and again in 1938, and in the latter connection, a far-reaching agreement with the United Kingdom in 1938, which went some way towards reversing the inward-turning policies of the Commonwealth.

Attempts were made at negotiation with Spain and Italy, though without success. Not even attempts were undertaken with Japan and Germany. A trade agreement with the Soviet Union in 1935, exchanging most-favoured-treatment for promises to purchase U.S. products up to a given amount, carried forward the Roosevelt policy of economic intercourse which had begun with diplomatic recognition in 1933. It was an empty gesture.

In addition to these actions, negative and positive, there was a movement away from involvement in world affairs, a ritualistic locking of the barn door after the horse was stolen. The Johnson Act of 1934, named after Senator Hiram Johnson, an isolationist from California, denied the right of countries which had defaulted on their war debts to borrow in United States markets. In August 1935, as Mussolini prepared to invade Ethiopia, the Congress passed the Neutrality Act forbidding the shipment of arms to either aggressor or victim. The legislation was strengthened after the outbreak of the Spanish Civil War a year later. 'The Unbrave New World'[8] was afraid of contamination by the Old.

The Axis countries

Hitler's accession to full power in March 1933 was a forecast of far-reaching changes in the German economic system. In Munich, in 1920, the National Socialist party had laid down a list of twenty-five points, largely economic and social, directed against capitalism, 'interest slavery', and the like, and in favour of colonies, land reform, pensions for old people and the development of the middle class through assistance to shopkeepers. A

8. An expression of Vansittart's; see *The Mist Procession, The Autobiography of Lord Vansittart*, Hutchinson, London, 1958, p. 467.

four-year plan announced in the spring of 1933 promised the rescue of the peasant and the worker, the latter by an attack on unemployment. Agriculture was to be reformed through the establishment of the *Reichsnährstand* (Food Estate), which controlled prices and then production. Unemployment was attacked through conscription (in March 1935), the development of parastatal bodies, such as the storm troopers and the S.A., and especially in spending on public works and armaments. But the anti-capitalism of the initial stages did not survive for long. The purge of 30 June 1934 was not economic in origin, but it none the less had the effect of moving party doctrine in a more conservative direction in respect of income distribution, if not of control of industry. Control was provided by the law of 27 February 1934, 'Gesetz zur Vorbereitung des organischen Aufbaus der deutsche Wirtschaft' (Law for the Preparation of the Organic Constitution of the German Economy), which laid out a criss-crossed pattern of industrial and regional *Überwachungsstellen* (Control Offices). Initially, these Control Offices regulated imports on the basis of goods quantities, but this task was eventually turned over to the Reichsbank and operated through foreign-exchange controls.

On 2 May 1933, the S.S. seized all offices of trade unions in Germany; officials were arrested, and union property was confiscated. The property was incorporated into the Nazi-controlled *Deutsche Arbeitsfront* (German Labour Front), which included entrepreneurs and professional men as well as workers. Wages and working conditions were regulated by *Treuhänder der Arbeit* (Labour Trustees), appointed for each district. The German Labour Front included Social Honour Courts to deal with abuses by employers or agitation by workers; and *Kraft durch Freude* ('Strength through Joy'), which organized workers and youth in holidays through taxes on workers' salaries. In particular, workers were required to carry a work book by which both their jobs and movements were controlled.[9]

Since an early task was to eliminate unemployment, the National Labour Service was established for a variety of projects ranging from agriculture, reclamation, road construction and,

9. Gustav Stolper, *The German Economy, 1870–1940*, Reynal & Hitchcock, New York: Allen & Unwin, London, 1940, Part 5.

ultimately, military installations. It was made compulsory in June 1935. Workers with agricultural training were dismissed and sent back to farms. All labour was frozen in its jobs in 1934. A campaign was undertaken to drive women from gainful employment and back to the hearth. These efforts, it was later thought, prevented Germany from undertaking full mobilization after 1938 and during the Second World War.[10]

Hjalmar Schacht fought hard to prevent deficit financing rising above a dangerous level until 1938, when he resigned. But spending for public works, including *Autobahnen*, was undertaken through special paper discounted by banks. The effect was rapidly to reduce unemployment from 6 million in October 1933 to 4·1 million a year later, 2·8 million in February 1935, 2·5 million in February 1936, and 1·2 million in February 1937. At the time when the Second Four-Year Plan was introduced by Hitler in a speech at Nuremberg in September 1936, and formally in October of that year by Herman Göring, anti-depression policy was a thing of the past. Women who had received marriage loans were allowed to take jobs. The forty-hour week was ignored, although the forty-eight-hour week did not come in until August 1938. In June 1938, the Compulsory Labour Decree (*Dienstverpflichtverordnung*) provided that any inhabitant of the Reich had to accept any work or vocational training assigned to him or her by the Labour Front.

The Second Four-Year Plan also turned policy definitely away from unemployment towards preparation for war. It still contained schemes for public buildings and *Autobahnen*, but the emphasis was on providing synthetic industries in rubber, oil, fats, etc., to protect Germany against blockade in time of war.

German foreign trade moved slowly during the period. Clearing and payments arrangements, begun to conserve scarce foreign exchange, were slowly developed into devices for obtaining real resources. The suggestion that Germany bought petroleum, grain and fattened hogs from south-east Europe in exchange for harmon-

10. Edward L. Homze, *Foreign Labour in Nazi Germany*, Princeton University Press, 1967, pp. 7 ff. See also Burton H. Klein, *Germany's Economic Preparations for War*, Harvard University Press, Cambridge, Mass., 1959, pp. 60 and 73.

icas and aspirin is exaggerated, as is the view that Germany used such clearing to manipulate the terms of trade strongly in her favour.[11] It is nevertheless true that Germany's monopsony position as an important market for the goods of south-eastern Europe together with the closing of the markets of France and Britain to these products meant that these countries were helped by selling their foodstuffs and raw materials to Germany on clearing account, and that they were willing to wait some time to get manufactured goods in exchange, often at high prices. German clearing arrangements with Latin America succeeded almost in bringing back trade to the levels of the 1920s. With Western Europe, the Commonwealth and North America, it remained at a low level, handicapped by the complex clearing arrangements.

The corporate state, undertaken in the February 1934 law, was already far advanced in Italy. Its proximate origin was the Rocco Law on Corporations of April 1926, named after the Minister of Justice. This established machinery for relations between confederations of employers on the one hand, and those for workers on the other, with the state occupying a position in the middle. Strikes and lockouts were forbidden, and contracts reached in bargaining were deposited with the Ministry of National Economy.

During the depression, Italy held the lira at a high level, but employed tariffs, quotas, prohibitions and subsidies to stave off the deflationary pressures from abroad through reduced exports and direct-price effects via appreciation. New loans to industry were to be provided by the Istituto Mobiliare Italiano (I.M.I.), founded in January 1933; cheap money was achieved through a refunding of the public debt, but business was asked to share orders and forbidden to expand plant without government approval. In January 1933, additionally, the Istituto per la Ricostruzione Industriale (I.R.I.) was created to assist the large banks by providing liquidity. Since these banks owned equities in major industrial concerns, I.R.I. found itself organizing industries into giant concerns which were easy to finance and plan. This was undertaken in shipping, steel, shipbuilding, machinery and

11. C. P. Kindleberger, *The Terms of Trade: A European Case Study*, Technology Press, Cambridge, Mass.: Chapman & Hall, London, 1956, pp. 114–22.

munitions.[12] Since much of Italian industry was conducted in miniscule firms, especially in the south, the effort at concentration consolidated Italy into a dual economy.

In October 1935, Mussolini launched his attack on Ethiopia. It proved fateful for the League of Nations, which sought to impose sanctions on the extension of credit to Italy and the provision of raw materials or munitions. It has been claimed that the sanctions failed because they were disregarded by the major petroleum companies.[13] Feis's account exonerates the large international oil companies, but makes it clear that the high prices for oil generated by the refusal of the business induced hundreds of small business operators to charter tankers and deliver fuel not only to Italy but also to Red Sea ports.[14] The United States was not a member of the League, and asked for the cooperation of American business over sanctions rather than requiring them to be observed. Lacking any strong lead from the United States or Britain, sanctions failed. By May 1936, the Ethiopian forces had been overcome and the League withdrew the sanctions that had never been effective. Their failure contributed to Japanese readiness to invade Manchuria in 1937.

Like Germany, Japan enjoyed uninterrupted expansion in the years 1934–6, with wages steady and prices rising at the rate of world prices. Unlike Germany, however, much of the impetus for the expansion came from the international margin as a result of the undervaluation of the yen. The terms of trade were strongly unfavourable rather than favourable, as was the case with Germany. Japanese internal spending was dominated by military disbursements. When the attempt was made at the end of 1936 to curb them after full employment had been reached, so as to prevent inflation, the Minister of Finance was assassinated by a military fanatic.

12. Shepard B. Clough, *The Economic History of Modern Italy*, Columbia University Press, New York, 1964, p. 249.

13. ibid., p. 254.

14. Herbert Feis, *Seen from E. A.: Three International Episodes*, Alfred A. Knopf, New York, 1947, pp. 305–8.

United Kingdom

The first major country to surpass its 1929 performance in industrial production was the United Kingdom, which reached 116 in the last quarter of 1934, compared with 114 in the last quarter of 1929 (1924 = 100). The fact reflects partly the efficacy of British recovery under the impact of depreciation and cheap money, and partly the weakness of the expansion of the 1920s. Unemployment declined only slowly from 17·6 per cent in 1932 to between 12 and 13 per cent in 1935. This was highly concentrated in depressed areas specializing in coal, shipbuilding and cotton textiles. In some of them, unemployment rose as high as 50 per cent. Recovery was especially strong in motor-cars, electrical industry, chemicals, together with housing, and in southern and south-western England, as opposed to Wales, south-west Scotland, Northern Ireland and the Clyde, Tyne and Mersey river areas.

A slow movement of population southwards and eastwards helped to relieve the depressed areas. The Special Areas (Development and Improvement) Act of 1934, amended in 1937, undertook to provide facilities for light industries in the areas, and to assist firms settling there. In 1935, the government brought pressure on Richard Thomas to build its new steel strip mill not in Lincolnshire, as economic considerations dictated, but in the depressed area of Ebbw Vale in South Wales.

In addition to the depressed industries and areas, and the verve of rising production in mechanical, electrical and chemical lines, the 1930s in Britain were characterized by a movement away from competition. 'Trade associations and price fixing were the rule in British industry between the wars ... the limited, exiguous, emasculated, etiolated competition of the 1930s was too little for good economic health ... and ... produced unenterprising habits.'[15] This was particularly the case with chemicals, soap, oil, wallpaper, tobacco and steel. The steel industry had obtained generalized protection in early 1932, and a special rate of $33\frac{1}{3}$ per cent in the spring of that year. The organization of the European

15. A. J. Youngson, *The British Economy, 1920–1957*, Allen & Unwin, London, 1960, pp. 133 and 134.

steel cartel in 1933, however, led to dumping in the British market, especially of basic Thomas steel. The industry turned to the Import Duties Advisory Committee for an increase in tariff to 50 per cent and was able to reach agreement with the European cartel for a limited import quota. By 1937, when the rearmament boom flourished, this quota was exceeded.

But the major economic success of the period was housing under the influence of government assistance, a substantial backlog, migration, lower building costs, cheap money, cheap food and development of the motor-car, which stimulated movement to the suburbs, and perhaps a change in tastes.[16] The boom increased the demand for building materials and household furnishings. As was noted in Chapter 8, the spillover into import demand was the basis for the spectacular recovery in Sweden.

British exports shifted, together with domestic production, from the staple trades – coal, ships, iron and steel and cotton textiles – to the new industries – electrical equipment, motor-cars, chemicals, etc. – which rose from 13·6 per cent of total exports in 1929 to 17·6 per cent in 1937.[17] The change received little help from long-term lending. Long-term loans for new money from 1931 to 1938 amounted to an annual average of £33 million, as compared with £117 million from 1924 to 1930, during much of which capital lending was restricted. A complete embargo on foreign loans was applied in June 1932. Shortly after the success of the War Loan conversion, the embargo was relaxed to permit domestic and Empire conversions, and in October 1932 it was still further dismantled to apply only to new issues for borrowers outside the Empire. In July 1934, sterling-area countries were encouraged to borrow for adding to reserves or for imports from Britain. The stimulus thus afforded to exports was limited. The Export Credit Guarantees Department, begun immediately after the war but reorganized thoroughly in 1928, was twice expanded from its original limit of £25 million, reaching £75 million in 1938. The terms under which export credits were guaranteed, or loans

16. See H. W. Richardson and D. Aldcroft, *Building in the British Economy between the Wars*, Allen & Unwin, London, 1969, *passim*.

17. A. E. Kahn, *Great Britain in the World Economy*, Columbia University Press, New York: Pitman, London, 1946, Table 8, p. 109.

provided, were improved through lowering rates and extending the period. But amounts were small – no more than £10 million a year.

Less developed countries

Within the British Commonwealth, economic recovery was assisted by the rise of prices in 1933 and 1934, especially in those countries which had depreciated against sterling. On a 1929 base, Australia and New Zealand had respectively reached the 80s and 95 by 1935. With the help of the sizeable increase in the price of gold and expansion in output – restrained, however, by a new tax system which encouraged the working of low-grade ore – prices in the Union of South Africa also reached the 80s. The recovery in British India prices was much less extensive – from 58 in March 1933 to 65 in 1935 and 1936. The performance in the Netherlands East Indies, which remained tied to the gold bloc through the Dutch guilder, was still worse. From a price level of 49·6 in March 1933 (on the basis of 1929 = 100), the index declined slowly to 46 in 1935 and 44 in 1936, despite the recovery in world prices.

In Latin America, the price experience of some countries like Argentina was assisted by both the depreciation of the peso and the drought in the United States, which created an export market for Argentine corn. Mexico and Peru restored prices and money income through cutting off imports by foreign-exchange controls and domestic inflation. The process was carried in Chile to the extent of doubling 1929 prices by mid 1936.

As Figure 2 (p. 88) shows, beginnings were made in this period in getting burdensome commodity stocks reduced in general, and especially in tin, wheat, cotton, silk and sugar. This was only to a slight extent accomplished through actual reductions in production. In raw materials, increased business activity led to increases in demand. In foodstuffs, population growth and increased incomes helped. In both groups attempts were made at international commodity agreements, which functioned for a time in wheat, sugar, rubber, tin and cotton, but were not sustained.

On the whole, however, with one or two exceptions, such as the Union of South Africa, the less developed countries had a diffi-

245

cult time in the 1930s. Unable to borrow to sustain their investment programmes, and with heavy burdens in debt service from low prices in gold currencies and sterling, their balances of payments remained under pressure. Foreign-exchange controls and depreciation persisted, and tariffs remained high, despite the attempt by the United States to bargain them down under the Reciprocal Trade Agreement Act. In many parts of Africa and Asia, the depreciation of the yen and the pushing of Japanese textile and other exports led to specific import controls to protect simple industry, and to safeguard the traditional markets of the metropoles of Britain and France. Recovery was hesitant, limited, unsatisfactory.

Like the Axis, the Soviet Union went its own way, largely cut off from the world economy, pursuing the collectivization of agriculture and the construction of heavy industry, and importing to build autarchy and freedom of dependence on raw-material imports. The motive was partly military defence and partly the protection of socialism against contagion from world depression. Soviet trade statistics are kept on an arbitrary basis, but show declining exports going from a monthly average of 180 million new (1935) roubles in 1932 (compared with 296 million at the peak in 1930) downward each year to 75 million in the early months of 1936. The change from old to new roubles in the latter year had no effect on trade, which is conducted on a negotiated basis and foreign prices. Expanded diplomatic and commercial relations with the West led to a rapid increase in record export trade after the middle of 1936.

In short, world recovery in 1934 and 1935 was limited and fragmented. It excluded the gold bloc.

11. The Gold Bloc Yields

The gold bloc

The gold bloc began to take shape at the time of the depreciation of sterling, when the central banks of Belgium, France and the Netherlands all suffered exchange losses. It was formally constituted in a meeting of 3 July 1933, when President Roosevelt's letter denouncing stabilization of the dollar effectively broke up the World Economic Conference. It had little cohesion and no organization. Some basis of tradition went back to the Latin Monetary Union of 1870, when the French, Belgian and Swiss francs were equivalents. This had been broken up by the First World War and the varying degrees of inflation and depreciation which followed. The Dutch and Swiss clung to gold at the old parity as an act of faith.[1] Having devalued by large amounts during the 1920s at substantial cost to the rentier classes, France and Belgium were determined to resist inflation. It was not clear whether Italy was a member or not.

For five years prior to 1931, France, the leader of the gold bloc, had been an independent monetary force. Its large gold reserves, buoyant trade and budgetary surpluses had made it impervious

---

1. But see G. M. Verrijn Stuart, 'The Netherlands during the Recent Depression', in A. D. Gayer (ed.), *The Lessons of Monetary Experience, Essays in Honor of Irving Fisher*, Farrar & Rinehart, New York: Allen & Unwin, London, 1937, p. 249: 'Until then [June 1933] I still hoped that some form of international understanding might lead to putting into effect a policy of "reflation within gold". The deplorable results shown by the London Economic and Financial Conference in the first month convinced me that the only way for the Netherlands to escape from the difficulties was to give up the gold base of the guilder and devalue.'

to the troubles that affected Germany, Britain and even the United States. But 1931, and especially 1933, changed all that. As the world broke up into sterling, dollar, blocked-currency and gold blocs, it was the last which went on to the defensive, embracing the difficult and, as it proved, impossible task of deflating to maintain its trade in balance and its gold reserves.

Deflation as a cure for disequilibrium

If recent history would not permit depreciation, and pride forbade exchange control (except in the case of Italy), the remaining remedy was deflation. Sauvy chooses to illustrate the overvaluation of the franc by retail prices in France and Britain, adjusted to an over-valuation of 22 per cent in February 1935, as shown in Figure 10.[2] The peak of overvaluation was reached in February 1934 at 26 per cent. The pressure on French exports was severe. Monthly average exports declined from 3,600 million Poincaré francs in 1930 to 1,500 million in 1932 and 1,300 million in 1935. Average monthly imports for the same period went from 4,400 million francs to 2,500 million and 1,700 million. The declines from 1932 to 1935 occurred despite the expansion of world trade. French exports of textiles, clothing and leather goods were hit more sharply than iron and steel or motor vehicles. Consumer categories suffered more from tariff and quota restrictions. But the price disadvantage was severe, since it proved impossible to reduce costs and prices to make up for the appreciation of the currency.

The patterns of attempts to deflate were similar. As prices declined, wholesale prices falling from 462 in 1931 to 407 in 1932, 388 in 1933, 366 in 1934, and 347 in 1935 (July 1914 = 100), successive governments would try to balance the budget by cutting expenditure, and especially by reducing payments to pensioners and veterans, and the wages of government employees. These

2. See Alfred Sauvy, *Histoire économique de la France entre les deux guerres*, II: *1931–1939*, Fayard, Paris, 1967, pp. 400–401 and 508–9. Sauvy is aware of the theoretical and practical difficulties of accurate measures of over-valuation and under-valuation of the exchange rate. The account given in this chapter relies heavily on Sauvy's detailed history of France in the 1930s.

efforts were strongly opposed. Pensioners, veterans and function-aries experienced money illusion, and regarded their incomes as determined by the money amounts received, taking no account of the decline in prices. Or those who understood that they had gained in real income through falling prices despite fixed incomes in francs, were unwilling to share with their less fortunate com-patriots. The social cement in the system was crumbling. From 1930 to 1935, disposable income declined from 331,000 million francs to 221,000 million in money terms, but only to 291,000

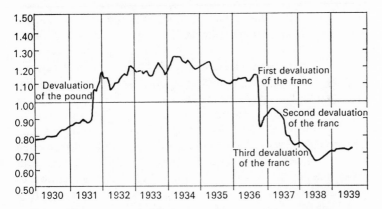

Figure 10. Relationship between French and English prices, 1930–39.

	1931	1932	1933	1934	1935	1936	1937	1938	1939
January	0·86	1·13	1·15	1·22	1·21	1·12	0·95	0·77	0·71
February	0·87	1·13	1·16	1·26	1·22	1·12	0·96	0·75	0·72
March	0·88	1·05	1·15	1·25	1·23	1·14	0·97	0·73	0·72
April	0·88	1·10	1·17	1·25	1·21	1·14	0·94	0·72	0·72
May	0·89	1·09	1·16	1·24	1·16	1·13	0·93	0·67	0·72
June	0·87	1·10	1·13	1·22	1·13	1·12	0·93	0·66	0·71
July	0·87	1·14	1·15	1·22	1·12	1·13	0·79	0·66	0·72
August	0·86	1·17	1·19	1·23	1·12	1·16	0·80	0·66	0·73
September	1·07	1·14	1·23	1·22	1·11	1·15	0·76	0·68	
October	1·04	1·20	1·20	1·19	1·10	0·86	0·73	0·68	
November	1·14	1·21	1·15	1·19	1·10	0·90	0·74	0·69	
December	1·18	1·18	1·17	1·20	1·12	0·92	0·75	0·71	
Average	0·93	1·13	1·16	1·22	1·15	1·07	0·85	0.70	0·73

million in real terms – 13 per cent real instead of 33 per cent nominal.[3] Pensioners' real income increased 46 per cent, that of government employees 18·9 per cent, weekly occupied workers 18·5 per cent (more in certain industries, such as coal). Landlords' real income went up 11·5 per cent. The main burden fell on the unemployed and on agriculture. The unemployed never reached very large numbers, amounting only to 500,000 receiving assistance in February 1935 on a rather restricted definition. This was perhaps because a million Polish, Italian and Algerian workers had left France or been rounded up and deported. In addition, many workers left the city for the farm, where, despite the decline in income – amounting to almost 32 per cent – it was possible to sleep and eat.[4] The reversal of the normal movement from countryside to city occurred widely in the world during the depression, and especially in the United States. An analogous return to familiar surroundings took place in net return migration from the Commonwealth to Britain.

The Minister of Finance would propose expenditure cuts, and occasionally new taxes. Sometimes these would pass. More often the government would fall. In 1932 and 1934 there were four governments; in 1933 three. In June 1935 Laval undertook to produce deflation by decree, as Brüning had in Germany four years before. He issued decrees in three groups in July, August and October.

Malthusianism

Apart from the attempts to reduce wages and pensions by decree, French governments to 1935 were obliged to worry about agriculture. For the most part, they followed policies which French economists described as 'Malthusian'. This term is unfair to the memory of Thomas Malthus, known elsewhere for his law of population and his pioneering insight into macroeconomic analysis. In the French context, Malthusian policies are those of raising prices by restriction, prohibition, subsidy, minimum prices

3. ibid., p. 575.
4. ibid., pp. 133, 135 and 137.

or other interference in the market process. The French revival of the ancient practice of prohibitions and quotas instead of tariffs, to make sure of cutting off imports, was Malthusian, as was the establishment of minimum prices for wheat and wine above the market-clearing level, leading to black markets in these two commodities. Steps to retire married women from the labour market, and to lower the retirement age for men, belong in the same category, together with the prohibition by a new law of a shoe plant projected by the Czech manufacturer, Bat'a, in March 1936, in an effort to protect the small shoe manufacturer and retail distribution.[5]

Malthusianism was an ancient tradition in France, which believed in the decent wage and the just price, and after the depreciations of sterling and the dollar sought to shut itself up by closing down on imports. Keynesianism, which was detected by Germans in 1931 and broadcast to the world in *The Means to Prosperity* of 1934, before the *General Theory of Employment, Interest and Money* of 1936, was not available in France as an alternative to Malthusianism. The French did not read Keynes, since he had shown himself unfriendly to her by writing *The Economic Consequences of the Peace* and had wrecked French chances of obtaining reparations from Germany. No French economist would study Keynes until time was to hang heavy on their hands during the German occupation.[6]

Belgium devalues

While French economists were advocating deflation, opposing both foreign-exchange control and devaluation, Italy defended itself with controls and Belgium devalued. Italy found itself unable to devalue because of Mussolini's pride in the currency,

5. ibid., p. 372.

6. Pierre Lalumière, *L'Inspection des finances*, Presses Universitaires de France, Paris, 1959, pp. 179 ff. This is an exaggeration, as there had been French translations published of *A Revision of the Treaty*, *Monetary Reform* and *Essays in Persuasion*. A translation of *The General Theory of Employment, Interest and Money* had been arranged in 1938. It was not finally produced, on account of the war, until 1942.

251

and unwilling, with high unemployment, to deflate. With increasing ties to Germany, with which it had clearing arrangements, it gradually defended the international-payments position with exchange control. The Belgian devaluation, which represented a real defection from the gold bloc, was taken in cold blood.

The contrast is with the British and United States depreciations: the one under pressure, the other off-hand or even quixotic, and both highly casual about the rate. In Belgium, the University of Louvain had organized an economics institute, led by Professors Dupriez, Baudhuin and Paul Van Zealand, and, among research assistants, Robert Triffin. A study of 1933 suggested that the Belgian franc was overvalued by some 25 to 30 per cent, and that deflation was impossible.[7] In September 1934, Professor Baudhuin took a post with the Treasury and privately advised it to devalue. In March 1935, in a public speech, he stated that devaluation was inescapable, and the only way to rescue the Belgian economy. This led to an outflow of capital, a government crisis, and a new cabinet, headed by Van Zealand. On 29 March Van Zealand sought and obtained emergency powers from the Belgian Parliament, and on 2 April he devalued by 28 per cent.[8] Prices bounded up from 54·5 in March to 68 at the end of the year and 75 a year later. Production, exports, gold stocks of the National Bank of Belgium all recovered. France was not moved.

The Popular Front

French workers demonstrated against the deflationary policies recommended by the experts and put into effect by Laval. Socialists joined with Communists in a Popular Front, and the general trade union merged with the Communist labour organization. There were strikes in shipyards, ports, truck plants and a general strike in the metals industry in the Paris region. The workers sat

7. See Robert Triffin, 'La théorie de la surévaluation monétaire et la dévaluation belge', in *Bulletin de l'Institut des Recherches Économiques de l'Université de Louvain*, IX, No. 1 (November 1937), pp. 3–36.

8. Sauvy, *Histoire économique de la France entre les deux guerres*, II, pp. 105–6.

in. This brought down the Sarrault government, which had taken over from Laval in January. During the course of the unrest, Hitler's *Wehrmacht* marched into the Rhineland and started its fortification.

The Popular Front had no real economic programme. It advocated control of trusts, repression of agricultural speculation, suppression of fraud, elimination of tax evasion, extension of the school-leaving age, respect for pensions and the rights of veterans, maintenance of social security, but especially the repudiation of deflation and the introduction of the forty-hour week. There was no mention of devaluation. The Socialists were prepared to contemplate it, the Communists vehemently opposed, stating it as contrary to the workers' interests. The implicit model was not spelled out. If there was any programme for recovery, it came from a view that the forty-hour week, with no change in pay, would contribute purchasing power sufficient to enable the economy to move upward. There was no provision for coping with the balance of payments, or the capital outflow stimulated by the sit-in strikes. It was as if the Popular Front had been dealing with a closed economy. As he took office, Blum promised that the country would not wake up one morning and find the hoardings covered with an announcement of devaluation. In his memoirs, Auriol, the Minister of Finance, suggested that foreign-exchange control would have suited the temperament of the Popular Front, but that nothing was ready, 30,000 million francs in gold had already left, it was necessary to have control of the credit mechanism and foreign-exchange control would have separated France from its western allies. In addition, he wrongly thought that foreign-exchange control implied devaluation, which the Communist allies opposed.[9] The opposition to devaluation at the start of the Popular Front has its modern parallel in the decision by the British Prime Minister, Harold Wilson, not to devalue in the autumn of 1964.

9. Vincent Auriol, *Hier et aujourd'hui*, Charlot, Paris, 1945, pp. 38–9, quoted by Sauvy, *Histoire économique de la France entre les deux guerres*, II, p. 200. For doctrinaire Marxist opposition to devaluation in Germany, see above, pp. 162–3.

The first step taken by the Popular Front was to force employers to sign the *Accord de Matignon* guaranteeing wage rises, a three-weeks' annual holiday with pay and the forty-hour week. Like the decision on devaluation, it has a modern parallel: the *Accord de Grenelle* of 1968 which raised wages after the disturbances of May and June in the universities and the accompanying general strike. Again like the decision on devaluation, it constituted a poor precedent.

The *Accord de Matignon* was a humiliation for the employers and a disaster for everyone. Wages were raised by 15 per cent for the lowest-paid workers, and by 7 per cent for the highest, with a 12 per cent average being representative of many plants. Holidays with pay and the forty-hour week also raised costs. Wholesale prices rose from 375 (on the 1913 base) in May to 420 in September, and retail prices from 76·4 (base 1930) to 80·5. Exports failed to recover after the strikes. The stock market declined, the capital outflow picked up. Devaluation was forced upon France. It was undertaken by agreement with the United States and Britain to prevent retaliation. The significance of the Tripartite Monetary Agreement for the international economic system will be discussed presently. For France and the rest of the gold bloc, it provided an international cover for a retreat from an impossible position which had been held for far too long.

After devaluation

In the Netherlands and Switzerland, like Belgium before them, limited devaluations corrected the overvaluation and allowed the economy to snap back into line with the rest of the world economy. Trade in the Netherlands rebounded vigorously, with exports rising from 45 million guilders a month in the first nine months of 1936 to 90 million by June 1937. Swiss recovery was almost as extensive, from 68 million Swiss francs to 123 million in September 1937. The Italians used the occasion to devalue the lira rate, adjust exports and imports upward, and reduce the force of foreign-exchange control.

In France, however, the forty-hour week became a symbol of the workers' pride and independence. Serious consideration was given to moving upward to a forty-five-hour week, especially as hours were lengthened in the German armament industry, ultimately going to fifty-four hours a week in aviation. This was rejected. The forty-hour week was extended to coal mines and metallurgical plants, which had originally been exempt.

It proved impossible to restore the trading position or the confidence of the rentier with the forty-hour week, or to quiet the worker without it. In March 1937, 10,000 million francs were sought as a loan, with a dollar guarantee. It failed to build confidence on the right. Another crisis of confidence and capital outflow led to gold losses in June. Blum again sought to govern by decree, was refused and left power; Chautemps took over as Premier and Bonnet as Minister of Finance. They turned the franc loose from the Monetary Law of 1 October 1936, with the result that it again declined below 4 cents. In March 1938, the Chautemps government proposed a modern statute of conditions of work, providing for collective bargaining, conciliation and arbitration, plus, at the demand of labour, escalation clauses in work contracts. It passed. Chautemps then asked for powers to restore the budget by decree. These were denied. The Chautemps cabinet was followed briefly by a second Blum cabinet. During this period, Hitler proclaimed the *Anschluss* and marched German troops into Austria. The Blum cabinet fell. Daladier took over, devalued the franc once again in May, and governed by decree. The last of four sets of decrees beginning in November 1938, after Munich, was prepared under the aegis of a new Minister of Finance, Paul Reynaud, a confirmed liberal. He reversed the trend.

Reynaud killed the five-day week, levied new taxes, adopted budgetary economies, instituted a more liberal régime for prices, credit and conditions of work. He especially attacked fiscal fraud. With the rate of the franc at 178 to the pound, a new convention between the Finance Ministry and the Bank of France revalued the latter's gold at 170 to the pound, transferring the profit to the Ministry. A threatened general strike fizzled out. Six thousand million francs of capital returned from abroad. Production picked up by leaps and bounds, with a 15 per cent rise between November 1938 and the following June. Too late, Reynaud served up a repetition of the economic miracle of Poincaré – one which a number of countries of Europe were to experience after the Second World War.

Sauvy claims that the malaise from 1936 to 1938 was entirely owing to the forty-hour week.[10] The idea was economically Malthusian, despite its positive social roots in the twelve- to thirteen-hour day of the nineteenth century. It was not perhaps worse than the doctrinaire view of the right on budgets. Sauvy's text is replete with balanced homilies of this kind: 'The right reduced expenses, but the deficit formed again; the left reduced the working day, but unemployment came back into existence.'[11]

To a certain extent, Sauvy is justifying his opinion at the time when, from a position in the bureaucracy, he vigorously opposed the forty-hour week in the face of opposition from his superiors. A somewhat later observer is disposed to believe that the forty-hour week can be useful as a short-run measure of spreading the work, but was wrongly applied in a country such as France, where unemployment was not substantial.[12] Within six months of the serious application of the law in September 1936, the economy had brought unemployment down to the amount appropriate for transitional needs. The forty-hour week then proved disastrous, but it was so in conjunction with other French policies of all political colours, especially the refusal to devalue and the insistence on budget balance. Léon Jouhaux noted that the forty-hour week would have had to be internationalized if it was to succeed. Twenty years later, Michel Debré said the same thing about French planning. Idiosyncratic remedies encounter difficulties in a connected world. The essence of the French difficulty, however, lay in the loss of social cohesion. Neither right nor left worked in terms of a national solution, but only in those of its own interest. The right was prepared to strike through tax fraud and capital export if it did not get its way; the left behaved identically with different weapons. Reynaud succeeded, under the rising threat of

10. Sauvy, *Histoire économique de la France entre les deux guerres*, II, *passim*, but esp. pp. 209, 297, 305 and 334.

11. ibid., p. 468; see also pp. 253, 269, etc.

12. H. W. Arndt, *Economic Lessons of the 1930s*, Frank Cass, London, 1944, p. 147.

Germany after Munich, partly because his policies were more liberal, but also because he attacked the forty-hour week indirectly by granting exceptions of fifty hours, and later sixty hours, to armament industries, and then to the industries supplying them. The principle of the forty-hour week was retained, its use abandoned. It did not survive the war.

The Tripartite Monetary Agreement

Sauvy dismisses the Tripartite Monetary Agreement curtly: the three central banks agreed to nothing.[13] Morgenthau said, 'If this goes through it is the greatest move taken toward peace in the world since the World War . . . It may be the turning point for again resuming [sic] rational thinking in Europe.'[14] Each view contains a grain of truth. The Tripartite Monetary Agreement committed the major powers to almost nothing, but constituted a significant step in rebuilding the international economic system.

Neither President Roosevelt nor his Secretary of the Treasury, Morgenthau, understood well what they were doing in the international monetary field. Roosevelt kept coming back to his message to the London World Economic Conference, which he thought should be the text and bible of United States monetary policy. When asked whether he was willing to sell gold to the British against dollars, he started a 'long harangue that he thought the United States should have a secret commodity index with which it could manage the dollar'.[15] Later he was fearful that the Tripartite Monetary Agreement might be interpreted as a departure from the monetary policy set out at the time of the London conference.[16] Morgenthau's opinions on the dollar veered about in chaotic fashion, if one is to believe his diary and his biographer. At one time he defends devaluation; at another, he states that it did not fail but offered no future benefits. He was not prepared

13. Sauvy, *Histoire économique de la France entre les deux guerres*, II, p. 224.
14. John Morton Blum, *From the Morgenthau Diaries*, vol. I: *Years of Crisis, 1928–1938*, Houghton Mifflin, Boston, 1959, p. 171.
15. ibid., p. 144.
16. ibid., p. 168.

to sacrifice any freedom in monetary policy that domestic developments might require, but recognized his responsibility for preventing competitive international devaluation and the disorder it
would involve. He told the press that American monetary policy
was on a twenty-four-hour basis, but urged stabilization, and
when the British responded to his stabilization feeler by saying
that it reserved the right to devalue for domestic reasons, he felt
encouraged.[17] Lacking any real understanding of the international
monetary mechanism, but excited by dabbling in esoteric affairs of
state, he over-reacted to the unfolding course of events; becoming
infuriated at a speculative attack on francs; making his blood
boil because the State Department (probably Feis) favoured an
exchange rate of $4·86; taking the credit for saving France with a
$33 million credit in May 1935; becoming shaky at the knees over
the draft of the Tripartite Monetary Agreement – a great victory
over Feis – because it was so important; and breaking out into a
cold sweat over a French suggestion that the American Treasury
should run its unconverted French balances up to $5 million or
$10 million, saying that it was like kiting a cheque.[18] The prize
example of misunderstanding and over-reaction was his denuncia-
tion of the Soviet Union for selling £1,200,000 in the New York
market and driving the rate down from $5·02 until the Treasury
stabilized the market at $4·91. This took place on 26 September
1936, a Saturday and a half-day, when London was closed and the
New York market thin. The Russians, Morgenthau claimed, were
trying to undermine the capitalist system, and he prevented it.
The Russians, in turn, indicated that they owed $6 million to
Sweden and were only trying to convert pounds to dollars before
the market fell, as was likely to happen if the return flow of funds
from London to Paris reversed the upward pressure on the pound.
Morgenthau claimed that the American Treasury would make a
profit on the transaction. When the market opened on Monday
at $4·86 – the rate the Department of State had advocated –
Morgenthau was unable to close out the £900,000 he had bought
at $4·91 with a profit. For years thereafter the $\frac{1}{4}$ per cent handling

17. ibid., pp. 125, 133, 138 and 142.
18. ibid., pp. 129, 132, 138, 167 and 455.

charge on gold bought and sold was credited to the account to eat up the loss. John Morton Blum contends that the Russians did not need dollars to pay dollars in Stockholm; they could have paid in pounds.[19] The political historian is on dangerous ground in rewriting old exchange contracts. Blum continues, '. . . or, as Morgenthau contended, they could have waited to convert the pounds until all the money markets were open'. But this would have meant a loss of 11 cents, or perhaps up to 16 cents, on each of £1,200,000. Morgenthau's understanding of the intricacies of international finance, and his enthusiasm for them, make trying reading, but the Tripartite Monetary Agreement was none the less a milestone.

The agreement provided very little in the way of cooperation. Each treasury, and much was made of the fact that the agreement ran between stabilization funds rather than central banks (though the detail was trivial except in institutional terms), would be prepared to execute support orders for the other and hold the exchange for twenty-four hours, when it could ask for conversion into gold. The United States was ready to make gold available against dollars, and the obverse for Britain and France when they were not on the gold standard. This was a technical facility of some value, relieving Britain, for example, of the need to deal in dollars via the London gold market and reliance on private arbitrage.

The French gained assurance that the United States and Britain would not indulge in competitive exchange depreciation, although the reversal of the capital flow out of Paris inevitably caused some adjustment in the pound rate, which had been allowed to rise when capital was coming out of Paris so as to divert much of the flow to New York and away from the high-priced pound. The French also had an international context in which to undertake a necessary domestic adjustment.[20]

19. ibid., p. 176.

20. This point is made in one of the few documents on the subject in the French diplomatic papers. See *Documents diplomatiques français*, 2ème série, III, Imprimerie Nationale, Paris, 1968, #240, Paris to Washington and London, 8 September 1936, p. 348. The reason, of course, is that the telephone had taken over from the telegraph.

The British did not agree to stabilize the pound. On the contrary, they said they had no intention of so doing. But for the first time after June 1933, exchange rates were discussed, technical arrangements made and international cooperation built in the monetary area. The agreement was the origin of the ultimate swaps, when the holdings of one another's currency, which in 1937 made Morgenthau break out into a cold sweat because it was like kiting a cheque, would be undertaken up to thousands of millions of dollars at a time.

The idea of central-bank cooperation to maintain exchange rates in the face of hot money was not new. In 1933, Jørgen Pedersen, Professor of Economics at the University of Aarhus in Denmark, put forward the idea in an offhand set of remarks at a study conference of the League of Nations, held in London two weeks before the World Economic Conference:

It ought to be possible to neutralize the effects of such a movement of [short-term] capital from one country to another – this flight of capital – by a pooling of the resources of the different Banks of Issue.
... If for instance, there had been perfect cooperation between the American Central Banking system, the Bank of France and the Bank of England in 1931, I do not see why Great Britain should have been forced off the Gold Standard at all. Perhaps she intended to be forced off the Gold Standard, in which case of course it was fortunate that it appeared, at least, to be so necessary ...
If we can ensure that cooperation between central banks will be possible in the future, then the movement of short-term capital does not seem to present any danger at all.[21]

In the discussion which followed, William Rappard, of the Institute of Advanced International Studies in Geneva, noted that the Federal Reserve Bank of New York and the Bank of France had opened credits in favour of the Bank of England. Pedersen replied that these were insufficient, that the banks which lent money to Britain did so in a half-hearted fashion. The Tripartite

21. League of Nations, Sixth International Studies Conference, a Record of a Second Study Conference on *The State and Economic Life*, held in London, 29 May–2 June 1933, International Institute of Intellectual Cooperation, Paris, 1934, pp. 132–3.

Monetary Agreement was also half-hearted, or perhaps only an eighth-hearted. But the statement in the Tripartite Declaration that the 'constant object of policy is to maintain equilibrium in international exchange and to avoid utmost disturbance there by monetary action' represented a fundamental change.

Morgenthau and Roosevelt were not the only personalities whose thoughts had evolved between 1933 and 1936. On hearing the President's message of 3 July 1933 to the World Economic Conference, Keynes had said, 'Roosevelt was magnificently right.' (It was suggested that he should have said, 'Roosevelt was magnificently left.') In the *Yale Review* for 1933 comes the famous quotation:

> Ideas, knowledge, science, hospitality, travel – these are the things which should of their nature be international. But let goods be home-spun whenever it is reasonable and conveniently possible, and above all, let finance be primarily national . . .[22]

By the spring of 1936, according to a report of Harry White, Keynes believed strongly that *de facto* stabilization was desirable, and possible through cooperation among treasuries.[23] This was a long way from the restoration of freer trade and international capital movements of the 1946 posthumously published article in the *Economic Journal*. It was also a long way from 1933.

22. J. M. Keynes, 'National Self-Sufficiency', *Yale Review*, vol. XXII, No. 4 (June 1933), p. 758.
23. Blum, *From the Morgenthau Diaries*, vol. I: *Years of Crisis, 1928–1938*, pp. 139–40.

12. The 1937 Recession

The 1936–7 boom

Production and prices, which had been rising evenly in 1934 and 1935, turned sharply upward in the second half of 1936. In the gold bloc, the movement was stimulated by depreciation, but this had no deflationary impact elsewhere as the world as a whole felt the stimulus of rising economic activity. The price movement was perhaps most pronounced in Japan, which had reached full employment through steady and rapid expansion from early 1932. It was nevertheless general.

In the United States, commercial loans had finally in March 1936 reversed their long decline from 1929. The upswing was further stimulated by the payment of $1,700 million in bonds as a bonus to the veterans of the First World War. President Roosevelt had twice vetoed congressional votes for the bonus, once in May 1935 and again in January 1936. On the second occasion, the Congress had passed the bonus over the veto, with a two thirds majority. Payment was effected on 15 June. The administration urged veterans to retain the bonds. Of them $1,400 million had been cashed and spent by the end of the year. This led to an upsurge in automobile production and residential housing.

A further stimulus to expansion was provided by the organizing campaigns of labour under the Wagner Act of 1935. Wage rates rose in bituminous coal in April 1936, and generally in manufacturing after October of that year. The rise in wages and prices, moreover, led industrialists to step up production before costs rose further. By mid 1937, gross national production had risen above the 1929 level. The rise was uneven: in consumers' non-durable goods, the 1929 peaks had been exceeded by 10 per cent; in residential construction, despite the fillip provided by the bonus, output remained 40 per cent below 1929, itself well under the peak of 1925. Other construction projects were 50 per cent below 1929. The surpassing of the overall output of 1929 was not a striking accomplishment in view of the increase in working population of some 10 per cent and increased productivity of perhaps 15 per cent. Nor was it to last.

In the spring of 1937, President Roosevelt expressed concern that speculation was becoming excessive, and commodity prices being bid up to heights which could not be sustained. According to the report of the Bank for International Settlements for May 1938:

Rubber producers are generally thought to be satisfied with a price of 9d. and in April 1937 the price reached 13d. For tin, £200 per ton is usually regarded as a fair price, but in the spring of 1937 it went above £300. It is believed that in Rhodesia, where conditions of copper production are most favourable, a profit can be made on copper at a price of £30 to £35 a ton, and the market price went to £80. As compared with the 9-cents-a-pound loan on cotton which had been granted in the United States, the market price touched 15 cents in March 1937. These examples could be multiplied many times.[1]

The results were brought about by increases in demand, as supplies grew rapidly. In 1937 the cotton crop in the United States hit a record peak of 19,000,000 bales. Export quotas for rubber and tin were enlarged from 60 per cent and 85 per cent at the beginning of 1936 to 90 per cent and 110 per cent of stated quotas, respectively. Tin, copper, zinc, rubber, cotton, wheat and sugar exceeded 1929 world output levels in 1937, and lead, wool and tea came close.[2]

1. Bank for International Settlements, Eighth Annual Report, covering the year ended 31 March 1938, p. 26. President Roosevelt's message of 14 April 1938 also reasoned in terms of 'fair prices', remarking that the price of copper had been pushed from 10–12 cents where production was profitable to 17 cents a pound – see *The Public Papers and Addresses of Franklin Delano Roosevelt*, vol. 7: *The Continuing Struggle for Liberalism*, Macmillan Co., New York, 1941, p. 223.

2. Bank for International Settlements, Eighth Annual Report, p. 27, which presents the following table:

The outcome was a rapid rise in exports and income in the bulk of the developing countries, especially for the twelve months after the summer of 1936. But much of the production and exports were for stocks. An investigation of the Cleveland Trust Company suggested that inventories of raw materials in September 1937 were 50 per cent above the level of 1929. They were out of line.

Gold dishoarding

The Tripartite Monetary Agreement was not only a signal for a rapid expansion of prices, wages and output. It led also to dishoarding of gold. European investors who had clung to gold because of distrust of currencies undertook to cash in and buy securities. Many of these were small savers. The Swiss National Bank reported that of 8,840 persons who turned in gold to its Zürich office between 30 September and 30 November 1936, 87 per cent had amounts under 500 Swiss francs and 46 per cent were for amounts of less than 100 s f. But the total amount of dishoarding was substantial. Much was invested in the United States. In addition, Europeans bought United States securities by drawing down dollar balances. Industrial common stocks rose from 121 in June 1936 (Standard Statistics index, 1926 = 100) to 130 in September 1936 and 152 in February 1937.

World production of primary commodities

Year	Tin	Copper	Lead	Zinc	Rubber
		(in thousand tons)			
1929	192	1,915	1,725	1,450	868
1932	99	886	1,162	778	709
1936	179	1,684	1,469	1,473	862
1937	199	2,141	1,642	1,620	1,140

Year	Cotton	Wool	Wheat (million bushels)	Tea (million pounds)	Sugar (thousand tons)
	(in million lb.)				
1929	12,700	3,915	3,566	968	27,340
1932	11,400	3,857	3,812	932	24,130
1936	15,000	3,713	3,491	844	28,670
1937	18,500	3,880	3,751	850	30,960

Gold continued to move to the United States. Instead of a reversal, such as one might have expected after the stabilization of European currencies, the movement dropped off after the heavy inflow of October 1936, the counterpart of capital flight preceding the agreements. But it did not halt. The amounts were becoming embarrassing. From the $6,800 million revalued figure of January 1934, the gold stock of the United States passed the $11,000 million mark in October 1936. Reserves in excess of Federal Reserve requirements reached $3,000 million, or half of total reserves, in November 1935 and again twice in 1936, before the summer increase in reserve requirements. This last action reduced excess reserves; they started back up.

In December 1936, the Treasury undertook a programme of gold sterilization to prevent further inflows of gold from adding to excess reserves, which had reached 50 per cent of the total. Sterilization was called for partly because the Stabilization Fund was incapable of offsetting the gold inflow, and partly because the open-market portfolio of the Federal Reserve System, at $2,430 million was required to provide income to cover the expenses of the system and could not therefore be reduced. The Exchange Equalization Account in Britain could finance a gold inflow because it was equipped with power to borrow sterling; when it bought gold it issued Treasury bills. The United States Stabilization Fund, however, possessed only gold. To get dollars to buy gold from abroad, it had to sell currently owned gold to the Federal Reserve System. The foreign gold might just as well be sold directly to the Federal Reserve. On this account, if it was useful to borrow the money from the market to hold gold out of the credit bases, the Treasury was obliged to undertake it since the Stabilization Fund had no authority to do so.

A few days before the programme of Treasury sterilization of gold, the Bank of England reduced the fiduciary issue of the Issue Department by £60 million, and replaced it with gold bought from the Exchange Equalization Account (E.E.A.). This indicated to the world that the E.E.A. was filled with gold, and had no margin of borrowing capacity.

In January 1937, the Federal Reserve Board again raised reserve requirements. On top of the 50 per cent increase of August 1936

265

was placed a 33⅓ per cent increase to take effect in two steps, half cn 1 March and the other half on 1 May 1937. The effect of the two decisions, and three distinct increases, was to double reserve requirements between July 1936 and May 1937. Central reserve city reserves on demand deposits went from 13 to 26 per cent; those on reserve cities from 10 to 20 per cent and country banks 7 to 14 per cent. The requirement on time deposits was raised from 3 to 6 per cent. The statement accompanying the decision referred explicitly to the $4,000 million in gold imports from the bank holiday in 1933 to the Treasury sterilization programme of December 1936.

The evident burden of gold imports into Britain and the United States gave rise to concern that the price of gold might be reduced. This led to more dishoarding. At the time of the Tripartite Declaration, gold hoarded in Europe amounted to $1,500 to $2,000 million, as estimated by the *Federal Reserve Bulletin*. Two thirds of this was held in London, largely for the accounts of nationals of countries other than Britain.[3] From September 1936 to July 1937, more than $1,000 million came out of these private hoards, and in so far as it was possible to estimate, largely from stocks held in London. During the winter and spring of 1937, dishoarding built up until, in March and April, small central banks, fearful that the price of gold would be reduced and they be caught with losses as in September 1931, joined in. The amounts were limited in the main to part of the gold held in stabilization funds, so that the published gold reserves of the national banks show a decline in these months only for the Swiss National Bank, which disclosed a reduction of only $22 million. By acting like private holders, however, the national banks of a number of the smaller countries underlined the distinction between the private national interest of the small country and the larger public interest of larger countries which, whether they wanted it or not, had responsibility for stabilizing the system.

At the height of the gold scare in April 1937, gold arbitrageurs were so certain of a cut in price that they were unwilling to risk their money for the five days it took, on average, to complete the transaction of buying in London and selling in New York. The

3. *Federal Reserve Bulletin*, vol. 23, No. 8 (August 1937), p. 704.

gold export point in London, involving a combination of sterling-dollar rate and sterling-gold price at which it was profitable to buy gold for shipment to New York and sale to the Treasury, dropped to a sizeable discount. This accentuated the dishoarding. Since the gold price held steady, the discount took the form of a rise in the sterling exchange rate, itself aided by economic and political disturbances in France which resulted in a renewed capital outflow.

In the autumn of 1936, the gold flow to the United States represented a movement of European money into American securities. It caused President Roosevelt to set up a committee of the Secretary of the Treasury, the chairman of the Board of Governors of the Federal Reserve System, and the chairman of the Securities and Exchange Commission, to explore methods of restricting the inflow of capital. Nothing came of it. In the spring of 1937, there was no European interest in securities. If anything, the prospect of a lower price for gold, as seen by the speculators, induced weakness in commodity and security markets, and Europeans tended to sell American securities. The movement was a simple one of selling gold for dollars.

The 'Golden Avalanche', as it was later called, produced a substantial literature for and against policy steps. There was widespread recommendation for a reduction in the gold price, whether on a negotiated basis internationally, as R. H. Brand recommended,[4] or by the United States alone, leaving to other countries the decision whether to change the gold price or allow their currencies to depreciate.[5] Short of such steps were proposals for regulating gold output and exports, reintroducing gold coins into circulation and introducing a two-price system for gold – one at $35 an ounce for central bank metal and the other, presumably lower, at whatever the market determined. As Secretary of the Treasury, Morgenthau went so far as to explore the possibility of negotiations with the Soviet Union on restricting the sale of gold to the West. His object was primarily political, and only

4. R. H. Brand, 'Gold: A World Problem', *International Conciliation*, No. 333 (October 1937), *passim*.

5. Frank D. Graham and Charles R. Whittlesey, *Golden Avalanche*, Princeton University Press, 1939, Chapter IX.

secondarily to 'ease the temporary decline in the international value of gold that occurred in the spring of 1937'.[6]

One objection to reducing the gold price was that, instead of the profits made from raising the gold price, there would be a loss. The technical aspects of this objection are disposed of by Nurkse, who suggests that such loss can easily be offset by some accounting device, such as the creation of a government debt to the central bank in place of the amount by which the gold reserves were marked down.[7] Feasible technically, such devices recommend themselves slowly to politically sensitive bodies, which give the public little credit for sophistication and doubt whether it can disregard a mere bookkeeping entry that raises the government debt.

President Roosevelt stated on 9 April 1937 that the United States had no plans to reduce the price of gold. This failed to calm the market. Among other reasons, the Bank for International Settlements uttered a Delphic statement about lowering the price of gold in the *Annual Report*, which appeared on 3 May.[8] The

6. John Morton Blum, *From the Morgenthau Diaries*, vol. I: *Years of Crisis, 1928–1938*, Houghton Mifflin, Boston, 1959, p. 467. Curiously enough, Morgenthau had nothing more to say about the gold scare, which surely was a central issue to the Treasury in the spring of 1937. His diaries are full of accounts of his differences with Governor Eccles of the Federal Reserve System about interest rates, which he appears to think had importance for the subsequent recession.

7. Economic Financial and Transit Department, League of Nations (Ragnar Nurkse), *International Currency Experience, Lessons of the Interwar Period*, League of Nations, Princeton, N.J., 1944, p. 133.

8. Bank for International Settlements, Seventh Annual Report, covering the year ended 31 March 1937, p. 56:

'It can hardly be doubted that at present a lowering of the price of gold would help to cope with the serious problems resulting from overabundant production. It would, however, cause certain difficulties with regard to valuation of existing gold reserves and the relative position of currencies (the latter, in so far as equilibrium has already been attained, should be disturbed as little as possible). It would, moreover, involve the danger of manipulation of currencies in the future, which would add an element of instability and distrust to the monetary structure.

'In the discussion of a reconstruction of the world's monetary system these various questions, difficult though they might be, cannot be avoided. Also from the point of view of the gold producers, it is important to establish

monthly inflow of gold which had reached $216 million in April 1937, the highest since the inflow of $219 million in October 1936 caused by the pressure on the gold bloc prior to the Tripartite Monetary Agreement, went to $262 million in June. This was the worst month, however, until Munich. The movement subsided in June, partly owing to weakness in raw-material prices, which was thought to discourage any official plan to reduce the gold price – if there were one, as seems entirely unlikely. In addition, the market was quieted by the action of the British in adding £200 million to the borrowing authority of the Exchange Equalization Account in June 1937: an indication, after imports of $1,200 million in 1936 and close to $210 million in the first half of 1937, that it expected to continue absorbing gold.

The American record does not indicate how seriously the question of a reduced gold price was taken. British Treasury files, however, show that its Washington representative had undertaken a series of discussions with Morgenthau in the spring of 1937, at Morgenthau's cottage in Georgia, without any of the United States advisers present. In these discussions Morgenthau raised the question of a tax on gold imports and of a reduction in the price of gold as a means of reducing imports. Bewley treated these proposals, together with others relating to limiting foreign purchases of United States securities, as 'only canvassing possible courses of action in the future'. He suggested in his report to London that Morgenthau was basically ignorant of financial matters, and more cautious in what he does than what he says, and that the proposals, which he had not thought out, would probably be dropped under the influence of his advisers.

The British Treasury was sufficiently stirred by the prospects, however, to elect to pursue the question further, and when Sir John Simon replaced Chamberlain at the Treasury, he cabled Morgenthau suggesting a visit by the top Treasury civil servant, Sir Frederick Phillips, in September. In the message, he stated that his mind was not made up on the subject of a reduction in the gold price, but that his first reactions were unsympathetic, given

---

conditions which will render gold continuously useful as a basis for currencies, instead of concentrating attention on immediate profits.'

the public's tendency to associate the reduced price of gold with deflation. He therefore proposed to do nothing for the immediate future.

When Phillips's instructions were drawn up in mid July, they did not rule out a reduction in the price of gold by concerted international action as a 'long-term possibility' in case of inflation; but given the need for higher commodity prices, it was not called for currently.

Morgenthau told Phillips in September 1937 that he got several callers a day with ideas on gold, but 'paid no attention to them'. The subject was not discussed in open meetings with Morgenthau, Riefler and Viner, but as Phillips left, Morgenthau privately informed him that he had just discussed gold with the President and that 'whatever course of action might be required in connection with gold imports, a lowering of the price of gold was definitely not part of it'. Phillips accepted this, according to British records, and concluded that Morgenthau's 'whole inclinations are against a change in the price and in favour of limiting output'.[9]

It is not clear from the record whether the lack of real consideration given to lowering the price of gold as a means of reducing the burden of absorbing the gold supply was the result of inattention, lack of imagination or the concern for the stability of the U.S. economy or for that of the world monetary structure indicated in the quotation from the B.I.S. report above. At the working level, economists in the Treasury Department, Federal Reserve Board and the Federal Reserve Bank of New York were producing proposals for an ultimate demonetization of gold, and suggestions of taxes and other devices to contain hot money. The former were hedged after September 1937, with the proviso that any reduction in the price of gold be postponed until the economy had recovered from recession. The latter were qualified with doubts as to their practicality. The Roosevelt committee on hot money met as late as April 1937 without producing useful proposals. By that time the problem had altered from one of slowing down the movement of European funds into the New York stock market to countering speculation against gold. But

9. British Treasury records, files of Sir Frederick Phillips, kindly summarized for me by D. E. Moggridge.

the interest and excitement in the gold scare at the bureaucratic level and in the financial press did not communicate itself to, say, *The Public Papers and Addresses of Franklin D. Roosevelt* or the *Morgenthau Diaries*. At the very least, Roosevelt and Morgenthau had learned enough about the international monetary system not to go off half-cocked with half-baked proposals, as they had in 1933. On a more generous interpretation, they and the British were prepared to ride out the destabilizing forces, no matter how uncomfortable, in the interest of maintaining relative exchange rates, which were broadly back to the 1929 pattern, and of stability of the international monetary structure. There are times, perhaps as in 1933, when it is appropriate to respond to the slogan later attributed to John Foster Dulles, 'Don't just stand there: do something.' On the other hand, there are also occasions when the system is best served by reversing it to, 'Don't just do something: stand there.'[10]

The Recession

Business had gone sideways from March to August 1937. A few prices, especially grains and cotton, had fallen. With a record crop, the price of cotton had dropped from 15 cents in March to 9 cents in August. Foreign trade was steady, with imports up more than exports. Markets were uneasy but calm. Then, in mid August, the stock market started off. In September, trading increased and prices fell precipitously. From 141 on 25 August, the Standard Statistics industrial index (based on 1926 as 100) went to 125 in two weeks. By the end of the month, it was 30 per cent below the March highs. On 13 September, the Open Market Committee took cognizance of the turn of events, and the possi-

10. This was the later conclusion of G. Griffith Johnson (but not of Graham and Whittlesey) in *The Treasury and Monetary Policy, 1933–1938*, Harvard University Press, Cambridge, Mass., 1939, p. 159:

'Apparently the most promising course is a waiting one ... in the hope of a rising price level ... a return of capital to France, a renewal of absorption in the Orient, ... and a restoration of international trade and lending. It may be argued that these happy conditions are unlikely to occur, but if that is so there is little that can be done now to solve the gold problem without bringing greater difficulties ...'

bility that the reduction of excess reserves of member banks from more than $3,000 million in July 1936 to less than $700 million in early August had had something to do with it. It requested the Secretary of the Treasury to release $300 million from the Inactive Gold Account set up under sterilization, and this was done. It helped but little. In October, the stock market declined still further, with a Black Tuesday on 19 October, bringing the industrial share average to 102. Commodity prices fell sharply, and so did industrial production. The Federal Reserve index of industrial production slipped from 116 of the 1923–5 average in the first eight months of August to 106 in September, 99 in October, 86 in November and 83 in December. Steel dropped from 85 per cent of capacity in August to 38 per cent of capacity in November and 26 per cent in December. This was the largest decline. The next largest occurred in cotton textiles, which fell from 143 per cent of the 1923–5 average in March, when three-shift working was normal, to 116 by August and 81 by December. Prices of farm products fell by 24 per cent between 3 April 1937 and the end of the year. Prices of durable goods did not decline substantially, but those of non-durables were off 10 per cent or so. All commodities fell in price by 8 per cent.

For a considerable time there was no understanding of what happened. Then it became clear. The spurt in activity from October 1936 had been dominated by inventory accumulation. This was especially the case in automobiles, where, as the result of fears of strikes, supplies of new cars had been built up. It was the same in steel and textiles – two other industries with strong C.I.O. unions. When it became evident after the spring of 1937 that commodity prices were not going to continue upward, the basis for the inventory accumulation was undermined, and first in textiles, then in steel, the reverse process took place. Long-term investment had not been built to great heights, and did not fall far. The steepest economic descent in the history of the United States, which lost half the ground gained for many indexes since 1932, proved that the economic recovery in the United States had been built on illusion.[11]

11. Monetarists may be interested in contemplating a quotation from the *Federal Reserve Bulletin* of June 1938, p. 437:

One particular deception had occurred in foreign trade. The excess of exports over imports in the United States accounts had been worked down from $478 million in 1934 to $235 million in 1935 and $33 million in 1936. In the first six months of 1937 there was an import surplus of $148 million. A considerable part of the increase in imports, however, was intended for stocks and was borrowed from future imports. In the second half of 1937, imports fell from a peak of $307 million in March 1937 to $209 million in December and $141 million at the bottom in July 1938. The export surplus for 1937 rose to $265 million and that for 1938 to $1,100 million. Foreign withdrawals of dollars after October 1936 were partly based on disillusionment with the New York stock market; in great measure, they went to pay for the United States export surplus. The widespread view that United States balance of payments was coming into adjustment proved false.

Some part of the recession – how much is debated – was the result of the sharp change in fiscal policy.[12] The 1936 deficit had been large. Swollen by the $1,700 million bonus payment, the excess of expenditure over receipts in the general and special accounts of the U.S. Treasury had been $4,600 million in fiscal 1936. In fiscal 1937 it was off to $3,100 million, and in fiscal 1938 down to $1,400 million. The decline in the deficit for calendar years was $2,200 million between 1936 and 1937.[13]

'The events of 1929 taught us that the absence of any rise in prices did not prove that no crisis was pending. 1937 taught us that an abundant supply of gold and a cheap monetary policy do not prevent prices from falling.'

12. The most detailed account, by Kenneth D. Roose, *The Economics of Recession and Revival, an Interpretation of 1937–38*, Yale University Press, New Haven, 1954, attributes more importance to the change in fiscal policy, and less to inventory accumulation, some considerable portion of which, he claims, was involuntary (p. 191). He also ascribes importance to the uncertainty of business expectations, based on the 'serious political conflict between the New Deal and business' (p. 238). This interpretation, however, was written at the height of faith in Keynesian doctrine.

13. Marriner S. Eccles, the chairman of the Board of Governors of the Federal Reserve System, refers in his memoirs to a $4,000 million impact of the change in government budget on disposable income between the first four months of 1936 and those of 1937. See his *Beckoning Frontiers, Public and Personal Recollections*, Alfred A. Knopf, New York, 1951, p. 295.

Whether the recession owed more to inventory accumulation and its reversal, tighter money – not actually tight – as a consequence of increases in reserve requirements, or to a sharp reversal in fiscal policy, it produced a change in the intellectual climate. Hitherto resisting the Keynesian revolution in analysis, the leading figures below the cabinet level became much more interested in the message of *The General Theory of Employment, Interest, and Money*. Whereas on 12 October Roosevelt was still urging congressional leaders to wipe out the predicted deficit in the budget for the fiscal year 1939, market collapse a week later produced a change of view.[14] In the Treasury, White, Oliphant, Magill and Selzer, but not Morgenthau, began to think in Keynesian terms. Apart from Eccles, Henderson, Hopkins and Currie were among the leaders.[15] The President was gradually won over. By 14 April a programme was worked out which embraced positive fiscal policy as a measure to stabilize the economy. It was announced in a message to the Congress and in a fireside chat on the same evening.

The dollar scare

While the recession ended the gold scare that the price of gold would be reduced, it gave rise to the opposite fear that the dollar would again be devalued. The prospect was not very real. In November, Morgenthau told Roosevelt that he was planning to assemble a group of people over the week-end to discuss gold – meaning a further undoing of the sterilization programme of December 1936. Misunderstanding him, Roosevelt said that he would not raise the price of gold.[16] That line of action was not contemplated. In a press conference on 18 February, discussing raising prices but especially restoring balance in relative prices, raising those which had fallen but not those which had been steady through the recession, he declared,

14. Blum, *From the Morgenthau Diaries*, vol. I, pp. 385–6.

15. Eccles, op. cit., p. 304, refers to the 'famous memorandum' of Lubin, Henderson and Currie on how the change in government spending produced the depression, which was written for a decisive White House meeting of 8 November 1937.

16. Blum, *From the Morgenthau Diaries*, vol. I, pp. 390–91.

Somebody else with a mind full of generalities will ask . . . 'Does this mean inflation?' No, the policy is to help restore balance in the price structure.

Somebody will say, 'Are we going to have further deflation [*sic*] of the dollar?' The answer is, 'No.'[17]

The dollar scare was neither serious nor prolonged. To a considerable extent it represented mainly the undoing of bear speculation against gold largely from Europe, and especially the United Kingdom, Switzerland and the Netherlands. Between the end of September and the end of the year $575 million were withdrawn from United States banks. But these large-scale movements of hot money did not upset the system. The increase in gold hoarding was easily met by ending the programme of gold sterilization which goal dishoarding had occasioned.

The recovery programme

The recovery programme of 14 April 1938 had a money-and-banking component: a reduction of reserve requirements by approximately $750 million effective from 16 April, and the discontinuance of the Treasury's inactive gold account, with its remaining amount of $1,183 million. The major proposal was to increase spending. Works Progress Administration funds were raised by $1,250 million for the largest amount. Next came $550 million to be loaned by the Treasury to states for public works, $450 million to be spent on public works by the Federal Government and $300 million available for loan by the United States Housing Authority. All in all, spending of over $2,000 million and loans to other spending bodies of almost $1,000 million were proposed. The budget implications explicitly involved acceptance of deficits. The Keynesian doctrine of spending for stability was finally accepted after having been resisted for seven years of depression by both Hoover and Roosevelt.

The commitment was both belated and faint-hearted, as Cary Brown has shown, in that casual impressions of the New Deal

17. *The Public Papers and Addresses of Franklin D. Roosevelt*, vol. VII, pp. 105–6.

greatly exaggerate its devotion to deficit spending.[18] Early deficits were reluctantly accepted as the result of shortfalls in taxes or expenditures which the administration had been unable to reduce. The recession was needed to demonstrate the efficacy of Keynesian ideas, which would make a deep national depression never again possible, and the commitment of the United States to steady support for the international system, such as it was, in one sort of disturbance and another.

The recovery from the recession lows took place quickly, though not as speedily as the recession which preceded it. In a note attached to the 14 April message to the Congress in his *Papers and Addresses*, Roosevelt included a table showing the decline from July 1937 to March and June 1938 and the recovery to August 1939 (Table 14). It sums up rather neatly how the recovery commenced unevenly in the spring of 1938, certain items, like construction, rising immediately, and others not reaching their lows until June; the uneven path of recovery; and the continued if gentle slide in prices. It does not indicate the part played in recovery in foreign orders for arms, as against domestic spending programmes. But it emphasizes the recession which was needed in addition to the depression to provide the intellectual basis for stabilizing the economy.

'The basic reason the depression lasted so long was, of course, the economic ignorance of the times.'[19] This answer, as we hope to have demonstrated, is inadequate on a world basis. It fits very well for the United States.

18. E. C. Brown, 'Fiscal Policy in the 'Thirties: A Reappraisal', *American Economic Review*, XLVI, No. 5 (December 1956), pp. 857–79.

19. Gilbert Burck and Charles Silberman, 'Why the Depression Lasted so Long', *Fortune*, vol. LI, No. 3 (March 1955), reprinted in Stanley Coben and F. G. Hill (eds.), *American Economic History: Essays in Interpretation*, J. B. Lippincott, Philadelphia, 1966, p. 496.

Table 14. Indexes of income, employment, production and other business activity of the United States, 1937–9 (adjusted for seasonal variation, except as noted).

	Base period	1937 July	1938 Mar.	1938 Jun.	1939 Aug.	(percent change) Jul. '37 Jun. '38	(percent change) Jun. '38 Aug. '39
Income payments	1929	89	81	79	85	−12	+8
Factory employment*	1923–5	111	91	84	96	−24	+14
Factory payrolls*	1923–5	105	78	71	90	−32	+26
Industrial production							
TOTAL	1935–9	120	84	81	104	−33	+28
steel		142	53	49	111	−65	+127
automobiles		144	57	49	84	−66	+71
cotton textiles		118	81	81	114	−31	+41
woollen textiles		97	53	68	106	−30	+56
shoes		108	93	88	107	−19	+22
Freight car loadings	1923–5	80	60	58	70	−28	+21
Construction contracts	1923–5	67	46	54	73	−19	+35
residential		44	33	42	67	−5	+60
other		86	56	64	78	−26	+22
Department store sales	1923–5	92	86	82	89	−11	+9
Wholesale prices*	1926	87·9	79·7	78·3	75·0	−11	−4

*Not adjusted for seasonal variation.

SOURCE: Franklin Delano Roosevelt, *The Public Papers and Addresses of Franklin Delano Roosevelt*, vol. VII, Macmillan Co., New York, 1941, p. 235.

13. Rearmament in a Disintegrating World Economy

In 1937, unlike 1929, there was no doubt where the trouble started. The recession originated in the United States. Moreover, in a world not closely knit by trade and payments, its impact was felt unevenly. After the up-coming war, Sir Dennis Robertson was to state that when the United States sneezed, Europe caught pneumonia. In 1937–8, the impact of the recession was mainly felt in the less developed countries. Busy preparing for war, Europe and Japan suffered no more than a few sniffles.

The industrial countries felt, first, a decline in security prices. This result was largely psychological. The nose-dive in New York made the world's capitalists uneasy, and some liquidation elsewhere was required to make good the liquidity lost on the New York Stock Exchange. With easy monetary policy, however, and substantial spending for public works, the dip did not develop into anything serious. In some markets, such as the Swiss, it did not occur at all.

There were two effects in foreign trade: (a) a loss in exports to the United States and to customers of the United States which were forced to cut back on imports because their exports to the United States had fallen; and (b) a reduction in the prices of imported raw materials. Prices of European and overseas commodities moved disparately. From 1928 to 1938, European import values as a whole fell from 100 to 73, constituting the trend. Extra-European commodities, such as cocoa beans, sugar, coffee, wool, cotton, fats and oils and silk, fell by more than the trend by percentages clustering around 40 per cent, whereas raw materials of European origin – wood pulp, coal, iron ore, iron and steel, cement – rose relative to trend by 45 to 75 per cent.[1] The divergence originated in the decline in United States' demand for the first group of commodities, and rapidly rising European expenditure for armaments, and for plants to build armaments, which affected the second.

Part of the improvement in Europe's terms of trade in 1938 over 1937 resulted from a decline in freight rates. This took place not at the expense of Europe's suppliers, but of shipowners, themselves largely European. The scramble for raw materials to be added to inventories in the United States, against the background of years of failure to replace ships, almost doubled the freight index between the first half of 1936 and the third quarter of 1937. Nine months later it had fallen 50 per cent. The decline of 35 per cent in the United States' demand for goods from 1937 to 1938 relieved the inflationary squeeze in shipping and helped to make overseas imports cheap again.

If it did not greatly disturb the industrialized countries, and aided them in a few respects, the United States recession was harsh on suppliers of raw materials. The price decline did not cumulate, as it had after 1929, and rearmament demand from Europe provided something of a cushion. To support prices, attempts were made to set in motion the machinery of export quotas, so laboriously constructed during the middle 1930s. It did not help greatly. The Pan American conference on coffee broke down in August 1937 before the recession struck in September, and Brazil gave up its attempt to stabilize the price of coffee the following November. Despite a rapid closing down of export quotas in rubber, tin, copper and wheat, prices fell sharply in these materials. The decline in United States consumption between January 1937 and January 1938 – illustrated by such figures as 30 per cent in silk, 35 per cent in cotton, 40 per cent in rubber, 60 per cent in tin and wool – proved too severe.

Nor did less developed countries receive help from a countercyclical revival of long-term lending. Instead of sending capital abroad, the United States was receiving it. The world economy

1. See C. P. Kindleberger, *The Terms of Trade: A European Case Study*, Technology Press, Cambridge, Mass.: Chapman & Hall, London, 1956, pp. 182–3.

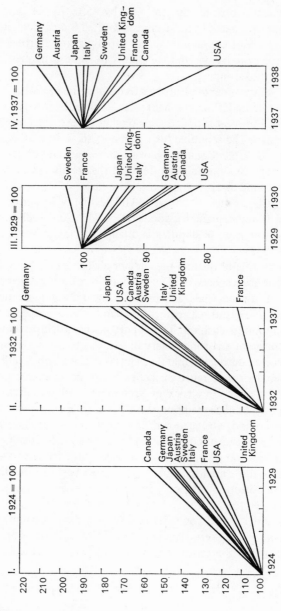

Figure 11. Changes in industrial production in selected countries, 1924–9, 1932–7, 1929–30 and 1937–8 (index numbers with specified bases).

SOURCE: League of Nations, *World Economic Survey, 1938–39,* Geneva, p. 107.

functioned poorly in trade, the capital market, and in payments. Separate countries were on their own.

The disarticulated world economy

The lack of coherence of the world economy in the 1930s is illustrated by changes in industrial production in the upswings of 1925 to 1929 and 1932 to 1937, on the one hand, and in the one-year declines from 1929 to 1930 and from 1937 to 1938. These are shown in Figure 11. On the upswing, the range of the selected countries runs from +12 per cent to +55 per cent in the 1920s, and +14 per cent to +120 per cent in the 1930s. On the downside, the spreads are +3 to −19 per cent and +8 to −22 per cent respectively.

The relationship of foreign trade to domestic production, measured by the ratio between the volume of imports and that of industrial production in 1938 as compared with 1929, held up for a few countries, notably France and the United States, but declined 10 per cent in Britain, nearly 20 per cent in Canada and 25 to 40 per cent in Japan, Germany and Italy.[2] Within the foreign-trade totals, moreover, trade was balanced less multilaterally. In 1928, according to Hilgerdt's calculations, bilateral balancing between exports and imports between pairs of countries on the average covered 70 per cent of merchandise trade, with about 5 per cent more covered by exports or imports of services or capital movements, and 25 per cent balanced multilaterally.[3] The drying up of the international capital market, tariff discrimination, foreign-exchange controls and clearing and payments arrangements sharply reduced the proportion of multilateral payments.[4]

2. League of Nations (James E. Meade), *World Economic Survey, 1938/39*, Geneva, 1939, p. 108.

3. See League of Nations (F. Hilgerdt), *The Network of World Trade*, Geneva, 1942, pp. 87 ff. Hilgerdt does not give a figure for the percentage bilaterally balanced in 1938 (nor the method of calculating the 1928 figure). Tables 44 and 48 and Diagrams 6 and 10 on pp. 77, 78 and 90, however, demonstrate the extent of shrinkage in regional multilateral clearing, and the fact is referred to throughout the text.

4. By the end of 1937, the number of clearing agreements had reached 170 – see League of Nations (James E. Meade), *World Economic Survey, 1937/38*, Geneva, 1938, p. 161.

Trade increasingly took place bilaterally, and to the extent it continued to be multilateral, was contained within bloc lines. The United Kingdom, for example, sold 62 per cent of its exports to the Commonwealth and sterling bloc in 1938, compared with 51 per cent in 1929, and bought 55 per cent of its imports within the bloc in the later year, as compared with 42 per cent in the earlier year. German trade with south-eastern Europe over the same period grew from 5 to 13 per cent in exports and from 4½ to 12 per cent in imports. The most remarkable shift took place in Japan's trade with the 'yen bloc' of Korea, Formosa, Kwantung and Manchuria, where exports rose from 24 to 55 per cent between 1929 and 1938 and imports from 20 to 41 per cent.[5]

Not only had the structure of trade altered. The adjustment mechanism no longer worked. Income changes produced disequilibrium in trade and payments rather than being induced in response to them. To the extent that adjustment was inescapable because of the lack of foreign-exchange reserves, it was brought about by tariffs, quotas and foreign-exchange controls. Tariffs were raised widely in 1938, reversing the liberalizing movement which had begun in 1937. The Hague Convention to lower tariffs among Scandinavian countries and Belgium and the Netherlands of 1937 was allowed to lapse the following year. One country after another tightened up exchange regulations, and where they were already tight a few countries added the death penalty, as did Germany in 1936 and Italy in 1939.

As already observed, the private capital market remained moribund. United States investors had had their fill of foreign bonds. Amortization and repayments exceeded the few new private issues. Some private loans within the Commonwealth were floated in London in 1936 and 1937 and a substantial Australian loan was raised in that market in 1938. For the most part, the British authorities kept restrictions on long-term lending, and after serious weakness in sterling in 1938, gradually limited all outflow of British funds, closing down forward facilities in December 1938 and purchases of foreign outstanding securities in April 1939. Government lending to replace the private capital

5. League of Nations, *Review of World Trade, 1938*, Geneva, 1939, pp. 34 and 35.

market found a beginning, but for expanding exports and employment, rather than to ease national adjustments to changing circumstances. The Export Credit Guarantees Department in Britain and the Export-Import Bank in the United States, both started before the 1937 recession, were expanded. In Britain a primary motive was to provide economic assistance to potential allies, and loans to the Turkish, Greek, Romanian, Chinese and Polish governments were undertaken, together with commercial credits to New Zealand importers. The Export-Import Bank expanded lending to Latin American countries, Poland and China to buy United States products. An Export-Import Bank loan of $20 million to Brazil to unfreeze commercial debts represented less a capital movement than a change from private to government ownership of foreign assets within the United States. An additional $50 million was made available to purchase additional goods. Of more enduring interest was a $50 million United States Treasury advance in March 1939 to the Brazilian government to establish a foreign-exchange fund and to assist in starting a central bank. This may be interpreted as merely a loan to sell United States exports to assist employment. Alternatively, it may be viewed as an early step in replacing the shattered private market for international lending on a governmental basis.

Rearmament

If the world economy was in dire straits, its polity was in worse. The Ethiopian War of 1935 had been followed by Japan's renewed attack on China in 1937, the Spanish Civil War, not to mention German military movement into the Rhineland in 1936, the *Anschluss* and Munich in 1938 and the occupation of Czechoslovakia in 1939. Britain started seriously to rearm. In 1937 it announced a five-year programme of expenditure for armaments of £1,500 million of which £400 million was to be financed by borrowing. Taxes were raised in the budget for the year ended 31 March 1938, and again in the following year. In February 1939 the limit for borrowing in the programme was raised from £400 to £800 million. By July 1939, the pressure was increased still further. The armament outlays for the fiscal year ending

31 March 1940 were lifted from £630 million to £750 million, of which £500 million was to be borrowed. Actual defence expenditure rose from £46 million in the second quarter of 1937 to £124 million two years later. These disbursements converted the economy from one of idle resources to scarcity, from falling prices to inflation, and gradually from resource allocation by competitive markets to the disequilibrium system of price controls, consumer rationing and supply allocations. Bottlenecks were attacked in a number of industries – not only armaments, but such ancillary lines as ship construction. A start was made to bringing new land under cultivation and accumulating seed, farm machinery and fertilizer as well as stocks of food. A stockpile of cotton was obtained by a government swap of cotton against rubber with the United States.[6]

The delays in getting defence spending under way in France were discussed in Chapter 11. No real progress was made until after Munich, when Paul Reynaud took over the Ministry of Finance under the Daladier government, won powers to govern by decree, reversed the policies of the Blum government and of Daladier's first Minister of Finance, and initiated a sharp upturn in French spending and production. National-defence industries that had been nationalized in August 1936, but slow to expand production, were galvanized into rapid action. In March 1939 a production service was begun in the Ministry of National Defence. In April, controls were imposed on transfers of labour, and limits set to profits in the armament industry. In May, the military was given power to requisition transport, redundant employees were reassigned from the railways, and war-risk insurance was established. Production rose rapidly, and with it hours of work.

Japan reached full employment by the middle of 1938. Three hundred million yen were transferred by the Bank of Japan to a revolving fund to finance raw-material imports for the export industries, and to disguise gold losses. A disequilibrium system of

6. Economists are confounded that history is replete with examples of errors of economic policy, as seen by contemporary analysts, which turned out to be useful. Among them was the U.S. farm policy which produced large supplies of redundant cotton and wheat during the depression which proved highly useful in war.

foreign-exchange controls, price controls and resource allocations followed.

A Supreme Autarky Commission, of that name, was established in Italy in October 1937 to emphasize withdrawal of another Axis member from the world economy.

Contemporary sources were vastly impressed by the German armament effort as displayed by volunteers with regular equipment in Spain, and by the *Wehrmacht*'s marches into the Rhineland, Austria and Czechoslovakia. Intelligence sources, together with public information, suggested that German military preparations had been under way since 1933 and that, as Hitler boasted, 90,000 million R M had been spent on armaments. The last statement was an exaggeration. As to the first, up to the occupation of the Rhineland in the spring of 1936, German rearmament was still small. In the three years to the end of March 1936, only 8,000 million R M had been spent, half of it in the last year. In the three following years, 32,000 million R M were spent (18,000 million in the last year), making 40,000 million R M in the six years to 31 March 1939. An accelerating rate of spending brought the total at outbreak of war to 50,000 million R M.[7] These figures include capital expenditures for armament plants and stockpiling of commodities, as well as material.

The move to intensive rearmament came in the summer of 1936, when Hermann Göring was appointed plenipotentiary of the Second Four-Year Plan with instructions to get ready for war in four years. No specific plan of military re-equipment has been found, nor was the overall four-year plan or its constituent elements, such as raw-material production, worked out well as a highly rational coordinated programme. Successes were achieved in a number of areas, such as agriculture, rubber (Buna-S) and aluminium, but output fell far short of targets in oil and iron ore, in which Germany remained heavily dependent on imports in 1939.

The German armament programme was held back by a *Blitzkrieg* strategy, by the resistance of financiers and industrialists and by an unwillingness to depart substantially from peace-

7. Burton H. Klein, *Germany's Economic Preparations for War*, Harvard university Press, 1959, pp. 16 ff.

time standards. German successes in the Rhineland, Austria, Czechoslovakia and Poland made the strategy of *Blitzkrieg* credible and rendered preparation for a drawn-out conflict unnecessary. The resistance of industrialists was economic, not political, and was expressed as an opposition to the substantial diversion of steel from existing uses to such roundabout purposes as iron-ore development. Not understanding that a nation can finance anything it can produce, Schacht fought armament expansion on financial grounds. By 1936, he had fallen into dis-favour over his cautious approach to raw-material development. Relieved as Minister of Economics in August 1937, he remained President of the Reichsbank until January 1939. A 3,000 million RM credit demanded of the Reichsbank was granted with great reluctance in 1937. He refused further credits after March 1938, which led to his dismissal.

But the basic reason for the limited character of the armament programme, given the aggressive intentions of the Nazi leadership, was its inability, and even unwillingness, to depart from peace-time norms. Consumption, investment in consumption industries and even government non-war expenditure passed previous peaks at the end of the decade.[8] There was no real mobilization of manpower or drastic extension of hours of work. Hitler was partly unwilling, partly unable, to achieve the mobilization required to back up his boasts.

Despite the discrepancy between talk and performance in armament, sufficient pressure was applied to the German economy to require it to develop a disequilibrium system. Hourly wages were frozen at the level of October 1933, prices at that of October 1936. The clearing system was extended from creditor countries and south-east Europe to Latin America. German relations with the world economy, like those of Japan and Italy, no longer responded to changes in money, prices or capital flows, but were highly controlled. Three of the leading ten industrial countries had largely withdrawn from the world economy.

8. Klein, *Germany's Economic Preparations for War*, p. 76.

Efforts to rebuild the world economy

Recovery had gone far enough in 1937 to lead governments outside the Axis and Communist countries to explore the means of rebuilding the world economy and ensuring against any renewed depression. This effort had at least three aspects. In April 1937, the British and French governments invited Paul Van Zealand, former Prime Minister of Belgium and a distinguished economist, to prepare a report on the possibility of removing obstacles to trade. This appeared in January 1938. In September 1937, a League of Nations Committee for the Study of the Problems of Raw Materials submitted its report to the Economic Committee of the League, which in turn reported to the Council in December of that year. Somewhat earlier, in June 1937, an International Labour Conference passed a resolution on international cooperation in the provision of information on public works, under which, and in collaboration with the Economic and Financial Organization of the League of Nations, which had been asked by the Assembly to examine measures for the prevention or mitigation of economic depressions, it convened an international conference on public works in June 1938.

As we saw earlier, the coordination of national expenditures for public works had been proposed from many sources, including the German heretical economists and the International Labour Office, for discussion at the World Economic Conference of 1933.[9] The flowering of Keynesian thought made the subject more timely. The spread of rearmament, on the other hand, made it impossible to accomplish anything. The twenty-five governments represented at the preparatory meeting of the International Public Works Committee in June 1938 limited themselves to recommending exchange of information on the planning, timing and finance of state expenditure on capital projects. Given the burgeoning expenditure for armament, this was the best that could be done. It was highly academic. Only after the Second World War was it found that the long lags in moving among the planning, design and execution stages made national counter-cyclical

9. See above, p. 206.

spending difficult to the point of impossibility, much less international coordination of national counter-cyclical spending. Later the International Bank for Reconstruction and Development was to insist that it could not carry out the provision of its charter which required it, *inter alia*, to time its development expenditures in anti-cyclical fashion.[10]

The report of the League Committee for the Study of the Problems of Raw Materials[11] is hardly distinguishable from the long line of official studies and reports on the raw-material problem which preceded and followed it[12] (eliminating, however, esoteric proposals for international compensation for terms-of-trade changes or tying the issuance of money to stocks of primary products). The difficulties of primary products were found in inelasticities of supply and demand; their solution through schemes which restricted production or exports or provided for stockpiling. Equal access was to be preserved, and consumer representation established on administrative bodies. In 1938, part of the difficulty in demand was lack of foreign exchange, while inelasticity of supply was partly the result of a need for foreign exchange on the part of producing countries, combined with a lack of availability of foreign loans. Like all such studies, that of the League Committee achieved no useful result, and for the same principal reason. At a given point in time producing and consuming countries find it difficult, if not impossible, to agree on prices which they are persuaded will be at a market-clearing level for an extended period. A period of rapid price decline, like that from September to December 1937, was particularly inappropriate as a moment to agree on a long-run equilibrium price. Where commodity schemes were in operation, export quotas were being

10. See International Bank for Reconstruction and Development submission to the Economic and Employment Commission of the United Nations, Press release No. 134, 11 May 1949. The question of anti-cyclical lending is nowhere discussed in *The International Bank for Reconstruction and Development, 1946–1953*, Johns Hopkins Press, Baltimore, 1954.

11. League document A. 27.1937. II.B.

12. See, for example, United Nations, *Commodity Trade and Economic Development*, Report by a Committee of Experts, New York, 1952; and Contracting Parties for the General Agreement on Tariffs and Trade, *Trends in International Trade*, Report by a Panel of Experts, Geneva, 1958.

reduced rapidly, but not sufficiently to prevent price declines. After the middle of 1938, the position was equally inauspicious for the opposite reason, that raw material prices were rising. Very quickly, however, as with the international coordination of public works, world rearmament and eventually war pushed the problem into the background.

The Van Zealand report on trade was equally academic, and partly for the same reason – rearmament. M. Van Zealand argued that tariffs should be reduced reciprocally, with concessions extended widely through the most-favoured nation clause; that quotas should be replaced by tariffs, or at the least tariff quotas; that the open door was needed in access to raw materials. He urged the gradual dismantling of clearing agreements, the removal of foreign-exchange controls by creditor countries to permit capital movements, and by debtor countries to the extent of financing foreign trade, even though control over other capital movements might need to be retained. The Bank for International Settlements might provide for the financing of trade by establishing a multilateral clearing arrangement, or a common fund used to finance international trade while exchange controls were in process of dismantlement. The ultimate means of control of hot money was the re-establishment of the gold standard. Means to that end would be to extend agreements under the Tripartite Monetary Agreement. Instead of guaranteeing exchange rates for twenty-four hours at a time, this should be done for six months. But the re-establishment of the gold standard was the final step in the restoration of the world economy, not the first.

Like the reports on public works and raw materials, the Van Zealand report received little attention, and partly, as indicated, for the same reason: the rapidly approaching war and the need to prepare for it. In addition, the sponsorship of France and Britain, and the intellectual leadership of a distinguished Belgian, were not sufficient. Action could come only from enlisting the forceful commitment of the United States. The United States was prepared to push ahead in lowering its own tariffs on a reciprocal basis, and to chip away at Empire preference. It had made a feeble beginning of international monetary cooperation in the

Tripartite Monetary Agreement, but with little real understanding of what was implied.[13]

Whether United States leadership in rebuilding the world economy would have been forthcoming without the war is a question which cannot be answered.[14] A start had been made, but there was little follow-up. The world was far from the powerful leadership felt during and after the war in the provisions for rebuilding the world economy embodied in the Atlantic Charter, Article VII of Lend-Lease, Dumbarton Oaks, Bretton Woods, Hot Springs, the Anglo-American Financial Agreement, the International Trade Organization and General Agreement on Tariffs and Trade, the Marshall Plan and Point IV. Not only was American initiative feeble and hesitant: there was no alternative to it. Even without the war, the exercise embodied in the League Committee on Raw Materials, the International Labour Office on coordination of public works and the Van Zealand report for reducing barriers to trade was doomed to remain academic.

13. As an illustration of how little he understood the international monetary system, take Morgenthau's suggestion that the Soviet Union should be invited to join the Tripartite Monetary Agreement – see John Morton Blum, *From the Morgenthau Diaries*, vol. I: *Years of Crisis, 1928–38*, Houghton Mifflin, Boston, 1959, p. 460.

14. That the initiative came from the United States, though with a quick response from Britain, is the theme of the opening chapters of Richard N. Gardner, *Sterling-Dollar Diplomacy*, revised edition, McGraw-Hill, New York, 1969. For an account of negotiations in London, see E. F. Penrose, *Economic Planning for the Peace*, Princeton University Press, 1953.

14. An Explanation of the 1929 Depression

We return to the original questions: what produced the world depression of 1929, why was it so widespread, so deep, so long? Was it caused by real or monetary factors? Did it originate in the United States, in Europe, in the primary-producing countries of the periphery, in the relations among them? Was the fatal weakness the nature of the international capitalist system, or the way it was operated, i.e. the policies pursued by governments? Were such policies, to the extent they were important, the consequence of ignorance, short-sightedness or ill-will? Were the depth and length of the depression a reflection of the strength of the shock to a relatively stable system, or a measure of the system's instability in the presence of a blow or series of blows of normal force (however measured)? Or to bring the issue back to the difference between Milton Friedman and Paul Samuelson, was the 1929 depression the consequence of United States monetary policy or a series of historical accidents? Inevitably in drawing the threads together there will be a considerable amount of confirmation of preconceptions. We are open to the accusation of having selected statistics, facts and incidents from the history of the decade which support a position chosen *a priori*. But we would claim that we have not knowingly suppressed any facts that do not fit the explanation which follows, nor ignored other explanations such as United States monetary policy (Friedman); misuse of the gold standard (Robbins); mistaken deflation (Keynes); secular stagnation (Hansen); structural disequilibrium (Svennilson); and the like. The chapter is entitled 'An Explanation' not 'The Explanation'.

The explanation of this book is that the 1929 depression was so

291

wide, so deep and so long because the international economic system was rendered unstable by British inability and United States unwillingness to assume responsibility for stabilizing it in three particulars: (a) maintaining a relatively open market for distress goods; (b) providing counter-cyclical long-term lending; and (c) discounting in crisis. The shocks to the system from the overproduction of certain primary products such as wheat; from the 1927 reduction of interest rates in the United States (if it was one); from the halt of lending to Germany in 1928; or from the stock-market crash of 1929 were not so great. Shocks of similar magnitude had been handled in the stock-market break in the spring of 1920 and the 1927 recession in the United States. The world economic system was unstable unless some country stabilized it, as Britain had done in the nineteenth century and up to 1913. In 1929, the British couldn't and the United States wouldn't. When every country turned to protect its national private interest, the world public interest went down the drain, and with it the private interests of all.

Asymmetry

If the world economy behaved symmetrically, there could be no world depression. A decline in the price of wheat might produce losses for farmers; it would, however, lead to gains in real purchasing power for consumers (shifts in real income from groups with different marginal rates of saving are ignored). Gold losses for one country would be deflationary, but gains for the recipient country would yield offsetting expansion. Contractive exchange appreciation would be matched by stimulating depreciation. The stock market could not absorb funds, since for every buyer that gives up money, there is a seller that gains it.

But symmetry is not the way of the world in all times and places, and not for the reason of interference by men with, say, the rules of the gold-standard game, or that New York as an international financial centre was inexperienced. It happened that in Britain, from 1873 to 1913, foreign lending and domestic investment were maintained in continuous counterpoint. Domestic recession stimulated foreign lending; boom at home cut it down. But the boom at home expanded imports which provided an export stimulus abroad in place of domestic investment with borrowed funds. Counter-cyclical lending stabilized the system.

In the 1920s, United States foreign lending was positively correlated with domestic investment, not counterpoised. The boom of the 1920s was accompanied by foreign lending; the depression of the 1930s saw the capital flow reversed. In his *The United States and the World Economy*, written in 1943, Hal Lary recorded the fundamental fact that the United States cut down on imports and lending at the same time. The cut in lending actually preceded the stock-market crash as investors were diverted from the boom in foreign bonds which followed the Dawes loan to the boom in domestic stocks dating from the spring of 1928. The deflationary pressure on Germany may be debated;[1] the pressure on the less developed countries at the periphery is clear cut.[2] As Table 1 (p. 56) shows, moreover, Britain joined the United States in reducing its lending in 1929 over 1928.

Maintaining a market for distress goods can be regarded as another form of financing. Free trade has two dimensions: (a) to adapt domestic resources to changes in productive capacities abroad, and (b) to maintain the import market open in periods of stress. The first is more readily done by a rapidly growing country which needs to transfer resources out of less productive occupations and is willing to embrace the competition of imports. By holding firm to free trade during depression at some short-run cost to resources in import-competing lines, the second provides a market for surpluses accumulated abroad. Britain clung to free trade from 1846 (or some year thereafter, such as 1860, when all tariffs but those for revenue had been dismantled) until 1916.

1. See Heywood W. Fleisig, 'Long-Term Capital Flows and the Great Depression: The Role of the United States, 1927–1933', unpublished dissertation, Yale University, 1968, *passim*, and Peter Temin, 'The Beginning of the Depression in Germany', *Economic History Review*, vol. xxiv, No. 2 (May 1971), pp. 240–48. Fleisig and Temin argue over the size of the shock to the system. If the system is basically unstable, this issue is downgraded in importance.

2. Heywood Fleisig, 'The United States and the World Periphery during the Early Years of the Great Depression', forthcoming in Herman van der Wee, ed., *The Great Depression Revisited*, Nyhoff, The Hague, 1972.

After 1873, she was not growing rapidly, but continued to adhere to free trade since her declining industries were exporters rather than import-competers. Her tenacity in adhering to free trade in depression may have been born of cultural lag and the free-trade tradition of Adam Smith, rather than of conscious service to the world economy.

The contrast is with the Smoot-Hawley Tariff Act of 1930. At the first hint of trouble in agriculture, Hoover reached for the Republican household remedy, as Schumpeter characterized it, in the face of a recommendation of the World Economic Conference of 1927 that nations of the world should adopt a tariff truce. The action was important less for its impact on the United States balance of payments, or as conduct unbecoming a creditor nation, than for its irresponsibility. The congressional rabble enlarged protection from agriculture to primary products and manufactures of all kinds, and Hoover, despite more than thirty formal protests from other countries and the advice of 1,000 economists, signed the Bill into law. This gave rise to (or at least did nothing to stop) a headlong stampede to protection and restrictions on imports, each country trying to ward off deflationary pressure of imports, and all together ensuring such pressure through mutual restriction of exports. As with exchange depreciation to raise domestic prices, the gain from one country was a loss for all. With tariff retaliation and competitive depreciation, mutual losses were certain. The formula of tariff truce and exchange stabilization proposed for the World Economic Conference of 1933 offered no positive means of raising prices or expanding employment. It would none the less have been significant as a means of slowing further decline. With no major country providing a market for distress goods, or willing to tolerate appreciation, much less furnish long-term capital or discounting facilities to countries suffering from payments difficulties, the fallacy of composition with the whole less than the sum of its parts ensured that deflation would roll on.

Initial conditions

The lack of leadership in providing discount facilities, anti-cyclical lending or an open market for goods rendered the system unstable. So did the heritage of war, and especially the combination of reparations, war debts, overvaluation of the pound and undervaluation of the French franc. One should perhaps add the German inflation of 1923, which made that country paranoid in its subsequent attachment to deflation. The structural dislocations of war in excess production of wheat, sugar and wool, plus ships, cotton textiles and coal, were of less consequence and could have been cared for fairly readily by the price system if macroeconomic stability could have been preserved. The financial distortions made such stability difficult if not impossible to sustain. A far-seeing leadership on the part of the United States might have been willing to waive war debts, but it would have been difficult to persuade the American voter of the merit of the course, especially when Britain and France were receiving reparations. Britain was willing to forego reparations, to the extent that war debts were written off – an attitude of limited self-denial – but the suggestion that the French could write off reparations, after having paid them in 1871 and 1819, and after four years of cruel war, is to ask too much from history.

The failure to achieve a system of equilibrium exchange rates must be set down, like budget-balancing in government accounts, at the door of economic ignorance. In the British case, the urge was to restore the *status quo ante*; it was aided by destabilizing speculation. The selection of an exchange rate for the French franc was addressed much more clinically – as it could be, since restoration of the old par was out of the question – but too little account was taken of the earlier export of capital and the need for an import surplus to transfer it inward as it returned to France. This can be regarded as economic ignorance of a second order. In combination with war debts and reparations, the disequilibrium rates made the underlying position weak. It is interesting, though perhaps idle, to contemplate whether the depression could still have been avoided, or mitigated by some substantial fraction such as two thirds, if the United States had managed to keep open its market, maintain long-term capital flowing and provide lending of last resort through discounting in crisis. One great difficulty was that while the market for goods might be kept open by vetoing congressional tariff proposals, and discounting undertaken through government or central-bank action, there was no way in which governments of the day could sustain international lending. Foreign loans were made by the market, or largely not at all. Lending could be stopped by government fiat, as the Capital Issues Committee did from time to time in London; it was impossible for government to get the private market to start after it had stopped. And to substitute government loans for the market on anything but an emergency-discounting basis called for machinery which was virtually non-existent. The Bank of France would direct President Luther of the Reichsbank to talk loans with private bankers. The Department of State could suggest that foreign governments talk to J. P. Morgan & Company. They could not produce loans. Leverage was weak.

British leadership

Not until 1931 was it clear that Britain could not provide the leadership. In the early 1920s, there were League of Nations programmes for the stabilization of the currencies of Austria and Hungary. These were to a considerable extent British in spirit, with help of experts from Scandinavia, the Low Countries and the Dominions, such as staffed the League of Nations Economic and Financial Section. Later the Dawes and Young Plans to settle German reparations were dominated by British experts, with Americans serving as front men to foster the British hope of tying reparations to war debts. By 1931, British capacity for leadership had gone. In small part it had been dissipated in puerile central-bank quarrels between Norman and Moreau, although much of the competition for domination over the smaller central banks of Europe was the product of Moreau's imagination. (Benjamin Strong tried hard to arbitrate these quarrels, and his death in 1928 was a loss for the stability of the system.) More significant was the burden of French sterling balances, which inhibited Britain as a lender of last resort. In the June 1931 crises, the climax of weakness was reached on the second Austrian loan for the *Kreditanstalt* when Norman offered 50 million schillings or $7 million as a loan for one week. At the World Economic Conference in 1933, it was clear that Britain had turned away from a leading world role, cultivating the Commonwealth and freedom to manage sterling, and largely leaving it to the United States to devise a world programme.

Lack of United States leadership

Revisionist historians, such as William A. Williams, insist that the United States undertook a leading world role under Charles E. Hughes as early as the Disarmament Conference of 1922.[3] It is difficult or impossible to find support for this position in the field of international economics, which supports the conventional wisdom of such historians as E. H. Carr, that 'in 1918, world leadership was offered, by almost universal consent, to the United States . . . [and] was declined'.[4] There was interest in the affairs of Europe in New York, in the Federal Reserve Bank of New York under Strong and Harrison, in the financial community represented by such people as Dwight Morrow, Thomas Lamont and Norman Davis. A few non-New Yorkers, such as Charles G. Dawes and Andrew Mellon, were brought into international finance and diplomacy. On the whole, however, the isolationism expressed by Henry Cabot Lodge in leading the rejection of the Versailles

3. See, for example, William Appleman Williams, *The Tragedy of American Diplomacy*, World Publishing Co., Cleveland, Ohio, 1959, *passim*, but esp. Chapter IV, 'The Legend of Isolationism'. Mr Williams, a Marxist revisionist historian, states (p. 123): 'Hoover did not grasp the fact that the depression was a sign of stagnation in a corporate economy which was born during the civil war and came to maturity in the decade from 1895 to 1905'; and (p. 128): '. . . from the fall of 1932 Roosevelt and Hull stressed the importance of foreign trade for domestic revival and expansion and for world wide relief of conditions which caused war and revolution'. It is difficult to see how a historian could ignore such evidence as the First Inaugural Address, cited earlier, to be able to make such a statement about Roosevelt.

4. Edward Hallett Carr, *The Twenty Years' Crisis, 1919–1939: An Introduction to the Study of International Relations*, Macmillan, London, 1939; 2nd edition, 1946, p. 234.

Treaty and United States adherence to the League of Nations typi-
fied the dominant sentiment. The United States was uncertain
in its international role. It felt that the British were shrewder, more
sophisticated, more devious in their negotiating tactics, so that
the United States came out of international conferences losers.
Stimson would have been willing to undertake a major discounting
operation to rescue the Reichsmark in July 1931. Hoover, Mellon
and (though from New York) Mills were opposed to sending
good money after bad, as discounting calls for. In 1933, James
Warburg, Moley and, presumably, Woodin and Roosevelt still
resisted sending good money after bad. Proposals for embryonic
international monetary funds were legion; and even Britain
presented one officially. They were uniformly turned down with
a lecture on how much the United States had already lost in unpaid war debts and the Standstill Agreement.[5] It was not until
1942 that Harry D. White began preparing a world plan for discussion at Bretton Woods – together with the plan of Lord
Keynes – a world plan for limited discounting.

Cooperation

Clarke's conclusion that central-bank cooperation was maintained
up to mid 1928 but failed thereafter has already been dealt with
in some detail. In summary, such cooperation on matters such as
hegemony over small central banks or the choice of an equilibrium
exchange rate was inadequate before 1926, and the Bank of
France supported the pound loyally (and expensively) in the late
summer of 1931. A deeper question is whether cooperation
as such would have been sufficient. In *America's Role in the*

---

5. Jørgen Pedersen blames the liquidity crisis of 1931 on the United States
for its failure to support the German mark, and, when that had been forced
to suspend gold payments, for its failure to underwrite sterling. See 'Some
Notes on the Economic Policy of the United States during the Period 1919–
1932', in Hugo Hegeland, ed., *Money, Growth and Methodology*, In Honor
of Johan Åkerman, Lund Social Science Studies, Lund, 1961, pp. 490–91.
This would be agreed today, and Professor Pedersen put it forward himself,
as noted earlier, in 1933. As he himself points out, however (p. 494), the
United States was acting with 'the normal prejudices of the period'.

World Economy,[6] Alvin Hansen prescribed for the United States policies of maintenance of full employment at home and co-operation with international efforts at freer trade, restoring capital movements, improvement of the world monetary system and so on. With the advantage of hindsight, it appears that more than cooperation was provided, viz. leadership, and that mere cooperation would not have built the institutions and policies of the Organization for Economic Cooperation and Development, Group of Ten, Bank for International Settlements, International Monetary Fund, International Bank, General Agreement on Tariffs and Trade, etc. As an acquaintance on the International Monetary Fund staff put it (admittedly to an American), if the United States does not take the leadership, nothing happens. Leadership may lack followership, and foolish or even sensible proposals may be defeated through lack of support. But the most sensible proposals emanating from small countries are valueless if they lack the capacity to carry them out and fail to enlist the countries that do. The World Economic Conference of 1933 did not lack ideas, as that of 1927 seems to have done. The one country capable of leadership was bemused by domestic concerns and stood aside.

One special form of cooperation would have been joint Anglo-American leadership in the economic affairs of the world. Economists usually agree that such arrangements, whether duopoly or bilateral monopoly, are unstable, and so do political scientists. Carr states explicitly that the hope for Pax Anglo-Saxonica was romantic and that Pax Americana 'would be an easier contingency'.[7] Vansittart, referring to the Standstill agreements and the German occupation of the Rhineland, wrote *à propos* of the World Economic Conference: 'When action was required two years earlier, the two governments [British and American] sheltered behind each other like the British and French governments three years later.'[8] With a duumvirate, a troika, or slightly

6. Alvin Hansen, *America's Role in the World Economy*, W. W. Norton, New York: Allen & Unwin, London, 1945.

7. Carr, *The Twenty Years' Crisis, 1919–39*, pp. 233–4.

8. Lord Vansittart, *The Mist Procession, the Autobiography of Lord Vansittart*, Hutchinson, London, 1958, p. 466.

wider forms of collective responsibility, the buck has no place to stop.

Changing leaders

Friedman and Schwartz make a great deal of the role in the great depression of the shift of monetary leadership in the United States from New York to Washington.[9] They suggest that this sounds far-fetched, since it is a 'sound general principle that great events have great origins', but note that small events at times have large consequences through chain reactions and cumulative force. The universality of the asserted principle seems dubious to this observer;[10] the observation that shifts of the locus of leadership give rise to instability does not. Had they not focused so exclusively on monetary conditions in the United States, Friedman and Schwartz might have noted the accentuation of the depression which came with the transfer of the presidency from Hoover to Roosevelt (occurring after the money supply had been greatly enlarged); and the still more significant (in my judgement) transfer of leadership in the world economy from Whitehall to the White House.

This notion of the instability of a financial system with two centres, or of one where leadership is in process of being dropped by one and picked up by another, is cited by Edward Nevin as crucial to the collapse of the gold standard in 1931. He quotes Sir Ernest Harvey's testimony before the Macmillan Committee: 'such leadership as we possess has been affected by the position which America has gained'; making a change in the ancient system as set out in the Macmillan Report, under which bank rate regulated the reserve position of the United Kingdom, and other countries adjusted their positions to that of Britain. He then went

9. Milton Friedman and Anna Jacobson Schwartz, *A Monetary History of the United States, 1867–1960*, Princeton University Press, Princeton, 1963, p. 419.

10. cf. Benjamin Franklin, *Maxims Prefixed to Poor Richard's Almanac*, Philadelphia, 1757, 'Little strokes fell great oaks', and 'A little neglect may breed mischief: for want of a nail the shoe was lost; for want of a shoe the horse was lost; for want of a horse the rider was lost'. The exception for cumulative feedback embraces the second quotation, but not the first.

on to say, 'Better that a motor car should be in charge of a poor driver than of two quite excellent drivers who are perpetually fighting to gain control of the vehicle.'[11] The analogy of two excellent drivers fighting for control of the wheel may be more graphic than apposite. The instability seems rather to have come from the growing weakness of one driver, and the lack of sufficient interest in the other. William Adams Brown, Jr, describes the gold standard of the period as 'without a focal point', meaning that it had two, but the conclusions of his monumental work do not dwell on this critical aspect of the world economy.[12]

Role of the small countries and France

One passenger in the vehicle which did not lack interest was France. And one group which lacked responsibility – to discontinue the metaphor, or perhaps they should be regarded as passengers in the back seat – consisted of the smaller countries: Belgium, the Netherlands, Switzerland and Scandinavia. The smaller countries can be disposed of first. They are sometimes blamed, as in Born's analysis, for having acted irresponsibly in, say, converting sterling into gold in the summer of 1931, or raising tariffs with alacrity after 1930. There is, however, no universally accepted standard of behaviour for small countries. On one showing, they lack power to affect the outcome of great events and are therefore privileged to look after the private national interest rather than concern themselves with the public good of stability in the world economy as a whole. On a somewhat higher ethical level, the small countries may be held Kantian Categorical Imperative, which enjoins them to act only in ways which can be generalized.

11. Edward Nevin, *The Mechanism of Cheap Money: A Study of British Monetary Policy, 1931–1939*, University of Wales Press, Cardiff, 1955, pp. 9n., 12 and 14.

12. William Adams Brown, Jr, *The International Gold Standard Reinterpreted, 1914–34*, National Bureau of Economic Research, New York, 1940, vol. II, p. 781: 'The essential difference between the international gold standard of 1928–29 and that of 1914 was that when the world returned to gold after the war it built its international financial system around a nucleus of London and New York, and not a single center.' The title of his Chapter 20 is 'The Experiment of a Gold Exchange Standard without a Focal Point'.

In such circumstances, of course, they would not have withdrawn credits from Austria in the spring of 1931, nor from Germany and Britain in the summer, nor from the United States in the autumn. The economist chooses between these standards perhaps on the basis of comparative cost. If the Netherlands had known the cost of leaving its sterling unconverted into gold, it seems unlikely that it would have done so, even at the risk of accelerating the collapse of the pound and deepening of the world depression. It may be that such countries as Sweden, Canada and New Zealand that set high standards of international conduct – in foreign aid, contributions to United Nations peacekeeping missions, etc. – do so solely from ethical reasons; or they may choose among occasions to take largely the opportunities which are relatively cheap. One may thus note that the small countries contributed substantially to the deflation by the speed with which they cut imports, depreciated, or converted sterling and dollars into gold, but find it hard to blame them for it.[13]

There is another aspect to the role of small countries: they could offer programmes for recovery because they knew that the major cost of programmes adopted would fall on other countries. Proposals for an embryonic international monetary fund in the Washington discussions preceding the World Economic Conference of 1933 were put forward by Poland, Turkey, Belgium, the I.L.O., and one was made by Britain, though this latter was quickly withdrawn when the United States frowned upon it. Lacking resources to make these schemes effective, small countries were reduced to advisory roles without conviction, even when the proposals were sound. An essential ingredient of followership is to convince the leader that he is the author of the ideas which require the use of his resources.

The case of France is different. France sought power in its

13. For an interesting political model of countries which are free-riders behind the leadership of others, see Norman Froelich and Joe A. Oppenheimer, 'I Get Along with a Little Help from My Friends', *World Politics*, vol. x xiii, No. 1 (October 1970), pp. 104–20. But note, p. 119, that leadership is rewarded in this model rather than made to pay for the privilege, as implied where the responsibilities of leadership are maintaining an open market for goods, a counter-cyclical export of capital and a mechanism for rediscounting in crisis.

national interest, without adequately taking into account the repercussions of its positions on world economic or political stability. Its intransigence in the matter of reparations or the attempt to attach political conditions to the second Austrian credit of June 1931 or the contemplated German loan of July of that year illustrate the position. Hurt in the depreciation of sterling in September, the Bank of France, under strong political pressure at home, converted its dollars into gold in the private national interest during 1931–2, all the while protesting its cooperation and concern for the interest of the United States. The rivalry between the Bank of France and the Bank of England over which should take over the leadership in restoring independence to central banks and stabilization of currencies in Eastern Europe would be pathetic, had it not run risks of instability for the system as a whole when the French threatened to withdraw balances from London.

Not quite big enough to have responsibility forced on it, nor small enough to afford the luxury of irresponsibility, the French position in the inter-war period was unenviable. It had the power to act as a destabilizer, but was insufficiently powerful to stabilize. 'Great Britain and the United States together were the active nucleus that replaced the single centre of pre-war days, but the position and policy of France actively affected their mutual as well as their joint relations to the outlying countries.'[14] In these circumstances France could be (and was) blamed for upsetting the system when she had no capacity to take it over and run it in the presence of two larger powers, one feeble, the other irresponsible.

Public v. private interest

Cynicism suggests that leadership is fully rewarded for its pains in prestige, and that no matter how much it protests its commitment to the public welfare, its fundamental concern is private. Bismarck insisted that free trade was the weapon of the dominant economy anxious to prevent others from following in its path. 'The white

14. Brown, *The International Gold Standard Reinterpreted, 1914–1934*, p. 785.

man's burden' is an expression used today only in mockery. A country like France deliberately setting out to achieve prestige suggests that those with a concern for problem-solving are either perfidious or self-deceiving. None the less there is a difference between accepting and declining responsibility for the way the system is run. The British accepted responsibility, although, as the 50 million schilling loan emphasizes, they were unable to discharge it. The French and the United States were unwilling to underwrite stability. Under Coolidge and Hoover, the United States refused to commit itself to any programme of foreign reconstruction or currency stabilization, leaving these questions to the Federal Reserve System.[15] There was hardly any improvement in Roosevelt's commitment to the world economy until timidly in 1936, at the time of the Tripartite Monetary Pact, and ultimately during the Second World War. Inside France, as between France and the other leading powers, 'all groups thought their opponents more united and dedicated than they were, and a concern for the general interest was virtually absent'.[16]

Unable to cope with the public good, the British more and more turned their energy to the private. Keynes's advocacy of a tariff and the refusal to contemplate stabilization after 1931 are examples. One may find a hint or two in the documents that the initiative came from the Dominions rather than Britain.[17] For a time, until well after the war, the British economics profession and public almost drew the lesson that each country should take care of itself without regard to external effects.

The point is illustrated in the memorandum written by Hubert Henderson at the British Treasury in 1943, entitled 'International

15. Lester V. Chandler, *Benjamin Strong, Central Banker*, The Brookings Institution, Washington, D.C., 1958, p. 255.

16. Alfred Sauvy, *Histoire économique de la France entre les deux guerres*, I: *1918–1931*, Fayard, Paris, 1965, p. 73.

17. See *Documents diplomatiques français, 1932–39*, 1er série (1932–1935), Tome III, Imprimerie Nationale, Paris, 1967, #470, Bonnet to Paul-Boncour, 9 July 1933, p. 871: 'One fact is evident: it is that Britain is not free. Its dominions and in particular Canada whose Prime Minister Bennett is a man of extraordinary violence have a predominant influence on her, to the point of modifying totally her opinion in the space of a few seconds.' This is doubtless hyperbole.

Economic History of the Interwar Period'.[18] This summarizes the crude view of the depression as resulting from nationalism and tariffs, the collapse of world trade, bilateralism and preferences and disregard of the advice of the League of Nations, leading to the conclusion that after the war there is need for the world to be more resolute in avoiding economic nationalism, and attempting to construct a freely working economic system with international credits, the reduction of trade barriers and the outlawry of qualitative regulation.[19] Henderson states that the history of the interwar period provides no support for this view. He opposes exchange depreciation: '... there can be little doubt that the depreciation of the pound was in part responsible for the sharper fall in gold prices, and disillusionment is general in the United Kingdom and still more in the United States on the power of exchange depreciation to promote national recovery'.[20]

But the conventional view is false in all essential respects. The old international order has broken down for good. Nothing but futility and frustration can come from the attempt to set it up again. Individual countries must be free to regulate their external economies effectively, using control of capital movements, quantitative regulation, preferences, autonomous credit policies, etc.[21]

This foot-dragging, which Keynes shared during the 1930s and until late in the war, is understandable. It misses the main lesson of the inter-war years, however: that for the world economy to be stabilized, there has to be a stabilizer, one stabilizer.

Counter-cyclical capital movements

Assume that the United States had not led the way to destroying the trade mechanism through the Smoot-Hawley Tariff of 1930, and that a discounting mechanism had been available to cope

18. See Hubert D. Henderson, *The Inter-war Years and Other Papers*, Clarendon Press, Oxford, 1955, pp. 236–95.

19. ibid., pp. 236 and 290.

20. ibid., pp. 260 and 262; see also p. 291: 'Of the various expedients which different governments employed in the 1930s, none produced more unfortunate results than deliberate exchange depreciation. It was the least helpful to the countries which tried it, and the most harmful to other countries.'

21. ibid., p. 293.

with 1931. There would still have been a serious depression, if perhaps not so prolonged, owing to the failure of counter-cyclical lending, and the absence of machinery such as the World Bank or foreign aid coordinated through the Development Assistance Committee (D.A.C.) of the Organization of Economic Cooperation and Development (O.E.C.D.), to replace the private market with public funds. It remains puzzling that the foreign capital market in New York (and to a much lesser degree in London) started to come back in the spring of 1930, after the stock-market crash, and then relapsed. There was no panic, and no alarm, but 'people felt the ground giving way under their feet'.[22] Arthur Lewis's explanation of the relapse in terms of the decline of prices is perhaps not wholly satisfactory, nor is the 'inexperience' of the New York capital market in international lending. They are all that is available. Even with anti-cyclical capital movements, there would have been a depression. With a flow of international capital positively correlated with business conditions in the lending country, the depression was inevitably severe. Add to this position, which was perhaps beyond the power of policy to correct in the existing state of knowledge, beggar-thy-neighbour tactics in trade and exchange depreciation, plus the unwillingness of the United States to serve as a lender of last resort in 1931, and the length and depth of the depression are explained.

There is one respect in which United States 'inexperience' in lending might be said to be relevant to the pattern of lending. A new lender is likely to behave differently from an old lender because of the wider array of investment opportunities available to it. Consider a country which has been long engaged in international investment. Its foreign loans are likely to follow what may be called a 'demand model', in which a given flow of savings is allocated between domestic and foreign uses depending upon the relative demands from them. A domestic boom diverts foreign loans to the home market. Depression at home and expansion abroad stimulates foreign lending. The result is a counter-cyclical pattern.

22. Joseph A. Schumpeter, *Business Cycles, A Theoretical, Historical and Statistical Analysis of the Capitalistic Process*, vol. II, McGraw-Hill, New York and London, 1939, p. 911.

When a country begins lending abroad for the first time, however, there are likely to be a host of unfilled opportunities for foreign loans. As savings become available, they are invested at home and abroad, simultaneously. The more profits at home in boom, the more foreign investment. This is a 'supply model', in which foreign lending depends on the availability of savings. Alteration between demand and supply models is evident in direct foreign investment. That it may apply to lending through foreign bonds is only a hypothesis. It would, however, explain why United States lending at the beginning of its career as a creditor was positively correlated with the domestic business cycle, whereas in Britain, the experienced lender, the pattern had been otherwise.

Relevance to the 1970s

Leadership is a word with negative connotations in the 1970s when participation in decision-making is regarded as more aesthetic. Much of the overtones of *der Führer* and *il Duce* remain. But if leadership is thought of as the provision of the public good of responsibility, rather than exploitation of followers or the private good of prestige, it remains a positive idea. It may one day be possible to pool sovereignties to limit the capacity of separate countries to work against the general interest; such pooling is virtually attained today in some of the functions needed to stabilize the world economic system, such as the Basle arrangements for swaps and short-term credits which, pending a world central bank, serve as a world rediscounting mechanism in crisis. In this area, and in the world agencies for maintaining freer trade and a liberal flow of capital and aid, however, leadership is necessary in the absence of delegated authority. That of the United States is beginning to slip. It is not yet clear that the rising strength of Europe in an enlarged European Economic Community will be accompanied by an assertion of leadership in providing a market for distress or aggressive goods, in stabilizing the international flow of capital or in providing a discount mechanism for crisis. Presumably the Basle arrangements for the last will endure. There are indications that the European market for goods will remain ample, except in agriculture, which is an important exception from a world viewpoint. There is still some distance to go to stabilize the flow of capital counter-cyclically.

As the United States economic leadership in the world economy falters, and Europe gathers strength, three outcomes are politically stable; three unstable. Among the stable outcomes are continued or revived United States leadership, after the exchange controls of 1963 to 1968 and the 1970–71 wave of protectionism have been reversed; an assertion of leadership and assumption of responsibility for the stability of the world system by Europe; or an effective cession of economic sovereignty to international institutions: a world central bank, a world capital market, and an effective General Agreement on Tariffs and Trade. The last is the most attractive, but perhaps, because difficult, the least likely. As between the first two alternatives, the responsible citizen should be content with either, flipping a coin to decide, if the third alternative proves unavailable, simply to avoid the undesirable alternatives.

The three outcomes to be avoided because of their instability are: (a) the United States and the E.E.C. vying for leadership of the world economy; (b) one unable to lead and the other unwilling, as in 1929 to 1933; and (c) each retaining a veto over programmes of stability or strengthening of the system without seeking to secure positive programmes of its own. The articles of agreement of the International Monetary Fund (I.M.F.) were set up to provide the United States with a veto over action which it opposed. In the 1969 reform which legislated the addition of Special Drawing Rights (S.D.R.s) to the monetary system, quotas of I.M.F. were adjusted to provide a veto to the E.E.C. as well. This leaves open the possibility of stalemate, as in the United Nations Security Council, when two major powers are unable to agree. In the circumstances of the Security Council there is a danger of regressive spiral into war; the analogue in the economic field is stalemate, and depression.

In these circumstances, the third positive alternative of international institutions with real authority and sovereignty is pressing.

Bibliography

ALDCROFT, D., *see* RICHARDSON, H. W., and ALDCROFT, D.

ALIBER, ROBERT, 'Speculation in the Foreign Exchanges: The European Experience, 1919–1926', *Yale Economic Essays*, vol. II, No. 1 (Spring 1962), pp. 170–245.

American Bureau of Metal Statistics, *Year Book of the American Bureau of Metal Statistics, 11th Annual Issue, 1930*, American Bureau of Metal Statistics, New York, 1931.

ANGELL, JAMES W., *The Recovery of Germany*, Yale University Press, New Haven, 1929; enlarged and revised edition, 1932.

ANGELL, JAMES W., *The Program for the World Economic Conference: The Experts' Agenda and the Document*, World Peace Foundation, Boston, 1933.

ARMSTRONG, HAMILTON FISH, 'France and the Hoover Plan', *Foreign Affairs*, vol. X, No. 1 (October 1931), pp. 23–33.

ARNDT, H. W., *The Economic Lessons of the 1930s*, Oxford University Press, London, 1944.

AURIOL, VINCENT, *Hier et aujourd'hui*, Charlot, Paris, 1945.

BAADE, FRITZ, 'Fighting Depression in Germany', in E. S. Woytinsky (ed.), *So Much Alive, The Life and Work of W. S. Woytinsky*, Vanguard Press, New York, 1962, pp. 61–9.

BAGEHOT, WALTER, *Lombard Street*, new edition, John Murray, London, 1917.

Bank for International Settlements, Annual Report for various years.

BASSETT, R., *Nineteen Thirty-One: Political Crisis*, Macmillan, London, 1958.

BAUDHUIN, FERNAND, *Histoire économique de la Belgique, 1914–1938*, 2 vols., Établissements Émile Bruyles, Brussels, 1946.

BAUER, P. T., *The Rubber Industry: A Study in Competition and Monopoly*, Harvard University Press, Cambridge, Mass.: Longmans, Green, London, 1948.

BELLMAN, HAROLD, 'The Building Trades', in *Britain in Recovery*, Pitman, London, 1938.

BENNETT, EDWARD W., *Germany and the Diplomacy of the Financial Crisis, 1931*, Harvard University Press, Cambridge, Mass., 1962.

BERNSTEIN, E. M., *see* Review Committee for Balance of Payments Statistics.

BEYEN, J. W., *Money in a Maelstrom*, Macmillan Co., New York, 1949; Macmillan, London, 1951.

BLUM, JOHN MORTON, *From the Morgenthau Diaries*, vol. I: *Years of Crisis, 1928–1938*, Houghton Mifflin, Boston, 1959.

BORN, KARL ERICH, *Die deutsche Bankenkrise, 1931, Finanzen und Politik*, R. Piper, Munich, 1967.

BOYLE, ANDREW, *Montagu Norman*, Cassell, London, 1967.

BRAND, R. H., 'Gold: A World Problem', *International Conciliation*, No. 333 (October 1937), pp. 663–77.

BROWN, E. C., 'Fiscal Policy in the 'Thirties, a Reappraisal', *American Economic Review*, vol. XLVI, No. 5 (December 1956), pp. 857–79.

BROWN, WILLIAM ADAMS, Jr, *The International Gold Standard Reinterpreted, 1914–1934*, 2 vols., National Bureau of Economic Research, New York, 1940.

BRÜNING, HEINRICH, *Reden und Aufsätze eines deutschen Staatsmanes*, edited by Wilhelm Vernekohl, Regensburg, Münster, 1968.

BRÜNING, HEINRICH, *Memoiren, 1918–1934*, Deutsche Verlags-Anstalt, Stuttgart, 1970.

BUNDY, MacGEORGE, *see* STIMSON, HENRY L., and BUNDY, MacGEORGE.

BURCK, GILBERT, and SILBERMAN, CHARLES, 'Why the Depression Lasted so Long', in Stanley Coben and F. G. Hill (eds.), *American Economic History: Essays in Interpretation*, J. B. Lippincott, Philadelphia, 1966, pp. 496–512; reprinted from *Fortune*, vol. LI, No. 3 (March 1955), pp. 84 ff.

BUTLER, WILLIAM F., 'Is Another Great Depression Possible?', unpublished memorandum, Chase Manhattan Bank, 28 April 1969.

CAIRNCROSS, ALEX K., *Home and Foreign Investment, 1880–1913*, Cambridge University Press, Cambridge, 1953.

CAMERON, RONDO E., *France and the Economic Development of Europe, 1800–1914*, Princeton University Press, Princeton, 1961.

CARR, EDWARD HALLETT, *The Twenty Years' Crisis, 1919–1939: An Introduction to the Study of International Relations*, Macmillan, London, 1939; 2nd edition, 1946.

CHANDLER, LESTER V., *Benjamin Strong, Central Banker*, The Brookings Institution, Washington, D.C., 1958.

CLARKE, STEPHEN V. O., *Central Bank Co-operation, 1924–31*, Federal Reserve Bank of New York, New York, 1967.

CLAY, Sir HENRY, *Lord Norman*, Macmillan, London, 1957.

CLOUGH, SHEPARD B., *The Economic History of Modern Italy*, Columbia University Press, New York, 1964.

Commercial and Financial Chronicle, various issues, 1933.

Commission of Inquiry Report into National Policy in International Economic Relations, *International Economic Relations*, University of Minnesota Press, Minneapolis, 1934.

Commodity Yearbook, 1939, Commodity Research Bureau, New York, 1939.

COPLAND, Sir DOUGLAS, *Australia in the World Crisis, 1929–1933*, the Alfred Marshall Lectures delivered in the University of Cambridge, October and November 1933, Cambridge University Press, Cambridge: Macmillan Co., New York, 1934.

COX, JAMES M., *Journey through My Years*, Simon & Schuster, New York, 1946.

CURTIUS, JULIUS, *Sechs Jahre Minister der deutschen Republik*, Carl Winter-Universitätsverlag, Heidelberg, 1948.

DEAN, VERA MICHELES, 'Austria: The Paralysis of a Nation', *Foreign Policy Reports*, vol. III, No. 22 (4 January 1933), pp. 256–66.

DÍAZ ALEJANDRO, CARLOS F., *Essays on the Economic History of the Argentine Republic*, Yale University Press, New Haven, 1970.

Documents diplomatiques français, 1932–1939, 1ᵉʳ série, 1932–5, Tomes I, II, III, Imprimerie Nationale, Paris, 1966; 2ᵉᵐᵉ série, 1936–9, Tomes I–IV, Imprimerie Nationale, Paris, 1967.

DOHAN, MICHAEL R., 'Soviet Foreign Trade, the N.E.P. Economy and Soviet Industrialization Strategy', doctoral dissertation, Massachusetts Institute of Technology, September 1969.

DUPLESSIS, J. C., *Economic Fluctuations in South Africa, 1910–1949*, Bureau of Economic Research, Stellenbosch, n.d. (1950 or 1951).

DUROSELLE, J.-B., *De Wilson à Roosevelt*, Colin, Paris, 1960.

ECCLES, MARRINER S., *Beckoning Frontiers, Public and Personal Recollections*, Alfred A. Knopf, New York, 1951.

The Economist, various issues.

EINZIG, PAUL, *International Gold Movements*, 2nd edition, Macmillan, London, 1932.

EINZIG, PAUL, *The Comedy of the Pound*, Kegan Paul, London, 1933.

EINZIG, PAUL, *Bankers, Statesmen and Economists*, Macmillan, London, 1935.

EINZIG, PAUL, *World Finance Since 1914*, Kegan Paul, London: Macmillan Co., New York, 1935.

BIBLIOGRAPHY

Federal Reserve Bank of New York files.

Federal Reserve Bulletin, various issues.

Federal Reserve System, *Banking and Monetary Statistics*, Washington, D.C., 1943.

FEDERN, WALTER, 'Der Zusammenbruch der Österreichischen Kreditanstalt', *Archiv für Sozialwissenschaft und Sozialpolitik*, 67 Band, 4 Heft (June 1932), pp. 403–35.

FEIS, HERBERT, *Seen from E.A.: Three International Episodes*, Alfred A. Knopf, New York, 1947.

FEIS, HERBERT, *The Diplomacy of the Dollar 1919–1939*, W. W. Norton, New York, 1950.

FEIS, HERBERT, *1933: Characters in Crisis*, Little Brown, Boston, 1966.

FERRELL, ROBERT H., *American Diplomacy in the Great Depression, Hoover-Stimson Foreign Policy, 1929–1933*, Yale University Press, New Haven, 1957.

FLEISIG, HEYWOOD W., 'Long-Term Capital Flows and the Great Depression: the Role of the United States, 1927–1933', doctoral dissertation, Yale University, 1969.

FLEISIG, HEYWOOD W., 'The United States and the World Periphery During the Early Years of the Great Depression', forthcoming in Herman van der Wee, ed., *The Great Depression Revisited*, Nyhoff, The Hague, 1972.

FOHLEN, CLAUDE, *Une Affaire de famille au XIX*ᵉ *siècle: Méquillet Noblot*, Colin, Paris, 1955.

FRANKLIN, BENJAMIN, *Maxims Prefixed to Poor Richard's Almanac*, Philadelphia, 1757.

FRIEDMAN, MILTON, and SCHWARTZ, ANNA JACOBSON, *A Monetary History of the United States, 1867–1960*, Princeton University Press, Princeton, 1963.

FRIEDMAN, MILTON, and SCHWARTZ, ANNA JACOBSON, *The Great Contraction*, Princeton University Press, Princeton, 1966; reprinted from Chapter 7 of *supra*.

FRIEDMAN, MILTON, *The Balance of Payments: Free Versus Fixed Exchange Rates*, American Enterprise Institute for Public Policy Research, Washington, D.C., 1967.

FRIEDMAN, MILTON, in *Newsweek*, 25 May 1970.

FROELICH, NORMAN, and OPPENHEIMER, JOE A., 'I Get Along with a Little Help from My Friends', *World Politics*, vol. XXIII, No. 1 (October 1970), pp. 104–20.

FUKAI, EIGO, 'The Recent Monetary Policy of Japan', in A. D. Gayer (ed.), *The Lessons of Monetary Experience: Essays in Honor of Irving Fisher*, Farrar & Rinehart, New York: Allen & Unwin, London, 1937, pp. 379–95.

FURNIVALL, J. S., *Netherlands India, A Study of Plural Economy*, Cambridge University Press, Cambridge, 1939.

GALBRAITH, J. KENNETH, *The Great Crash, 1929*, Houghton Mifflin, Boston: Hamish Hamilton, London, 1955.

GARDNER, RICHARD N., *Sterling-Dollar Diplomacy*, revised edition, McGraw-Hill, New York, 1969.

[Contracting Parties for the] General Agreement on Tariffs and Trade, *Trends in International Trade*, Report by a Panel of Experts, Geneva, 1958.

GILBERT, MILTON, *Currency Depreciation*, University of Pennsylvania Press, Philadelphia, 1939.

GORDON, ROBERT A., *Business Fluctuations*, 2nd edition, Harper & Row, New York, 1952.

GRAHAM, FRANK D., and WHITTLESEY, CHARLES R., *Golden Avalanche*, Princeton University Press, Princeton, 1939.

Green's Commodity Market Comments, 21 October 1970.

GRIGG, P. J., *Prejudice and Judgement*, Jonathan Cape, London, 1948.

GROTKOPP, WILHELM, *Die grosse Krise, Lehren aus der Überwindung der Wirtschaftskrise, 1929/32*, Econ-Verlag, Düsseldorf, 1954.

GUTHRIE, JOHN A., *The Newsprint Industry: An Economic Analysis*, Harvard University Press, Cambridge, Mass., 1941.

HABERLER, GOTTFRIED, *Prosperity and Depression*, League of Nations, 1937.

HAHN, L. ALBERT, *Fünfzig Jahre zwischen Inflation und Deflation*, J. C. B. Mohr (Paul Siebeck), Tübingen, 1963.

HANSEN, ALVIN H., *Full Recovery or Stagnation*, W. W. Norton, New York: A. & C. Black, London, 1938.

HANSEN, ALVIN H., *America's Role in the World Economy*, W. W. Norton New York: Allen & Unwin, London, 1945.

HARRIS, C. R. S., *Germany's Foreign Indebtedness*, Oxford University Press, London, 1935.

HARRIS, SEYMOUR E., *Exchange Depreciation: its Theory and History, 1931–35, with some Consideration of Related Domestic Policies*, Harvard University Press, Cambridge, Mass., 1936.

HASIB, ABDUL, *Monetary Negotiations in the World Economic Conference*, Publications of the Faculty of Arts, Muslim University, Alijar, 1958.

HENDERSON, HUBERT D., *The Inter-war Years and Other Papers*, Clarendon Press, Oxford, 1955.

HENDERSON, H. D., *see also* KEYNES, J. M., and HENDERSON, H. D.

313

HILGERDT, F., *see* League of Nations (F. Hilgerdt).

HOBSBAWM, E. J., *Industry and Empire: an Economic History of Britain since 1750*, Weidenfeld & Nicolson, London: Pantheon, New York, 1968.

HODSON, H. V., *Slump and Recovery, 1929–37*, Oxford University Press, London, 1938.

HOMZE, EDWARD L., *Foreign Labor in Nazi Germany*, Princeton University Press, Princeton, 1967.

HOOVER, HERBERT, *The Memoirs of Herbert Hoover*, vol. III: *The Great Depression, 1929–1941*, Macmillan Co., New York: Hollis & Carter, London, 1952.

HOUSE, E. M., and SEYMOUR, CHARLES, *What Really Happened in Paris: the Story of the Peace Conference, 1918–1919*, Charles Scribner's Sons, New York, 1921: Hodder & Stoughton, London, 1921.

HUGHES, HELEN, draft manuscript on economic history of Australia.

HULL, CORDELL, *The Memoirs of Cordell Hull*, 2 vols., Macmillan Co., New York: Hodder & Stoughton, London, 1948.

HURST, WILLARD, 'Holland, Switzerland and Belgium and the English Gold Crisis of 1931', *Journal of Political Economy*, vol. XL, No. 5 (October 1932), pp. 638–60.

International Bank for Reconstruction and Development, Press Release No. 134, 11 May 1949.

The International Bank for Reconstruction and Development, 1946–1953, Johns Hopkins Press, Baltimore, 1954.

IVERSEN, C., 'The Importance of the International Margin', in *Explorations in International Economics: Notes and Essays in Honor of F. W. Taussig*, McGraw-Hill, New York, 1936.

JACOBSSON, PER, *Some Monetary Problems, International and National*, Oxford University Press, London, 1958.

JOHNSON, G. GRIFFITH, Jr, *The Treasury and Monetary Policy, 1933–1938*, Harvard University Press, Cambridge, Mass., 1939.

JONES, JOSEPH M., Jr, *Tariff Retaliation, Repercussions of the Hawley-Smoot Bill*, University of Pennsylvania Press, Philadelphia, 1934.

KAHN, A. E., *Great Britain in the World Economy*, Columbia University Press, New York: Pitman, London, 1946.

KAHN, R. F., 'The Relation of Home Investment to Unemployment', *Economic Journal*, vol. XLI, No. 2 (June 1931), pp. 193–8.

KEESE, DIETMAR, 'Die volkswirtschaftlichen Gesamtgrössen für das Deutsche Reich in den Jahren 1925/36', in *Die Staats- und Wirtschaftskrise des Deutsches Reiches, 1929/1933*, Ernst Klett, Stuttgart, 1967, pp. 35–81.

KEYNES, J. M., *The Economic Consequences of the Peace*, Macmillan, London, 1919; Harcourt Brace, New York, 1920.

KEYNES, J. M., and HENDERSON, H. D., *Can Lloyd George Do it?* The Nation and Atheneum, London, 1929.

KEYNES, J. M., *Treatise on Money*, 2 vols., Macmillan, London: Harcourt Brace, New York, 1930.

KEYNES, J. M., 'An Economic Analysis of Unemployment', in Q. Wright (ed.), *Unemployment as a World Problem*, Norman Wait Harris Lectures for 1931, University of Chicago Press, Chicago, 1931, pp. 3–42.

KEYNES, J. M., *Essays in Persuasion*, Macmillan, London, 1931; Harcourt Brace, New York, 1932.

KEYNES, J. M., 'National Self-Sufficiency', *Yale Review*, vol. XXII, No. 4 (June 1933), pp. 755–69.

KEYNES, J. M., *The Means to Prosperity*, Macmillan, London: Harcourt Brace, New York, 1933.

KEYNES, J. M., *The General Theory of Employment, Interest and Money*, Macmillan, London: Harcourt Brace, New York, 1936.

KINDLEBERGER, C. P., 'Competitive Currency Depreciation between Denmark and New Zealand', *Harvard Business Review*, vol. XII, No. 4 (July 1934), pp. 416–27.

KINDLEBERGER, C. P., *The Terms of Trade: A European Case Study*, Technology Press, Cambridge, Mass.: Chapman & Hall, London, 1956.

KINDLEBERGER, C. P., *International Economics*, 4th edition, Irwin, Homewood, Ill., 1968.

KLEIN, BURTON H., *Germany's Economic Preparations for War*, Harvard University Press, Cambridge, Mass., 1959.

LALUMIÈRE, PIERRE, *L'Inspection des finances*, Presses Universitaires de France, Paris, 1959.

LARY, HAL B., *The United States in the World Economy: the International Transactions of the United States During the Interwar Period*, U.S. Government Printing Office, Washington, D.C., 1943.

LAUTENBACH, WILHELM, *Zins, Kredit und Produktion*, J. C. B. Mohr (Paul Siebeck), Tübingen, 1952.

League of Nations (Bertil Ohlin), *The Course and Phases of the World Economic Depression*, League of Nations, Geneva, 1931.

League of Nations, *Balance of Payments, 1930*, League of Nations, Geneva, 1932.

League of Nations, Sixth International Studies Conference, a Record of a Second Study Conference on 'The State and Economic Life',

Held in London, 29 May–2 June 1933, International Institute of Intellectual Cooperation, Paris, 1934.

League of Nations (James E. Meade), *World Economic Survey, 1937/38,* League of Nations, Geneva, 1938.

League of Nations (James E. Meade), *World Economic Survey, 1938/39,* League of Nations, Geneva, 1939.

League of Nations, *Review of World Trade, 1938,* League of Nations, Geneva, 1939.

League of Nations (F. Hilgerdt), *The Network of World Trade,* League of Nations, Geneva, 1942.

League of Nations (Ragnar Nurkse), *International Currency Experience, Lessons of the Interwar Period,* League of Nations, Princeton, N.J., 1944.

League of Nations, *Economic Stability in the Post-war World, Report of the Delegation on Economic Depression,* League of Nations, Geneva, 1945.

League of Nations, *Statistical Yearbook,* various issues, Geneva.

League of Nations, *Monthly Bulletin of Statistics,* various issues.

LEITH-ROSS, Sir FREDERICK, *Money Talks, Fifty Years of International Finance,* Hutchinson, London, 1968.

LEWIS, Sir WILLIAM ARTHUR, *Economic Survey, 1919–1939,* Allen & Unwin, London, 1949; Blakiston, Philadelphia, 1950.

LÜKE, ROLF E., *Von der Stabilisierung zur Krise,* Polygraphischer, Zürich, 1958.

LUNDBERG, ERIK, *Instability and Economic Growth,* Yale University Press, New Haven, 1968.

LUTHER, HANS, *Vor dem Abgrund, 1930–1933: Reichsbankpräsident in Krisenzeiten,* Propyläen, Berlin, 1960.

MALACH, VERNON W., *International Cycles and Canada's Balance of Payments, 1921–33,* University of Toronto Press, Toronto, 1954.

MALENBAUM, WILFRID, *The World Wheat Economy, 1885–1939,* Harvard University Press, Cambridge, Mass., 1953.

MANTOUX, ÉTIENNE, *The Carthaginian Peace or the Economic Consequences of Mr Keynes,* Charles Scribner's Sons, New York, 1952.

MARCUS, EDWARD, *Canada and the International Business Cycle, 1927–39,* Bookman Associates, New York, 1954.

MEADE, JAMES E., *see* League of Nations (James E. Meade).

MENNE, BERNHARD, *The Case of Dr Brüning,* Hutchinson, London, 1943.

MEYER, RICHARD H., *Banker's Diplomacy: Monetary Stabilization in the Twenties,* Columbia University Press, New York, 1970.

MINTZ, ILSE, *Deterioration in the Quality of Foreign Bonds Issued in the*

United States, 1920–1930, National Bureau of Economic Research, New York, 1951.

MITCHELL, BROADUS, *Depression Decade, From New Era through New Deal, 1929–1941*, Rinehart & Winston, New York, 1947 (Harper & Row edition, New York, 1969).

MODIGLIANI, FRANCO, *see* NEISSER, HANS, and MODIGLIANI, FRANCO.

MOGGRIDGE, D. E., *The Return to Gold, 1925: The Formulation of Policy and its Critics*, Cambridge University Press, Cambridge, 1969.

MOLEY, RAYMOND, with the assistance of ROSEN, ELLIOTT, *The First New Deal*, Harcourt Brace & World, New York, 1966.

MOLL, J. TH., *see* NEYTZELL DE WILDE, A., and MOLL, J. TH.

MONTGOMERY, ARTHUR, *How Sweden Overcame the Depression, 1930–1933*, Stockholm, 1938.

MOREAU, ÉMILE, *Souvenirs d'un gouverneur de la Banque de France, histoire de la stabilisation du franc (1926–28)*, Génin, Paris, 1954.

MORGANSTERN, OSKAR, *International Financial Transactions and Business Cycles*, Princeton University Press, Princeton, 1959.

MORGENTHAU, HENRY, *see* BLUM, JOHN MORTON.

MORISON, ELTING E., *Turmoil and Tradition: A Study of the Life and Times of Henry L. Stimson*, Houghton Mifflin, Boston, 1960.

MOULTON, HAROLD G., and PASVOLSKY, LEO, *War Debts and World Prosperity*, The Brookings Institution, Washington, D.C., 1932.

NEISSER, HANS, *Some International Aspects of the Business Cycle*, University of Pennsylvania Press, Philadelphia, Pa., 1936.

NEISSER, HANS, and MODIGLIANI, FRANCO, *National Incomes and International Trade, A Quantitative Analysis*, University of Illinois Press, Urbana, 1953.

NÉRÉ, J., *La Crise de 1929*, Colin, Paris, 1968.

NEVIN, EDWARD, *The Mechanism of Cheap Money: A Study in British Monetary Policy, 1931–1939*, University of Wales Press, Cardiff, 1955.

NEWBOLD, J. T. W., 'The Beginnings of the World Crisis, 1873–1896', *Economic History*, vol. II, No. 7 (January 1932), pp. 425–41.

New York Times, various issues.

NEYTZELL DE WILDE, A., and MOLL, J. TH., assisted by GOOSZEN, A. J., *The Netherlands Indies During the Depression, a Brief Economic Survey*, J. M. Meulenhoff, Amsterdam, 1936.

NICHOLS, JEANNETTE P., 'Roosevelt's Monetary Diplomacy, 1933', *American Historical Review*, LVI, No. 2 (January 1951), pp. 295–317.

NIVEAU, MAURICE, *Histoire des faits économiques contemporains*, 2ème édition, Presses Universitaires de France, Paris, 1969.

317

NOYES, ALEXANDER DANA, *The Market Place, Reminiscences of a Financial Editor*, Little Brown, Boston, 1938.

NURKSE, RAGNAR, 'International Monetary Equilibrium', *Essays in International Finance*, International Finance Section, Princeton University, No. 4 (April 1945), reprinted in American Economic Association, *Readings in the Theory of International Trade*, Blakiston, Philadelphia, 1949.

NURKSE, RAGNAR, see League of Nations (Ragnar Nurkse).

OHLIN, BERTIL, see League of Nations (Bertil Ohlin).

OPPENHEIMER, JOE A., see FROELICH, NORMAN, and OPPENHEIMER, JOE A.

PASVOLSKY, LEO, see MOULTON, HAROLD G., and PASVOLSKY, LEO.

PATRICK, HUGH T., 'Some Aspects of the Interwar Economy', paper prepared for the VIth Seminar of Conference on Modern Japan, Dilemmas of Growth in Prewar Japan, held in Puerto Rico, 2–7 January 1968.

PEDERSEN, JØRGEN, 'Some Notes on the Economic Policy of the United States during the Period 1919–1932', in Hugo Hegeland, ed., *Money, Growth and Methodology*, In Honor of Johan Åkerman, Lund Social Science Studies, Lund, 1961, pp. 473–94.

PENROSE, E. F., *Economic Planning for the Peace*, Princeton University Press, Princeton, 1953.

PERROT, M., *La Monnaie et l'opinion en France et en Angleterre, 1924–36*, Colin, Paris, 1955.

PIGOU, A. C., *Aspects of British Economic History, 1918–1925*, Macmillan, London, 1948.

REDDAWAY, W. B., 'Was $4·86 Inevitable in 1925?', *Lloyds Bank Review*, No. 96 (April 1970), pp. 15–28.

REUSS, FREDERICK G., *Fiscal Policy for Growth without Inflation: the German Experiment*, Johns Hopkins Press, Baltimore, 1963.

Review Committee for Balance of Payments Statistics, Report to the Budget Bureau, *The Balance of Payments Statistics of the United States, A Review and Appraisal* (E. M. Bernstein Report), U.S. Government Printing Office, Washington, D.C., 1965.

RICHARDSON, H. W., *Economic Recovery in Britain, 1932–39*, Weidenfeld & Nicolson, London, 1967.

RICHARDSON, H. W., and ALDCROFT, D., *Building in the British Economy between the Wars*, Allen & Unwin, London, 1969.

RIST, CHARLES, 'L'Expérience de 1926 et la franc d'aujourd'hui', in J. Lacour-Gayet *et al.*, *Monnaie d'hier et de demain*, Éditions SPID, Paris, 1952.

ROBBINS, LIONEL, *The Great Depression*, Macmillan, London, 1934.

ROEPKE, WILHELM, *Crises and Cycles*, William Hodge, London, n.d. (?1936).

ROOSE, KENNETH D., *The Economics of Recession and Revival, an Interpretation of 1937–38*, Yale University Press, New Haven, 1954.

ROOSEVELT, FRANKLIN D., *The Papers and Addresses of Franklin D. Roosevelt*, vol. II: *The Years of Crisis*, Random House, New York, 1938; vol. VII: *The Continuing Struggle for Liberalism*, Macmillan Co., New York, 1941.

ROSEN, ELLIOTT, *see* MOLEY, RAYMOND, with the assistance of ROSEN, ELLIOTT.

ROSTOW, W. W., 'The Strategic Role of Theory: A Comment', *Journal of Economic History*, vol. XXXI, No. 1 (March 1971), pp. 76–86.

ROTHSCHILD, K. W., *Austria's Economic Development Between the Wars*, Muller, London, 1947.

RUEFF, JACQUES, 'Sur un point d'histoire: le niveau de la stabilisation Poincaré', *Revue d'économie politique*, 69e année (mars-avril 1959), pp. 168–78.

RUEFF, JACQUES, Preface to MOREAU, ÉMILE, *Souvenirs d'un gouverneur de la Banque de France*, Génin, Paris, 1954.

SAFARIAN, A. E., *The Canadian Economy in the Great Depression*, University of Toronto Press, Toronto, 1959.

SALTER, Sir ARTHUR, *Recovery, the Second Effort*, Bell, London: Century, New York, 1932.

SALTER, LORD, *Memoirs of a Public Servant*, Faber & Faber, London, 1961.

SALTER, Sir ARTHUR, *Slave of the Lamp*, Weidenfeld & Nicolson, London, 1967.

SAUVY, ALFRED, *Histoire économique de la France entre les deux guerres*, Tome I: *1918–1931*, Fayard, Paris, 1965; Tome II: *1931–1939*, Fayard, Paris, 1967.

SAYERS, R. S., 'The Springs of Technical Progress in Britain, 1919–1939', *Economic Journal*, vol. LX, No. 238 (June 1950), pp. 275–91.

SCHACHT, HJALMAR H. G., *The Stabilization of the Mark*, Allen & Unwin, London, 1927.

SCHACHT, HJALMAR H. G., *The End of Reparations*, Jonathan Cape, London: Jonathan Cape and Harrison Smith, New York, 1931.

SCHACHT, HJALMAR H. G., 'Germany's Colonial Demands', *Foreign Affairs*, vol. XV, No. 2 (January 1937), pp. 223–34.

SCHACHT, HJALMAR H. G., *My First Seventy-Six Years*, Allan Wingate, London, 1955; published in the U.S. under the title *Confessions of 'The Old Wizard'*, Houghton Mifflin, Boston, 1956.

SCHATTSCHNEIDER, E. E., *Politics, Pressures and Tariffs: A Study of Free Private Enterprise in Pressure Politics as Shown by the 1929–30 Revision of the Tariff*, Prentice-Hall, New York, 1935.

SCHLESINGER, ARTHUR M., Jr, *The Age of Roosevelt*, vol. II: *The Coming of the New Deal*, Houghton Mifflin, Boston, 1959; Heinemann, London, 1960.

SCHMIDT, CARL T., *German Business Cycles, 1924–1933*, National Bureau of Economic Research, New York, 1934.

SCHMIDT, PAUL, *Statist auf diplomatischen Bühne, 1923–45*, Athenaeum-Verlag, Bonn, 1949.

SCHUMPETER, JOSEPH A., *Business Cycles: A Theoretical, Historical and Statistical Analysis of the Capitalistic Process*, 2 vols., McGraw-Hill, New York and London, 1939.

SCHWARTZ, ANNA JACOBSON, *see* FRIEDMAN, MILTON, and SCHWARTZ, ANNA JACOBSON.

SCHWARTZ, JORDAN, *1933: Roosevelt's Decision: the United States Leaves the Gold Standard*, Chelsea House, New York, 1969.

SEYMOUR, CHARLES, *see* HOUSE, E. M., and SEYMOUR, CHARLES.

SHAPLEN, ROBERT, *Kreuger, Genius and Swindler*, Alfred A. Knopf, New York, 1960; André Deutsch, London, 1961.

SILBERMAN, CHARLES, *see* BURCH, GILBERT and SILBERMAN, CHARLES.

SIMPSON, AMOS E., *Hjalmar Schacht in Perspective*, Mouton, The Hague, 1969.

SKIDELSKY, ROBERT, *Politicians and the Slump, The Labour Government of 1929–1931*, Macmillan, London, 1967.

SOBEL, ROBERT, *The Great Bull Market: Wall Street in the 1920s*, W. W. Norton, New York, 1968.

State, Department of, *Foreign Relations of the United States*, U.S. Government Printing Office, Washington, D.C., various issues.

STIMSON, HENRY L., and BUNDY, MacGEORGE, *On Active Service in Peace and War*, Harper & Bros., New York, 1947.

STOLPER, GUSTAV, *German Economy, 1870–1940, Issues and Trends*, Reynal & Hitchcock, New York: Allen & Unwin, London, 1940.

STUART, G. M. VERRIJN, 'The Netherlands during the Recent Depression', in A. D. GAYER (ed.), *The Lessons of Monetary Experience: Essays in Honor of Irving Fisher*, Farrar & Rinehart, New York: Allen & Unwin, London, 1937, pp. 237–58.

STUCKEN, RUDOLF, *Deutsche Geld- und Kreditpolitik, 1914 bis 1963*, J. C. B. Mohr (Paul Siebeck), Tübingen, 1964.

STURMTHAL, ADOLF, *The Tragedy of European Labour, 1918–1939*, Columbia University Press, New York, 1943. Gollancz, London, 1944.

SVENNILSON, INGVAR, *Growth and Stagnation in the European Economy*, Economic Commission for Europe, United Nations, Geneva, 1954.

SWERLING, BORIS C., *see* TIMOSHENKO, VLADIMIR P., and SWERLING, BORIS C.

TAYLOR, HENRY C., and TAYLOR, ANNE DEWEES, *World Trade in Agricultural Products*, Macmillan Co., New York, 1943.

TEMIN, PETER, 'Three Problems in Economic History', *Journal of Economic History*, vol. XXXI, No. 1 (March 1971), pp. 58–75.

TEMIN, PETER, 'The Beginning of the Depression in Germany', *Economic History Review*, vol. XXIV, No. 2 (May 1971), pp. 240–48.

THOMAS, BRINLEY, *Monetary Policy and Crisis: A Study of Swedish Experience*, Routledge, London, 1936.

TIMOSHENKO, VLADIMIR P., *World Agriculture and the Depression*, University of Michigan, Ann Arbor, 1953.

TIMOSHENKO, VLADIMIR P., and SWERLING, BORIS C., *The World's Sugar, Progress and Policy*, Stanford University Press, Stanford, 1957.

TREVIRANIS, GOTTFRIED REINHOLD, *Das Ende von Weimar, Heinrich Brüning und seine Zeit*, Econ-Verlag, Dusseldorf, 1968.

TRIANTIS, STEPHEN, *Cyclical Changes in Trade Balances of Countries Exporting Primary Products, 1927–33*, University of Toronto Press, Toronto, 1967.

TRIFFIN, ROBERT, 'La théorie de la surévaluation monétaire et la dévaluation belge', in *Bulletin de l'Institut des Recherches Économiques de l'Université de Louvain*, IX, No. 1 (November 1937), pp. 3–36.

TUGWELL, REXFORD G., *The Brains Trust*, Viking Press, New York, 1968.

United Nations, *Commodity Trade and Economic Development*, Report by a Committee of Experts, New York, 1952.

VANSITTART, LORD, *The Mist Procession, the Autobiography of Lord Vansittart*, Hutchinson, London, 1958.

WALKER, E. RONALD, *Australia in the World Depression*, P. S. King, London, 1933.

WARBURG, JAMES P., *The Long Road Home, the Autobiography of a Maverick*, Doubleday, Garden City, New York, 1964.

WICKER, ELMUS R., *Federal Reserve Monetary Policy, 1917–1933*, Random House, New York, 1966.

WILLIAMS, DAVID, 'London and the 1931 Financial Crisis', *Economic History Review*, second series, vol. XV, No. 3 (April 1963), pp. 513–28.

BIBLIOGRAPHY

WILLIAMS, WILLIAM APPLEMAN, *The Tragedy of American Diplomacy*, World Publishing Co., Cleveland, Ohio, 1959.

WOYTINSKY, W. S., *Internationale Hebung der Preise als Ausweg der Krise*, Leipzig, 1931.

WOYTINSKY, W. S., 'International Measures to Create Employment: A Remedy for the Depression', *International Labor Review*, vol. XXV, No. 1 (January 1932), pp. 1–22.

WOYTINSKY, W. S., *Stormy Passage, a Personal History through two Russian Revolutions to Democracy and Freedom, 1905–1960*, Vanguard Press, New York, 1961.

YOUNGSON, A. J., *The British Economy, 1920–57*, Allen & Unwin, London, 1960.

Index